the Dream World of
H. P. LOVECRAFT

the Dream World of
H. P. LOVECRAFT

HIS LIFE, HIS DEMONS, HIS UNIVERSE

DONALD TYSON

Llewellyn Publications
Woodbury, Minnesota

First Edition
First Printing, 2010

Cover art and interior illustration © Marc Sasso
Cover design by Kevin R. Brown
Editing by Brett Fechheimer
Llewellyn is a registered trademark of Llewellyn Worldwide Ltd.

Library of Congress Cataloging-in-Publication Data
Tyson, Donald, 1954–
  The dream world of H. P. Lovecraft : his life, his demons, his universe / Donald Tyson.
— 1st ed.
    p. cm.
  Includes bibliographical references and index.
  ISBN 978-0-7387-2284-9
  1. Lovecraft, H. P. (Howard Phillips), 1890–1937. I. Title.
  PS3523.O833Z88 2010
  813'.52—dc22
  [B]

                            2010022863

Llewellyn Publications
A Division of Llewellyn Worldwide Ltd.
2143 Wooddale Drive
Woodbury, MN 55125-2989
www.llewellyn.com

Printed in the United States of America

OTHER BOOKS BY DONALD TYSON

The Messenger
(Llewellyn, 1990)

Ritual Magic: What It Is & How To Do It
(Llewellyn, 1992)

Three Books of Occult Philosophy (editor)
(Llewellyn, 1992)

Scrying for Beginners
(Llewellyn, 1997)

Enochian Magic for Beginners: The Original System of Angel Magic
(Llewellyn, 2002)

Familiar Spirits: A Practical Guide for Witches & Magicians
(Llewellyn, 2004)

The Power of the Word: The Secret Code of Creation
(Llewellyn, 2004)

1-2-3 Tarot: Answers in an Instant
(Llewellyn, 2004)

Necronomicon: The Wanderings of Alhazred
(Llewellyn, 2004)

Alhazred: Author of the Necronomicon
(Llewellyn, 2006)

Portable Magic: Tarot Is the Only Tool You Need
(Llewellyn, 2006)

Soul Flight: Astral Projection & the Magical Universe
(Llewellyn, 2007)

Grimoire of the Necronomicon
(Llewellyn, 2008)

Runic Astrology
(Llewellyn, 2009)

The Fourth Book of Occult Philosophy (editor)
(Llewellyn, 2009)

The 13 Gates of the Necronomicon
(Llewellyn, 2010)

LOVECRAFT FAMILY TREE

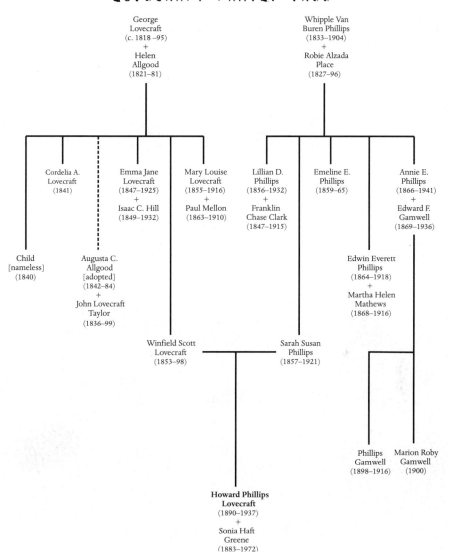

George
Lovecraft
(c. 1818–95)
+
Helen
Allgood
(1821–81)

Whipple Van
Buren Phillips
(1833–1904)
+
Robie Alzada
Place
(1827–96)

Cordelia A.
Lovecraft
(1841)

Emma Jane
Lovecraft
(1847–1925)
+
Isaac C. Hill
(1849–1932)

Mary Louise
Lovecraft
(1855–1916)
+
Paul Mellon
(1863–1910)

Lillian D.
Phillips
(1856–1932)
+
Franklin
Chase Clark
(1847–1915)

Emeline E.
Phillips
(1859–65)

Annie E.
Phillips
(1866–1941)
+
Edward F.
Gamwell
(1869–1936)

Child
[nameless]
(1840)

Augusta C.
Allgood
[adopted]
(1842–84)
+
John Lovecraft
Taylor
(1836–99)

Edwin Everett
Phillips
(1864–1918)
+
Martha Helen
Mathews
(1868–1916)

Winfield Scott
Lovecraft
(1853–98)

Sarah Susan
Phillips
(1857–1921)

Phillips
Gamwell
(1898–1916)

Marion Roby
Gamwell
(1900)

**Howard Phillips
Lovecraft**
(1890–1937)
+
Sonia Haft
Greene
(1883–1972)

CONTENTS

9

GENTEEL DECAY   189

10

THAT IS NOT DEAD...   209

To the impersonal dreamer belongs all infinity—
he is lord of the universe and taster of all the beauties of the stars.

— H. P. LOVECRAFT

Introduction

THE IMPERSONAL DREAMER

The purpose of this biography of H. P. Lovecraft is to show the role dreams played in the genesis of his fiction, and how the mythology he evolved in his body of work became the basis for a system of modern esoteric practice. Lovecraft's importance as a writer of horror tales has been well established. It is time now to reveal his importance as a visionary, and perhaps even as a prophet for the coming age.

It is easy enough to write a book detailing the basic facts of Lovecraft's life, because his letters provide a record of his activities and thoughts on almost a daily basis. Few lives have been so thoroughly self-documented. Indeed, all the essential facts of his life are here in the following pages, but facts alone are not enough. To really understand Lovecraft, it is necessary to venture beyond the physical events of his life and into the psychic events of his dreams. He was a man at war with himself, yet strangely unaware of the conflict. There were really two Lovecrafts—the man awake, and the man asleep.

Awake, Lovecraft was the consummate rationalist, disdaining to believe or even seriously consider any existence in defiance of the established laws of science. From early childhood he dismissed the possibility of the afterlife and the soul. He held in contempt all forms of religion and mysticism. Although he was born a Baptist, he was never a practicing Christian. As a young boy, he asked so many awkward questions in Sunday school that he was excused by his teachers from attending classes. The occult seemed to him no more than a silly waste of time. He called himself an agnostic for most of his life, but toward the end was referring to himself as an outright atheist.

It might naturally be supposed that a man of such opinions lacked imagination. Nothing could be less true. Asleep, he wandered through a vast pleasure palace of dreams, the variety and complexity of which would have baffled Shahrazad. His dreamlands were filled with great rivers, decayed country villages, forgotten temples, oceans upon which sailed ornate galleons bound for ancient ports, cities of gilded domes and spires, vast mountain ranges, and measureless caverns beneath the earth. Lovecraft discovered in childhood that he could move through these scenes in a conscious way as a roving, disembodied perceiver, or could enter them as a dream character and play a part in their unfolding.

Lovecraft's memory was far superior to that of a normal person. This is demonstrated in his letters by his ability to recall the minutiae of his daily activities years after the fact. That power of memory was not confined to his waking life but extended to his dreams. Not only were his dreams uncommonly detailed and vivid, but he was able to remember almost all of their detail with absolute clarity upon awaking, and, if he wished, to convey some of this vividness through words on the page. It was his desire to preserve his stranger and more intense dreams that impelled Lovecraft to begin writing stories. He had experimented with fiction in his youth, but it was not until he began to record his dream scenes that he became the Lovecraft we know today, a man of uncanny and horrific visions.

Lovecraft the rationalist dismissed the importance of his dreams, and of the stories based upon them. He pretended to himself that they were no more than a facile entertainment, a way of distracting the mind from the tedium and pointlessness of material existence. The reality was a bit different—Lovecraft wrote out his dreams because he felt compelled to do so, for the sake of his own sanity. Many of his nightmares terrified him. He would sometimes experience the same scenes, interact with the same monstrous beings, over and over in sleep. Writing the dreams down was his way of exorcising them. By making them external, he took conscious control over their unfolding in a way that he never quite managed in sleep.

He took pleasure in reliving the intense fear of his dreams while awake—what he referred to as their cosmic horror. His waking life lacked excitement and emotion. Outwardly he was the most prosaic of human beings. But by writing down his dreams he was able to carry over from his sleeping life to his waking life some of the intense excitement of his dreams, and nowhere was the intensity greater than in his nightmares. He craved the memory of this emotional high almost as an addict craves a drug.

Lovecraft was more than merely a dreamer. Night after night he engaged in intuitive astral projection. He became consciously aware in at least some of his more vivid dreams, and gained a measure of control over his perception of those dream dramas. He was never able to control their outcome, and that is why he wrote them down—to control them. Today we might prefer to say that Lovecraft engaged in lucid dreaming, but whichever term is used, the meaning is the same. He was aware of himself within his dreams.

Some of the things he carried back with him from sleep and recorded in his fiction have a disquieting power over readers. There is a sense of reality about them that is not often found in genre fiction. It is not so much that we believe the scenes he describes in his stories are literally real, but rather that we sense that the things he based his stories on have a kind of reality on some nonphysical plane of existence that Lovecraft visited while dreaming. His *Necronomicon*, his vast cavern realms, his undersea cities, and above all his Old Ones, speak to us on a level that is below the level of conscious deliberation. They have the power of mythology—not the mythology we know from ancient and dead civilizations, but the bright, hard force of a living mythology, a mythology that does not yet realize that it is mythic.

Lovecraft's mythology was termed the *Cthulhu mythos* by August Derleth, but this is generally acknowledged to be a poor term for it. Prior to this coining, Derleth wanted to call it the *Hastur mythos*, after an obscure mention of this name by Lovecraft, which Derleth turned into a major character in his own fiction. Lovecraft himself self-mockingly referred to it as his *Yog-Sothothery*, a reference to one of his Great Old Ones, Yog-Sothoth. He also made mention of his "Arkham cycle," referring to the invented Massachusetts town of Arkham that is central to so much of his fiction. In this confusion, some critics simply talk about the Lovecraft mythos, but in my own writings I prefer to use the term *Necronomicon mythos*, because it is the *Necronomicon* that is most central to Lovecraft's mythology—not Cthulhu, not Arkham, not Yog-Sothoth, and certainly not Hastur.

The *Necronomicon* is what Lovecraft is best known for among the general public. It is both a book of dreams and a dream book. Lovecraft glimpsed it in his dreams, in old bookshops on sagging shelves, and in the libraries of ancient private houses—a large book with a black leather cover much riddled with wormholes and worn by centuries of handling. The very title itself, *Necronomicon*, appeared to Lovecraft in a dream, and he recorded it without the slightest understanding of what the word means. Later while awake he attempted to make sense of the word, which is obviously Greek, and translated it to the best of his limited ability as "An Image of the Law of the Dead."

Lovecraft also glimpsed in his dreams the mad Arab, Abdul Alhazred, the original writer of this strange book that never existed in this world until Lovecraft dreamed it, and he saw the lost cities of Arabia where Alhazred, the poet of dreams, learned the dread secrets that are printed on its water-stained and mildewed pages—the secrets that drive men mad. The book has no physical reality in this waking world, and no one knows its true contents, yet it is Lovecraft's greatest creation, and its power over the imagination only grows stronger with each passing year. It is for this reason that I call Lovecraft's mythology the *Necronomicon* mythos.

This is a biography of Lovecraft, and when people think of Lovecraft or write about him, there are several aspects of his nature that are usually passed over in silence out of respect for Lovecraft the man, or love for his works. For one thing, he was odd—not odd in the usual sense, but truly alien from the rest of the human race. He was always the outsider. Unlike many of those outside the circles of popular society who gaze at them longingly and seek to break in, Lovecraft had no interest in other human beings, and very little use for them. He regarded other people as elements of the general landscape, with the same lack of involvement with which he regarded stones and trees. They added a bit of background color, and that was about all they meant to him. In company he was charming and affable, and was generally well liked by those who knew him on the personal level, but for Lovecraft himself, human interactions were of no importance. He simply did not care deeply about other people.

Another aspect of his nature seldom discussed is his astonishing selfishness, which may be related to his lack of real interest in other human beings. Lovecraft was not a cruel man—quite the contrary, he was kind to a fault—but he had no capacity of sacrifice for others. As a child, he was spoiled beyond all reason, and as an adult he continued to expect everything in life to be handed to him on his terms. He persisted in this irrational expectation even when events had long since disproved it. He would do things his way, and be damned to the consequences. It was the attitude of a toddler not yet forced by life to do what is tedious and unpleasant, and in many ways Lovecraft never matured emotionally beyond this level.

The least palatable aspect of Lovecraft's character was his lifelong, deeply ingrained bigotry and racism. It evolved when he was a teenager and a young man, during the five-year period when he withdrew from the world and became a virtual recluse. Succinctly stated, Lovecraft hated on principle anyone who was not Anglo-Saxon. In his letters, he mentions on numerous occasions and in great detail his contempt and detestation for blacks, Asians, Jews, Arabs, Turks, Poles, Italians, and the Irish. He writes of the superiority of the "Aryan race" with such fervor that it comes as no surprise to learn of his approval during the 1930s of the Nazis and their views. When he was forced to live for a two-year period near Red Hook, a neighborhood of Brooklyn much frequented by immigrants, the experience almost drove him insane.

I have not spared Lovecraft the man in this examination of his life and his beliefs, but in the end the value of his work transcends his personal limitations. The man is gone, and the work remains. In spite of his mental instability, his antisocial nature, his archaic affectations, his emotional immaturity, and his overt racism, he created a mythic world that continues to captivate the imagination of millions of readers, and has spawned countless films, songs, stories, books, comics, pictures, toys, and role-playing games.

Perhaps even more significant, in the longer term, is the birth of a new kind of magic based on the *Necronomicon* mythos. This system of practical occultism has not yet reached maturity, so it is impossible to predict how it will evolve. Like the mythos itself, it is alive, and as with any living thing it keeps changing. Lovecraft would have laughed with bemusement had he been told that a few decades after his death, serious occultists would evoke his Old Ones to tangible presence in ritual circles, but that it what is happening today. Magic precedes mysticism, and it may be that we are seeing the birth pains of a new religion for the modern age, a materialistic faith that maintains the actual existence, in some distant dimension of reality, of the Old Ones and their minions.

The material in this book is arranged in a way it is hoped will relieve monotony for the reader. Chapters of straight biography alternate with chapters devoted to an analysis of Lovecraft's personality and his writings. Those who wish merely to know the details of Lovecraft life will find most of them in the odd-numbered chapters, and in the timeline at the back of the book. The even-numbered chapters contain an examination of how the events in Lovecraft's life affected him both as a human being and as a creative artist, along with an interpretation of the meaning of his dreams and the significance of his work to the modern West.

SILVER SPOON

*M*idnight on Angell Street, Providence, Rhode Island, in the autumn of 1896. In an upstairs bedroom of the great clapboard Phillips mansion, a six-year-old boy lies flat on his back in bed, staring sightlessly through the impenetrable darkness, a quilt clutched under his prominent chin. The clink of a coal in the cast-iron hall stove outside his door makes him flinch, but he does not blink, even though his eyes sting and water from the effort to force them open. Outside the closed window, a mournful wind sighs through leafless maples. The boy barely hears. His mind is fixed on one thing—to stay awake, no matter how hard the effort, no matter what the cost. He dare not let his attention wander, not even for an instant. But he is so very tired. His eyelids droop.

They come, as they always do, sliding up the window sash and stepping noiselessly into his room, darkness against darkness, naked bodies edged with flickering sliver light that defines their shapes. Slanted pairs of blood-red eyes bob in the black like ghostly lanterns as they surround his bed. Never do they utter a word—how could they, for they have no mouths. Membranous wings lie folded close against their backs. Slender barbed tails flick the air restlessly. Without a rustle, they draw the covers off his bed. He sees them as if floating in the air above—sees his own body shiver on the sheet, unable to move, *unable to scream. It has happened so many times, but its inevitability only makes the horror worse.*

Long black fingers clutch at the flesh of his belly, lifting him, twisting him through the opened window and into the night sky, over the rooftops, high above the church steeples of the city. The stars turn and roll beneath him as the creatures pass him back and forth, their touch an insidious tickling sensation that penetrates through his skin and into his flesh, setting his teeth on edge. Faster, higher, for an eternity they carry him on flapping, leathern wings, until the familiar New England landscape is transformed into something alien and terrifying. He glimpses skylines of strange domed cities and silhouettes of alien temples to unknown gods. He is carried still higher, and the ground merges with the darkness. There is only the wind in his ears and the unendurable tickle of taloned fingers.

They fly on forever. The boy has no way to mark the passage of time. At last, a faint glow at the edge of the sky reveals an endless mountain range of closely ranked, needle-sharp peaks beneath him, stretching to the horizon in all directions. The clutch of the creature slips from his belly, and he screams in terror, but before he can fall far, another of the things catches him up. They begin to cast him back and forth for sport, dangling him with one claw. The peaks of the mountains threaten below. At last, tiring of their amusement, they allow him to drop, flying off through the darkness and leaving him to plummet with nothing but the rushing wind for a companion. The peaks loom up, great swords of stone, as he tumbles screaming—

If it can ever be said of anyone that he was born with a silver spoon in his mouth, it can aptly be said of Howard Phillips Lovecraft. In Lovecraft's case the spoon was solid English sterling and was made by the venerable Gorham and Company, silversmiths of Providence, Rhode Island, for which his father, Winfield Scott Lovecraft (1853–98), worked at the time of his son's birth as a commercial traveler, selling the company's wares to shops. However, this metaphorical spoon was not purchased by his struggling salesman father but by his wealthy grandfather, the industrialist Whipple Van Buren Phillips (1833–1904), who was destined all too soon to become young Lovecraft's surrogate father.

It was providential indeed that Lovecraft was born in the spacious three-story Phillips family mansion at what was then 194 Angell Street, where the street intersects Elmgrove Avenue, in the district of College Hill on the prosperous eastern side of the bucolic New England university city of Providence. The happy memories impressed during early childhood created in Lovecraft's heart an abiding love for both the imposing Phillips homestead and for the city of his birth that would endure throughout his life. No matter how far he traveled, he always returned to Providence, and it was in Providence that he died and is buried.

Lovecraft might easily have been born elsewhere. His mother, the headstrong and emotionally unstable Sarah Susan Phillips (1857–1921), had married beneath her station. Her husband, who had worked as a lowly blacksmith during the 1870s before taking his traveling sales position with Gorham, was incapable of giving her the kind of lifestyle to which she had become accustomed in the bosom of the Phillips family. Nor were Winfield's prospects for inheritance favorable—his father, George Lovecraft (c. 1818–95), of Mount Vernon, New York, was a salesman who earlier in life had worked as a harness maker. Susie, as she preferred to be called, resigned herself to leaving the Phillips family fold and moved with her husband to Dorchester, Massachusetts, immediately after her marriage, to make a new life.

The marriage may have been a matter of discord within the Phillips household.[1] Susie married Winfield Lovecraft on June 12, 1889, in St. Paul's Episcopal Church at Boston, not at Providence, even though it is traditional that the bride's family fulfill the obligations of the wedding ceremony. It is perhaps significant that the newlyweds chose not

to settle in Providence—they may have wanted to put distance between themselves and Susie's disapproving parents and sisters. Nonetheless, when the time came to give birth to Howard, Susie was prevailed upon to returned to the family mansion, presumably to better
ensure her medical care and comfort during the birth and her recovery
from labor, and it was in the Angell Street house that Lovecraft was
born, on August 20, 1890, at nine in the morning.

The newlyweds did not stay long at the Phillips house, but moved
back to the suburbs of Boston, where they rented accommodations in
Dorchester. For a time in the spring of 1892 they vacationed in Dudley,
Massachusetts, with one of Susie's friends, the schoolteacher Miss Ella
Sweeney, who remembered that Susie could not bear to sit down for
even an hour in the dining room because she fretted so much about
the welfare of her young son upstairs. When Ella tried to take Lovecraft for a walk, Susie told her to stoop down because she was afraid
that her friend would dislocate her son's shoulder. This over-protectiveness, which is not uncommon in some mothers toward their first-
born, increased rather than diminished as the years passed.

Money must have been tight for the Lovecrafts. Toward the end of
1892 they were prevailed upon to board in Auburndale, a suburb of
Boston, at the Vista Avenue house of Susie's schoolgirl acquaintance,
the prominent and somewhat eccentric poet Miss Louise Imogen
Guiney (1861–1920), during which period they planned the construction of their own new house outside of Boston, which sadly was destined never to be built. Poetry seldom pays well. Miss Guiney, a spin-
ster who was four years younger than Susie Lovecraft, lived alone with
her mother, apart from their servants. The Lovecrafts needed a cheap
place to stay, and Miss Guiney needed a source of income—that was
the only binding tie.

Among Little Howard's earliest memories is an impression of the
large Saint Bernard dogs that Miss Guiney kept as pets and named

after great figures in English literature, particularly one shaggy dog named Brontë that would walk beside his baby carriage while his mother pushed him around the streets. The dog would allow Lovecraft to place his tiny fist into its vast mouth, and growled whenever anyone strange approached the carriage.

The mother of the poet called Lovecraft "Little Sunshine" because of the long, golden ringlets that cascaded to his shoulders, a name her daughter adopted for him. The amiable if somewhat controlling Miss Guiney took to drilling Lovecraft in verse memorization, and had him stand up periodically before her friends and give little recitals. She also trained him, as she might have trained a parrot, to respond in a loud and cheerful voice to her question, "Whom do you love?" with the words "Louise Imogen Guiney!"[2] Lovecraft remembered sitting on the knee of a great figure in American letters, Oliver Wendell Holmes, Sr., in the Guiney drawing room—Holmes was a frequent visitor to the Guiney residence.

Other early memories were those of his father, which he would cherish later in life since they were the only memories of the elder Lovecraft that he was ever to be permitted to form. In 1934 he wrote in a letter, "I can just remember my father—an immaculate figure in black coat and vest and grey striped trousers. I had a childish habit of slapping him on the knees and shouting, 'Papa, you look just like a young man!' I don't know where I picked that phrase up; but I was vain and self-conscious, and given to repeating things which I saw tickled my elders."[3]

The elder Lovecraft appears in a family photograph taken in 1892.[4] He is posed standing beside his seated wife, who holds their infant son on her knee, a slightly bored expression on his handsome face, or perhaps a look of impatience. He is clean-shaven apart from a forest of whiskers sprouting from his upper lip, and his well-oiled hair has the same wave in it that is evident in Lovecraft's long ringlets. By contrast, the smile on his wife's lips is wire-thin and looks strained. Her hair is done up in a bun on top of her head, as was the custom of the time. The only one of the three who appears to be enjoying the experience is young Howard, who positively beams with self-importance and the inner joy that can only come to a young child who finds himself the center of adult attention.

Alas, his happiness was soon destined to be interrupted, if but temporarily. In April of 1893 while on a sales trip to Chicago, Winfield Lovecraft began to hallucinate in his hotel room, crying out in a loud voice that his wife was being assaulted on the floor above.[5] At the time, Susie was nowhere near Chicago. He had to be restrained for his own protection. He was conveyed to Butler Hospital in Providence and institutionalized on April 25. He remained in this mental hospital for over five years until his death on July 19, 1898, when Lovecraft was only seven years old. Lovecraft was never taken to the hospital to visit his father, nor was he ever informed of the true nature of his illness. In later life he always maintained that his father had died from a paralyzing stroke that had induced a coma from which he never awoke. No doubt this was the story told to him by the Phillips family.

The available evidence suggests that the elder Lovecraft became psychotic due to syphilis, and suffered what was known as general paresis of the insane, or paralytic dementia, a consequence of the advance of the third and final stage of this horrifying disease. As a salesman traveling from town to town across New England, staying in different hotels, he would have had ample opportunity to contract this venereal disease from a prostitute. At the time there was no cure, or even a reliable test—the Wassermann diagnostic test was developed in 1906, and the first effective treatment, involving the administration of an arsenic compound, was not developed until 1910. Given the period of years that can elapse between the contraction of the disease and obvious symptoms of insanity, it is probable that Winfield Lovecraft was already infected when he married Susie Phillips. It can be passed on from mother to child congenitally. However, there is no solid evidence that she or her child suffered from syphilis.

The madness and permanent removal to an institution of a father would have been a tragedy of heart-wrenching sadness in the life of most two-year-old boys, but for Lovecraft it marked the transition back into the wealth and security of the Phillips household, and the beginning of the happiest period of his life. After institutionalizing her husband, Susie Lovecraft went home to live with her parents. It must have been humiliating to have to drag herself back in this fashion to the family fold, but she had little alternative—her husband had not left her any significant savings, and given her social position she could scarcely take the job of a clerk or a laborer. Some time after Winfield Lovecraft was placed in Butler Hospital, his father, George Lovecraft, sent to young Howard the Lovecraft family library. These books seem to have been Lovecraft's only legacy from his paternal grandfather.

Even so, Lovecraft had very little to complain about. He had literally fallen into the ample lap of luxury, that lap belonging to his doting grandfather Whipple, who adored the boy. The Phillips mansion on Angell Street had fifteen rooms and was on three levels—the four permanent house servants lived on the attic level. Within the extensive grounds was a fountain, an orchard, shade trees, and behind the main house a combination stable and carriage house that held the family carriage and living quarters for the coachman who cared for the horses. The vacant lot adjoining the property was soon appropriated by Lovecraft as his personal kingdom, along with the entire back garden. Lovecraft would later write of this period in his childhood, "My array of toys, books, and other youthful pleasures was virtually unlimited."[6]

Whipple Van Buren Phillips was a man of endless energy and ambition. If he did not become one of America's great robber barons of the nineteenth century, it was not for lack of trying. His father was killed on November 20, 1848, only two days prior to Whipple's fifteenth birthday, in an accident at the grist mill he had built on the headwaters of the Moosup River in Foster, Rhode Island. His mother had died earlier that same year, so Whipple suddenly found himself an orphan. In 1852 he went to live with his uncle James in Delavan, Illinois, but he returned to Foster the following year for reasons of climate, a decision that was to prove fortunate. In 1855 he was able to buy the general store in Foster, and on January 27 of the following year he married his first cousin, Robie Alzada Place (1827–96). Their first child, Lovecraft's aunt Lillian Delora Phillips (1856–1932), was born less than three months after the wedding,[7] on April 20, which suggests that the marriage was not entirely a free decision on Whipple's part.

It is reasonable to speculate that a significant portion of the money to buy the store came from Robie's dowry. The newlyweds took occupancy of a house that had been built by Robie's father, Stephen Place. The general store prospered, and in two years Whipple sold it at a profit and used the proceeds to essentially buy up the entire village of Coffin's Corner, in the western part of Rhode Island. He build a new house for himself, a grist mill, an assembly house for the community, and cottages for his employees at the mill. Around 1859 he moved his family to Coffin's Corner, which he later renamed with the less mortuary title of Greene. He joined the Freemasons and even had a Masonic Hall constructed in the community, where he served as postmaster from 1860 until 1866. From 1870 to 1872 he represented Coventry in the Rhode Island General Assembly.[8]

In 1873 he sold his mill and other interests in Greene, and moved the center of his real estate and land speculation business to Providence, where he had for some years maintained an office. He settled on the west side of the town at 276 Broadway, but in 1881 he had what was to become the family residence constructed at 194 Angell Street (the lot was renumbered 454 Angell Street when Lovecraft was five or six, but the original house was torn down in 1961), on an elevated terrace of ground so that it looked down upon the surrounding properties. It may seem a bit grandiloquent to refer to the clapboard, three-level house of many gables as a mansion,[9] but by the standards of the day, which were modest, it was an impressive enough place to call home, as much for its extensive grounds as for the house itself. Writing in 1916 to Rheinhart Kleiner, one of his many correspondents, Lovecraft would refer fondly to the house as "one of the handsomest residences in the city—to me, the handsomest—my own beloved birthplace!"[10]

To gain some appreciation for Lovecraft's sudden change in fortune, it is necessary to know that he was the only child in the great house on Angell Street, which, apart from the stabilizing authority his grandfather and the occasional presence of his uncle Edwin Everett Phillips (1864–1918), who got married when Lovecraft was just three years old, was a house of women. In addition to his son, Whipple had sired three daughters who lived to adulthood (a fourth died in childhood), and as yet only Susie had found—and lost—a husband. The full weight of the smothering maternal attentions of his mother, his grandmother, and his two still-unwed aunts, to say nothing of the maids, descended around young Lovecraft like a storm of scented rose petals.

His mother was determined to keep him dressed in smocks like a little girl, and continued to curl his long hair into golden ringlets until the age of six, when Lovecraft finally refused to put up with it any longer. While the barber was cutting her son's hair, she sat beside the chair and wept bitter tears. This custom of dressing boys as girls was not uncommon during the period, and may have been done as a superstitious way of turning evil aside from young boys, the underlying rationale being that girls were not as highly valued, and therefore were less likely to attract malicious envy.[11] When Lovecraft rode his tricycle, Susie would walk along beside him to ensure that he never fell and bruised himself.[12] To say he was mollycoddled would be an understatement. He was the center of his small but luxurious universe, and must have assumed himself to be the very sun in the heavens, since he brought smiles of joy to all who looked upon him.

At the end of the nineteenth century, Providence was a very pleasant place indeed for the only child of a wealthy family of white Anglo-Saxon Baptists. The Phillips family could trace its lineage in the New World back to the Massachusetts Bay Colony founded in 1630. Even the less socially prominent Lovecraft family was of good old English stock. Lovecraft was always inordinately vain about his racial heritage. He liked to boast that he was pure English on both sides of his bloodline, but took special pride in being only the second generation of the Lovecrafts born on American soil—his paternal grandparents and all earlier generations were born in England. He grew up with the understanding that the entire episode of the American Revolution had been an unfortunate mistake, but that there was no reason to hold a grudge against the Mother Country because of it.

Young Lovecraft spent much of his early years playing on the grounds of the Phillips house and in the adjoining vacant lot, once his mother relented sufficiently to let him out of her sight. The family coachman, an Irishman named Kelly, who lived in a three-room apartment in the upper part of the stable with his wife, built for him during 1894 and the year following a kind of playhouse in the vacant lot, and helped the child construct an elaborate play railway system that ran over both properties. Lovecraft called the playhouse his "Engine House" and took pride in having put together the mock steam engine for his railway himself, "by mounting a sort of queer boiler on a tiny express-waggon."[13] Around 1900, when financial constraints forced his grandfather to sell the horses and carriage, and release the coachman from his employ, the empty stable became Lovecraft's private playground and he extended his railway into it.

With the help of neighborhood children, he also constructed a mock fortified Alaskan village he called New Anvik in the vacant lot— the name was derived from the 1895 children's book *Snow-shoes and Sledges* by the writer Kirk Munroe, a sequel to his popular Alaskan adventure *The Fur-Seal's Tooth*, published the previous year. This became part of Lovecraft's imaginary world, which he clung to far longer than most boys. After he and his mother were forced by the death of Whipple Phillips in 1904 to move up the road to a slightly less grand house at 598 Angell Street, not far from the corner of Butler Avenue, Lovecraft reconstructed New Anvik in another empty lot beside the new address, and continued to play in the dirt in his fantasy village. Not until 1907, when he was a high school student of seventeen years of age, did he finally admit to himself that he had grown too old for playing make-believe in the yard. With great reluctance he turned his elaborate constructions over to the care and enjoyment of a younger boy who lived nearby. Remembering the event, he wrote in a letter in 1920, "Big boys do not play in toy houses and mock gardens, so I was obliged to turn over my world in sorrow to another and younger boy who dwelt across the lot from me."[14]

Lovecraft's interior fantasy life was every bit as rich as the play-world he constructed in the vacant lot next to the Phillips mansion. When he was still quite young, it became evident that he was precocious. He learned the alphabet at two years of age, and began to give little poetry recitals for anyone who would listen. The attentions of the poet Louise Imogen Guiney just prior to his second birthday helped focus his interest on verse. At that age he was without self-consciousness and delighted to show off his talents to adults. By age three he had learned to read *Grimm's Fairy Tales* on his own—Lovecraft later asserted that by the age of four he could read with ease. In 1895, he discovered the *Arabian Nights*. It became his favorite book of stories. He developed a passion for all things Arab. He dressed himself as an

Arab, surrounded himself with furnishings that had an Arab look, and took to calling himself Abdul Alhazred.

Exactly how Lovecraft came to adopt this obscure name, which is now famous as the name of the supposed author of his apocryphal *Necronomicon*, is not known with certainty, because Lovecraft himself did not remember the details. He gave the impression in a letter to his editor Edwin Baird, written in 1924, that he had conceived the name himself: "At one time I formed a juvenile collection of Oriental pottery and objects d'art, announcing myself as a devout Mohammedan and assuming the pseudonym of 'Abdul Alhazred'—which you will recognize as the author of that mythical *Necronomicon* which I drag into various of my tales."[15] Many years later, in a 1932 letter to Robert E. Howard, Lovecraft indicated that it may have been suggested to him by the family lawyer and friend, Albert Baker: "I can't quite recall where I did get the name Abdul Alhazred. There is a dim recollection which associates it with a certain elder—the family lawyer, as it happens, but I can't remember whether I asked him to make up an Arabic name for me, or whether I had merely asked him to criticize a choice I had otherwise made."[16]

Another epoch in Lovecraft's early literary evolution was his discovery in 1896 of Greek mythology. This occurred first when he came across copies of Nathaniel Hawthorne's *Wonder Book* and *Tanglewood Tales*, and then with his reading of a simplified version of Homer's *Odyssey* in the Harper Half-Hour Series, which his Aunt Lillian had in her library. But it was his discovery of *The Age of Fable, or Stories of Gods and Heroes* by the Massachusetts author Thomas Bulfinch, a kind of primer on Greek myths for American schoolboys first published in 1855, that irrevocably turned his face from the sands of Arabia to the groves of Arcadia. Immediately the *Arabian Nights* were forgotten, and Lovecraft embraced the stories of Greek Paganism as passionately has he had formerly reveled in the wonder tales of the djinn. He became a complete Hellenist, going so far as to make small offerings on a Pagan altar he had set up in his playground.

This led to one of the more significant events in his early life, although its importance is often missed by Lovecraft's commentators. He later described the circumstances in his brief essay, "A Confession of Unfaith," written in 1921. It is worth quoting this passage in full, because it has bearing on the side of Lovecraft we will examine together in later chapters, his esoteric and paranormal side.

> When about seven or eight I was a genuine pagan, so intoxicated with the beauty of Greece that I acquired a half-sincere belief in the old gods and nature-spirits. I have in literal truth built altars to Pan, Apollo, Diana, and Athena, and have watched for dryads and satyrs in the woods and fields at dusk. Once I firmly thought I beheld some of these sylvan creatures dancing under autumnal oaks; a kind of "religious experience" as true in its way as the subjective ecstasies of any Christian. If a Christian tell me he has felt the reality of his Jesus or Jahveh, I can reply that I have seen the hoofed Pan and the sisters of the Hesperian Phaëthusa.[17]

He began to visit the classical art museums of Providence and Boston to look at Greek art, started collecting plaster reproductions of the gods and goddesses, learned the Greek alphabet, and acquired largely by his own efforts the rudiments of the Latin language. Just as he had adopted a new name when he submerged himself in all things Arab, so now he took upon himself the name Lucius Valerius Messala, which although it was Roman, not Greek, signified for Lovecraft the awakened wonders of classical mythology.

The taking on of a new name is a deliberate magical act of death and rebirth, by which the old, mundane life is abandoned and a new esoteric life is embraced. It is used in this way by many religious and occult organizations. For example, when a woman becomes a Catholic nun, she abandons her birth name and takes on a new name that represents her new life as a bride of Christ. European witches were sometimes said in the testimonies of the witch trials to use a secret cultic name at their gatherings, and it is the custom for modern witches to adopt a magic name, just as it is the custom for ritual magicians to receive a new name when they enter an occult lodge such as that of the Hermetic Order of the Golden Dawn. Hence the magician Aleister Crowley was known for a time as Frater Perdurabo.

It is significant that Lovecraft instinctively undertook this ritual of death and magical rebirth, not once but twice during his early childhood. At age four he assumed the name Abdul Alhazred and with it took on the magical identity of an Arab, and at age six he underwent the same deliberate occult transformation and adopted the name and identity of a Roman. There is no reason to suppose that Lovecraft was ever instructed in these name-rituals of transformation. The practice of magic is not imposed from without but arises from within. This is the enduring strength of magic—it does not need to be taught. Lovecraft was a natural adept, even though he did not know it and would have laughed at the idea later in life.

In 1896 he had already begun to compose his own original poetry and short pieces of prose fiction. Although there is no doubt that he was a prodigy, he was not in the class of, say, a Mozart—his childish productions have scant merit, other than the young age of their composer. As Samuel Johnson once remarked about a dog walking on its hind legs, "It is not done well; but you are surprised to find it done at all." Lovecraft's youngest surviving composition dates from 1897, the earlier pieces having been lost or destroyed. It is a bit of rhyming verse in eighty-eight lines titled "The Poem of Ulysses," consisting of a paraphrase of the abridged version of Homer's *Odyssey*, with which he was then familiar.

The following year, in 1898, one of the more significant events in his young evolution as a writer occurred, when he discovered the stories of Edgar Allan Poe. Lovecraft would forever after regard Poe as the greatest master of the horror story. In his highly influential critical essay, "Supernatural Horror in Literature," he later wrote of Poe, "to him we owe the modern horror-story in its final and perfected state."[18] What Lovecraft particularly appreciated about Poe was his lack of sentimentality.

> Poe, on the other hand, perceived the essential impersonality of the real artist; and knew that the function of creative fiction is merely to express and interpret events and sensations as they are, regardless of how they tend or what they prove—good or evil, attractive or repulsive, stimulating or depressing, with the author always acting as a vivid and detached chronicler rather than as a teacher, sympathizer, or vendor of opinion.[19]

When he came to write such stories as an adult, Lovecraft consciously imitated Poe's style on several occasions, and always strove to be the impersonal observer he so admired in Poe. He remarked in one of his innumerable letters, "Since Poe affected me most of all horror-writers, I can never feel that a tale starts out right unless it has something of his manner. I could never plunge into a thing abruptly, as the popular writers do. To my mind it is necessary to establish a setting and avenue of approach before the main show can adequately begin."[20]

Imitation was an inherent tendency in Lovecraft that he fell prey to repeatedly in his career. He was highly impressionable. When he came under the influence of a writer he particularly admired, he could scarcely resist the urge to copy that writer's style. The pattern would repeat itself when he discovered in 1919 the collection of fantasy stories *A Dreamer's Tales* by Edward John Moreton Drax Plunkett, 18th Baron of Dunsany (1878–1957). For a time he sought to imitate Lord Dunsany's florid prose. The results were only partially successful, and are not the most highly acclaimed of Lovecraft's body of work. Imitation is almost always a mistake for any creative artist. To a lesser degree, the same thing occurred in 1923 when Lovecraft first encountered the stories of Arthur Machen.

It is perhaps worth noting that in the year Lovecraft discovered Bulfinch and Greek mythology, his grandmother died; and in the year he discovered Poe, his insane father died in Butler Hospital; and in the year he discovered Dunsany, his mother was committed to Butler Hospital after suffering a nervous breakdown. A severe mental and emotional shock can render the mind receptive to suggestion. This natural human response is utilized in the process of enforced conditioning, or brainwashing, to implant new beliefs or to root out old beliefs. Lovecraft's worship of the Greek gods, and his attempts to imitate Poe with an almost slavish devotion, and later Lord Dunsany, may have been caused in part by an enhanced impressionability brought about by the severe mental stress of his grandmother's death, his father's death, and his mother's institutionalization.

Lovecraft's fascination for strange and terrifying stories was not limited to Poe. He read whatever came to hand. His grandfather Whipple, noticing this early interest, began to compose original Gothic tales for the boy, based on the writings of Horace Walpole, Matthew Gregory Lewis, Anne Radcliffe, and other English writers of the late eighteenth century whose fiction was heavily laced with creaking doors, mysterious portraits, claps of thunder, suits of armor that moved, dungeons, ghostly apparitions at windows, shadows in the mist, and similar truck that we would consider cliché today. Lovecraft wrote concerning these extemporaneous compositions of his grand-father: "He obviously drew most of his imagery from the early gothic romances—Radcliffe, Lewis, Maturin, etc.—which he seemed to like better than Poe or other later fantasists. He was the only other person I knew—young or old—who cared for macabre and horrific fiction."[21]

The extensive Phillips library, supplemented by the books Love-craft had received from his paternal grandfather as a legacy, became his playground of the mind while he remained at 454 Angell Street. At an unnaturally young age he graduated from children's books to adult works on literary criticism, political commentary, and what was then known under the collective term *belles lettres*—inconsequential little essays on art, daily life, and sundry other topics of general interest. The English writers of the late eighteenth century, both in poetry and in prose, particularly appealed to his rational and orderly mind. He read the poetry of Pope, the essays of Addison, and a jumbled host of political commentaries, religious tracts, biographies and travel books of that periwigged age. He even sampled its novels, but did not much like them. We can only imagine with sympathy young Lovecraft's at-tempts to plod through the volumes of Samuel Richardson's *Pamela*, an eighteenth-century novel singularly lacking in cosmic horror.

Given his general impressionability, it is not surprising that Love-craft began to imitate the manner and style of the writers of the eight-eenth century. This early affectation of antique English speech and English prose was to remain with him for decades, although it gradu-ally diminished with time. Only in the last phase of his life was he able to shake it off, and even then he would often fall into the use of archaic spellings or constructions in his letters as a way of emphasizing a point or injecting a bit of wit.

Lovecraft's boyhood interests were not completely devoted to fantasy and literature. In 1898, the same year he discovered the won-ders of Edgar Allan Poe, he gave a public violin recital for family and friends. His violin studies began when he was seven and continued for approximately two years. He also sang for the family from time to time. Despite these signs of some early talent, he was never greatly interested in music in any form later in life. Also in this eventful year he developed an interest in chemistry. A family friend, Professor John Howard Appleton, who taught chemistry at nearby Brown University, presented the boy with his own beginner's text in chemistry, *The Young Chemist*. Lovecraft studied it avidly and began to conduct smelly experiments, no doubt to the dismay of his mother and aunts.

However, it was not chemistry that became his second great passion after English literature, but astronomy, which Lovecraft began to study in 1902. The sheer vastness of time and space that was opened in his mind by astronomy filled him with wonder and a certain dread that was similar to the feeling of dread produced by the stories of Poe. He became aware, as only those who study astronomy can, of the frightening insignificance not only of our species and its history, but of the entire planet on which we dwell, and indeed of the solar system we inhabit. The vastness of scale that occurs in astronomy has no equal in any other field of human learning. Not even religion dares to intimate in its wildest flights of fancy the inconceivable gulfs of space and time that are revealed by the study of the heavens.

He wrote of this discovery in his autobiographical essay "A Confession of Unfaith":

The most poignant sensations of my existence are those of 1896, when I discovered the Hellenic world, and of 1902, when I discovered the myriad suns and worlds of infinite space. Sometimes I think the latter event the greater, for the grandeur of that growing conception of the universe still excites a thrill hardly to be duplicated. I made of astronomy my principal scientific study, obtaining larger and larger telescopes, collecting astronomical books to the number of 61, and writing copiously on the subject in the form of special and monthly articles in the local daily press. By my thirteenth birthday I was thoroughly impressed with man's impermanence and insignificance, and by my seventeenth, about which time I did some particularly detailed writing on the subject, I had formed in all essential particulars my present pessimistic cosmic views. The futility of all existence began to impress and oppress me; and my references to human progress, formerly hopeful, began to decline in enthusiasm.[22]

On February 12, 1903, Lovecraft purchased his first book about the stars, *Lessons in Astronomy* by Charles Augustus Young. Until then he had been making do with whatever other texts he could find, but chiefly relying on a copy of Elijah Hinsdale Burritt's venerable *Geography of the Heavens*, which he had inherited along with other astronomical books upon the death of his maternal grandmother in 1896. Robie Phillips was an educated woman who had studied astronomy at the Smithville Seminary, a Baptist teachers' college founded in 1839 in North Scituate, Rhode Island, which was renamed the Lapham Institute in 1863. It was probably her edition of Burritt that sparked Lovecraft's initial fascination with the night sky. Writing to Maurice W. Moe in 1915, Lovecraft called this book "the most prized volume in my library."[23]

As in all other things, his mother humored his sudden mania for astronomy by buying for him, in the summer of 1903, an astronomical refractor telescope with a 2.25-inch objective lens. This was probably the diameter of the actual aperture of the lens—it may have been nominally listed as a 2.5-inch lens, but it is customary for a portion of the edge of the lens to be obscured by the lens mounting, which renders its actual aperture slightly less than its nominal aperture. In a letter to Rheinhart Kleiner that is dated November 16, 1916, Lovecraft referred to this instrument as "a 2-½" astronomical telescope."[24]

Lovecraft used his first telescope mainly to study the surface features of the moon and, of all things, Venus, which is usually not of great interest to young amateurs because it is featureless. However, Lovecraft was captivated by the sheer mystery of it. Concerning his early obsession with astronomy, he wrote to Maurice Moe in 1915, "Not one clear night passed without long observation on my part, . . ."[25] Lovecraft would go on to acquire two more telescopes, the final one a 3-inch Bardon refractor that he purchased from Montgomery Ward for fifty dollars, and used until 1936.[26]

However, his astronomical viewing was not limited by his own telescopes. While still quite young, he was given free access to the 13-inch refractor that was housed at Ladd Observatory, a part of Brown University. The head of the astronomical department and director of the observatory, Professor Winslow Upton, was a close friend of the Phillips family. The observatory is located about a mile from where Lovecraft lived, on the top of what was then known locally as Tin-top Hill, due to the presence of a cone of bright tin suspended from the top of a tall oak tree at 205 Doyle Avenue, which was used as a location marker by surveyors and mariners (the tree was cut down in 1907). Later, the apocryphal story evolved that the hill got its name from discarded tin cans that glinted in the sunlight. Lovecraft would push his bicycle up Doyle Avenue to reach the telescope, and coast down the hill all the way home. He wrote that he could go and come at will, so it appears that his mother had no objection to him staying out of the house until all hours of the night, provided she knew what he was doing.

This interest in astronomy gave rise to Lovecraft's first serious and sustained nonfiction productions, astronomical articles that he began writing for his own privately circulated periodicals. He soon found himself submitting them to professional newspapers on a regular basis. On July 6, 1906, he was given an old Remington typewriter, and continued to produce the finished drafts of all his work on this machine until his death. Lovecraft hated to type, and always composed with a pen or pencil in longhand, but he recognized the necessity for a writer to submit his work in a typed format. In that same year, at age fifteen, he began writing a weekly astronomy column for the *Pawtuxet Valley Gleaner*, and a monthly column for the *Providence Tribune*. The *Pawtuxet Valley Gleaner* went out of business in December, but his column in the *Tribune* continued into 1908.

The following year, in his capacity as writer of astronomical articles for the *Tribune* newspaper, Lovecraft met the professional astronomer Percival Lowell, who had traveled from his home at Flagstaff, Arizona, to lecture at Sayles Hall, Brown University. Lovecraft's friend Professor Upton introduced him to Lowell before the lecture. The self-conscious Lovecraft was so terrified that the great man would express anger at disparaging remarks Lovecraft had made in his newspaper articles concerning Lowell's controversial ideas about the canals of Mars, that Lovecraft scarcely knew what he said and was relieved when the interview ended. He only realized much later that Lowell had probably never even seen the articles.

Astronomy was a serious pursuit for Lovecraft. He intended for many years to make it his lifelong profession, not realizing that he was inherently unsuited to it by his very nature. What fascinated him was the mystery and strangeness of space, the intellectual romance of the unknown, not the actual science of astronomy. He remarked in a letter written in 1918 that it used to frustrate him greatly that he could not view the far side of the moon (which is always turned away from the Earth) through his telescope[27]—he ached to know what lay on the other side, which no one at that time had ever seen. Later in life, in his novel *The Dream-Quest of Unknown Kadath*, he would describe the far side of the moon of his imagination. The reason he studied unvarying Venus so tenaciously was his hope of making some new and strange discovery through its obscuring veil of clouds.

What he failed to appreciate at the time is that the profession of astronomy is made up of exacting and tedious observations, coupled with complex mathematical calculations. The fleeting moments of discovery are interspersed by years of stupefying repetition. Lovecraft had no patience to persist in any work that did not interest him at the moment he was doing it, and in spite of his early signs of literary precocity, he was to learn in high school that he was uncommonly poor at algebra. Any professional astronomer needs to excel in mathematics. Lovecraft was a mystic and a dreamer, not a scientist, but as yet he had not arrived at this realization, and to a large degree, he never would.

In the spring of 1908 Lovecraft's boyhood ended with a resounding crash that was to reverberate throughout the remainder of his life. He dropped out of high school and went into a period of almost complete seclusion that lasted for five years. During this withdrawal he avoided all unnecessary human contact and did essentially nothing, other than to entertain himself with various diversions. He slept during the day, lay around the house in his bathrobe, and only left the house late at night when he could walk the streets unseen. The mental breakdown that precipitated this great hiatus remains the single most perplexing mystery of Lovecraft's life, which his biographers have never ceased to speculate and argue about.

This abrupt rejection of human society did not occur in a vacuum, but was a consequence of Lovecraft's boyhood experience, which was not nearly so idyllic as the incidental examination we have just undertaken would suggest. In the next chapter we will look at the dark side of Lovecraft's early years, and how they may have conspired to bring about his mental and emotional collapse as a teenager.

2
RICH AND STRANGE

The bright watercolor impression sketched in the preceding chapter of young Lovecraft's life is an idyllic pastoral. Despite the shock of his father's madness, his early years seem almost too perfect. He was coddled and protected, the center of adult attention with no other child for competition, his every utterance applauded, his every action a source of wonder and amusement. He had all the rich food he could eat, fine clothes to put on, the best in medical care, private tutors, and servants to respond to his every whim. Almost everyone in his small world loved him, and those who may have had mixed feelings about his greatness—the other boys in the neighborhood with whom he played in the vacant lot—could be controlled by limiting his interactions with them.

As is true of all sketches, this interpretation of Lovecraft's childhood is two-dimensional, and paper thin. Beneath the surface of his placid life lurked madness, nightmare, and a growing horror that had its germination from the black seed of his grandmother's death in 1896, and reached its full narcoleptic flowering in his mental breakdown of 1908. The breakdown did not occur in isolation, but was the culmination of a series of life experiences coupled with Lovecraft's singular temperament, so unlike the temperament of other children. For Lovecraft was not the normal, happy little boy he appeared to be on the surface. He was in many ways as unnatural as the changelings he would later write about in his story "Pickman's Model," who were inserted into the cribs of unsuspecting families in place of normal infants. His inherent strangeness was unprepared to cope with the steadily accumulating shocks of his young life.

The first such shock was the removal of his father to the insane asylum. Under other circumstances this might have proved devastating, but it happened when he was only two years old, and the immediate consequences were all positive, from his childish point of view. He went from relative poverty to a life of luxury, from having only his mother fuss over him to being the center of an entire mansion full of adoring adults. His mother probably did her best at the time to conceal her distress from her young son. He was later told that his father had suffered a stroke due to the mental strain of overwork, and he believed it. So young a child would not have been in a position to consider the more sinister explanation of syphilis.

The first true black cloud on the clear horizons of Little Sunshine's life came in the form of his grandmother's death in 1896, which plunged the entire Phillips household into mourning. For Lovecraft, the transformation in his private world must have been apocalyptic. Overnight, all the smiles turned to tears. No longer was he the center of attention every minute of the day. The adults ignored him as they talked amongst themselves in hushed voices. The house went into mourning, which at the end of the nineteenth century was no small transformation. Everyone was forced by custom to wear black for an extended period of time, both before and after the funeral. The house itself would have been draped in black crêpe, with various other symbols of death such as a wreath hung in conspicuous places.

The effect of this transformation on the hyper-impressionable five-year-old Lovecraft was profound. Robie had kept her distance from the child, which was not uncommon for women of her social class during that period of history—she never shared her interest in astronomy with Lovecraft by taking him outside under the night sky and pointing out the constellations—but in spite of this emotional distance, which lessened the severity of his grief, he sucked up the general funeral atmosphere of the house like a poison. Twenty years later he would write in a letter, "the death of my grandmother plunged the household into a gloom from which it never fully recovered. The black attire of my mother and aunts terrified and repelled me to such an extent that I would surreptitiously pin bits of bright cloth or paper to their skirts for sheer relief."[1]

There is something infinitely pathetic about this small child's attempt to recapture the world he had lost, a world that until his grandmother's death he must have assumed that he controlled with absolute authority. Suddenly, it had changed beyond recognition, and there was nothing he could do to return it to its former condition. The death occurred in the bleakness of winter, on January 26. Although it was the custom not to place the corpse into the ground when the earth was frozen and covered with snow, around the beginning of February there would have been a service at the funeral home with Lovecraft in attendance, and it seems probable that he would have been shown the Phillips' family plot in Swan Point Cemetery where the corpse was to be conveyed.

There is nothing quite like an old New England graveyard for weird atmosphere of the Charles Addams variety. Lovecraft must have viewed with awe the stone angels, ornate carvings, wrought-iron railings, naked windblown trees, and the varied shapes of the gravestones and crypts. At any rate, the shock of his grandmother's death had rendered his mind receptive, opening it to accept profound new impressions, and this was the impression it was given. Little wonder that a few short months later he would embrace as an antidote to this winter melancholy the stories and poetry of Greek mythology.

A more direct consequence of his grandmother's death was the nightmares. They began while the house was still in mourning, and continued with varying degrees of intensity throughout the remainder of his life, although their content would change over time. Gone forever was Little Sunshine, stolen away by shadows. The earliest nightmares of the frightened and bewildered five-year-old boy that was left in his place concerned a species of flying horror made all of darkness. Lovecraft wrote in a letter, "And then it was that my former high spirits received their damper. I began to have nightmares of the most hideous description, peopled with things I called 'night-gaunts'—a compound word of my own coinage."[2]

Lovecraft suspected that the night-gaunts might have been suggested to his impressionable mind by an engraving by Gustave Doré in an illustrated deluxe edition of Milton's *Paradise Lost*, which he had come across not long before the nightmares began. The image to which he referred shows the black silhouette of a bat-winged Lucifer falling from the starry night sky to the globe of the world far below. Lovecraft described these night-gaunts as lean, black, and rubbery to the touch, with barbed tails, horns, and bat-like wings. Their most horrifying feature was their complete lack of faces. In effect, they were living shadows.

We can only imagine what Carl Jung might have made of them, drawn up as they were from the deepest abyss of young Lovecraft's subconscious. Jung wrote: "Filling the conscious mind with ideal conceptions is a characteristic feature of Western theosophy, but not the confrontation with the shadow and the world of darkness. One does not become enlightened by imagining figures of light, but by making the darkness conscious. The latter procedure, however, is disagreeable and therefore not popular."[3]

The nightmares of living darkness varied in their details, but the general content was always the same. The night-gaunts, who came in flocks of up to fifty at a time, tickled Lovecraft's stomach as he lay in bed, before seizing Lovecraft out of his bed by the stomach and lifting him into the gray air while they pinched and poked him. They carried him into the sky, playfully flinging him from one to the other like a rag doll so that Lovecraft feared at every moment that he would tumble down to his death. They did this silently, for they had no voices. As he passed over the landscape so far below, Lovecraft glimpsed the towers of "dead and horrible cities" unlike any in the waking world. Toward the end of the dream Lovecraft found himself carried high above a mountain range of closely clustered mountains with needle-sharp peaks that thrust upward menacingly. Then the night-gaunts abruptly dropped him, so that he tumbled and fell for miles through the air, faster and faster with every passing moment—but just before his body was impaled on one of these sharp peaks, Lovecraft awoke.

This repeating nightmare, as childish as it may seem to an adult, terrified Lovecraft to such an extent that he did everything in his power to avoid falling asleep. Of course this attempt proved futile. Night after night they came, snatching him from his bed and carrying him far away to release him high above the threatening peaks. Lovecraft gained the conviction, he knew not from where, that these creatures lived in burrows that honeycombed a high mountain in some unknown region. These nightmares continued to plague him for a full five years. Other terrifying dreams would mingle with the nightmares of the night-gaunts, and other horrors would eventually replace them, but no nightmares Lovecraft would ever suffer throughout the rest of his life would fill him with such complete and abject fear.

When his father, Winfield Lovecraft, finally died on July 19 of 1898, the emotional impact on the seven-year-old boy must have been much less than the shock of his grandmother's passing two years before, since he had not seen his father during the entire period of his institutionalization at Butler Hospital. The viewing of the corpse, if indeed the morticians were able to render his father's syphilis-ravaged face presentable through the use of cosmetics and wax, would have been for Lovecraft the viewing of a stranger only dimly relatable to a few memory vignettes. In death, Winfield Lovecraft proved to be a better provider than he had been in life—he left his wife an estate of ten thousand dollars.[4] He was buried in the Phillips' grave plot at Swan Point Cemetery. Whipple Phillips would probably have preferred that it were otherwise, but he wished to protect the feelings of his daughter and grandson, and to avoid scandal. This time the ceremony had a summer backdrop of green grass and softly rustling leaves, but the gravestones around the family plot would have seemed more familiar to Lovecraft than the face of his own father.

The family deaths in Lovecraft's early life all seem to mark transitions in his interior mental topography. The death of his grandmother was followed by his nightmares of the night-gaunts and his discovery of Greek mythology. The death of his father was followed not long after by the first of what may be called, for want of a better term, his mental episodes, and the discovery of Edgar Allan Poe. Lovecraft would later describe the first mental episode as a "near-breakdown,"[5] but he never specified its details, so it is difficult to determine what it may have signified. Another "near-breakdown" occurred in 1900, but what may have provoked the second episode remains unclear.

In the autumn of 1898, at the late age of eight years, he began to attend the Slater Avenue primary school. Lovecraft later wrote of this event, "Hitherto it had been deemed unwise to subject so irritable and sensitive a child to discipline of any sort."[6] He was placed in the highest grade, and had little difficulty coping academically due to his facility with reading and writing and his prior studies. However, his attitude was what might be described as abysmal. Lovecraft's attendance at school during the 1898–99 year was spotty; and on those days he deigned to go to school at all, he punctuated his presence with sneering arguments with his teachers.

It must be concluded that Lovecraft was a spoiled rich brat, accustomed to getting his own way in all things, and to doing whatever he liked, any time and any way he wanted to do it. He admitted as much himself later in life in his letters. "Being a 'spoiled child' I had but to ask, and it was mine,"[7] he wrote to his friend Alfred Galpin. To J. Vernon Shea he confessed, "The fact is, I was actually spoiled—having just about everything I wanted."[8]

The shock of that first year of school was the emotional equivalent of the *Titanic* running into the iceberg. With supreme arrogance and certainty of his own superiority over his teachers and fellow students, Lovecraft refused to change his ways. As a result, he was not in attendance at Slater Avenue when school resumed in the fall of 1899. Lovecraft biographer L. Sprague de Camp wrote, "Whatever the reason—neurotic illness, bullying, his mother's frantic over-protectiveness, or some combination of these—he was taken out of school."[9]

Lovecraft's rebellion against his teachers at the Slater Avenue primary school might be put down to excessive authoritarian zeal on the part of the teachers, as Lovecraft later asserted, were it not for his inability to accept the authority of his Baptist Sunday school teachers. At around this time he was placed in the Sunday school class at the First Baptist Meeting House, not far from the Phillips mansion on College Hill. The Bible lessons he was taught made no sense to his young mind, and he felt scant reluctance at pointing out their logical shortcomings to his teachers, nor at asking disruptive and even impertinent questions during class. It was soon agreed that the best course would be to exempt young Lovecraft from Sunday school entirely.

Of his Sunday school expulsion, Lovecraft later wrote, "The absurdity of the myths I was called upon to accept, and the sombre greyness of the whole faith compared with the Eastern magnificence of Mahometanism, made me definitely an agnostic; and caused me to become so pestiferous a questioner that I was permitted to discontinue attendance."[10] In rosy retrospective interpretation, Lovecraft casts himself in the role of the bold seeker of truth unintimidated by ignorant authority, but the reality is a bit more prosaic—that of a spoiled brat who would not sit and listen with the rest of the children, but was so disruptive in classes that he was permitted to leave and not asked to return.

Clearly, the problem lay not with the schools, nor with the teachers, but with Lovecraft. Lovecraft did not attend school at all from 1899 to 1901. In the midst of this three-year hiatus he suffered his second "near-breakdown" about which we know so little. How much of the decision not to force the boy to go to school was based on his mother's concern about his mental health, and how much was due to Lovecraft's own willful arrogance, may only be conjectured. Another attempt was made to send Lovecraft to school in the fall of 1902, but it met with similar unfortunate results. The boy who thinks he knows everything learns nothing. Lovecraft must have been completely impossible to teach.

Later in life, Lovecraft would claim that he had detested the rigid and, as it seemed to him, arbitrary system of authority that was imposed at the Slater Avenue school, and rebelled against his teachers by being surly and sardonic toward them. The reality seems much less Promethean. Lovecraft, the spoiled grandson of a wealthy and powerful industrialist, was accustomed to getting his own way in everything, and simply did not enjoy being told what to do. In this rebellion he was abetted by his childhood friend Chester Pierce Munroe (1889–1943), who allowed Lovecraft to lead him down the garden path to similar acts of smirking disobedience.

The two closest and virtually the only friends Lovecraft had as a child were Chester Munroe and his brother Harold Bateman Munroe (1891–1966), who lived some four blocks away from Lovecraft's house and attended the Slater Avenue school. It was at school during the fall of 1902 that Lovecraft first met them. He called this relationship with the Munroe brothers "my only childhood friendship."[11] He does not seem to have classified the other children who helped him to construct his little play world of New Anvik as friends, by his own definition, so it must be presumed that he thought of them merely as acquaintances, or perhaps as day laborers.

Biographers of Lovecraft have asserted that his childhood was happy, but to form only one friendship (Lovecraft thought of the Munroe brothers as a unit) is not the sign of a happy childhood. Indeed, when writing of his early childhood prior to attending school, Lovecraft remarked, "You will notice that I have made no reference to childish friends and playmates—I had none! The children I knew disliked me, and I disliked them."[12]

He did not attend Slater Avenue when school began the following autumn, but instead received private instruction. Whipple Phillips was a wealthy man, and even though that wealth showed signs of declining, enough of it remained for him to hire private tutors for Lovecraft over the 1903–04 school year. It will not surprise anyone to learn that Lovecraft had disputes with his tutors and harbored bitterness toward them. One of them was named A. P. May. As biographer S. T. Joshi relates, on January 3, 1904, a mock advertisement was placed in the *Rhode Island Journal* pretending to be by the tutor himself, and seeking employment. In this genuinely petty and poisonous advert, which could rightly be characterized as a libel, May is described as a "10th rate Private Tutor" offering "Low Grade Instruction at High Rates." The advert concludes, in sneering capitals, "HIRE ME. I CAN'T DO THE WORK BUT I NEED THE MONEY."[13] If indeed this advert was placed by Lovecraft, as seems likely, it was probably the single most contemptible thing he ever did.

Throughout these on-again, off-again school years, Lovecraft was troubled by persistent facial grimaces and spasms, which he found himself unable to suppress, try as he might. As Lovecraft put it, "My face was full of unconscious and involuntary motions now and then— and the more I was urged to stop them, the more frequent they became."[14] This problem persisted into adulthood, but was often dormant later in his life. Lovecraft's mother assumed that the condition was caused by ingrown facial hairs.[15] The usual presumption among his biographers is that Lovecraft was exhibiting signs of mental stress, although Joshi speculated that he may have suffered from the physiological disorder known as chorea minor,[16] which was Lovecraft's own opinion. However, chorea minor involves involuntary movements of the entire body and affects speech, and Lovecraft does not seem to have suffered these symptoms. There are two somewhat more esoteric explanations that must be considered.

The first consideration involves psychic receptivity or mediumship—what we today call channeling. It is possible that a spirit was attempting to speak through Lovecraft. When a spirit medium establishes initial contact with a spirit that attempts to communicate through the medium, the body of the medium often undergoes various involuntary physical movements. When communication is attempted by means of the planchette or through automatic writing, these movements are usually in the hands and arms, but when communication is attempted by voice, they initially manifest in the form of facial grimaces and inarticulate sounds, as the spirit seeks to perfect its control of its human host. This is often observed among charismatic

Christians when they "speak in tongues." Although the faithful believe themselves possessed by the Holy Spirit rather than by lesser spiritual beings, the physical phenomena are the same.

These involuntary movements can be subtle or quite violent. The prominent spirit medium of the late eighteenth century, Reverend William Stainton Moses, writing in his 1879 book *Spirit-Identity*, described how his body was conditioned for automatic writing: "My right arm was seized about the middle of the forearm, and dashed violently up and down with a noise resembling that of a number of paviors at work. It was the most tremendous exhibition of 'unconscious muscular action' I ever saw. In vain I tried to stop it. I distinctly felt the grasps, soft and firm, round my arm, and though perfectly possessed of senses and volition, I was powerless to interfere, although my hand was disabled for some days by the bruising it then got."[17]

The second consideration as to the possible source of Lovecraft's facial grimaces has to do with the nature of kundalini energy, an esoteric force sometimes personified as a goddess that feels like electric fire flowing through the nerve channels of the body, once it has been awakened from its sleeping place at the base of the spine. All of those who awaken kundalini fire experience involuntary movements of the body, as the energy, which seems to possess self-awareness, stimulates the body in various places by turns. Such involuntary movements may occur in the limbs or in the face. It is impossible to predict where they will manifest and equally impossible to stop them when they begin to occur. They are usually of relatively brief duration—a period of weeks or months—which would seem to argue against this source for Lovecraft's facial tics, but they may persist longer when the circulation of kundalini in the body is deliberately frustrated.

Both of these esoteric phenomena, the stirring of mediumistic receptivity, and the awakening and circulation of kundalini fire, are connected with suppressed sexual energy. The sexual force that is not permitted to flow forth in the usual way, by the emission of semen, finds other hidden outlets by stimulating latent mediumship, or awakening kundalini fire, the movement of which through the channels of the body is always accompanied by various occult abilities—among them psychic perception.

Lovecraft discovered the mysteries of sex when he was eight years old, by studying illustrated medical books in the Phillips' library. He was not impressed by the human reproductive process, which struck his young mind as vulgar and unpleasant. "The whole matter was reduced to prosaic mechanism—a mechanism which I rather despised or at least thought non-glamorous because of its purely animal nature and separation from such things as intellect and beauty—and all the drama was taken out of it."[18]

In view of his revulsion against sex, it is likely that at least for the early part of his adolescence he attempted to avoid masturbation. This abstinence would have had the effect, unforeseen by Lovecraft, of heightening his mediumistic abilities, and perhaps also of stirring sleeping kundalini fire to life within him, with its accompanying psychic effects.

Persistent involuntary facial tics and grimaces were not the only nervous mental problem that afflicted Lovecraft. From childhood he was tormented by a curious phobia for large, enclosed spaces, such as caverns or concert halls. He described it as a strange combination of claustrophobia (fear of enclosed spaces) and agoraphobia (fear of open spaces). There is actually a name for this fear—*kenophobia*, the fear of voids or empty spaces. This may be one reason so many of his horror stories involve subterranean gulfs and caves. The concept of a hollow Earth, which he probably encountered during his Theosophical studies later in life, must have terrified him. In his story "The Mound," three vast gulfs are described beneath the Oklahoma plains, one atop the other, each cavern large enough to contain an entire alien civilization with its cities and temples. Merely to think of descending into these underground open spaces would have chilled Lovecraft's blood.

Another medical affliction Lovecraft suffered was an inability to endure cold. Whether this was physical or psychological is difficult to judge. If it had its roots in Lovecraft's imagination, it manifested itself in his flesh. When he was forced to endure temperatures below 20°F, he lapsed into unconsciousness. His cryophobia, or fear of the cold, would later find expression in his short story "Cool Air." Again, in this tale we see Lovecraft externalizing his childhood fears, as a way of gaining at least a temporary control over them. When he came to write his novel *The Dream-Quest of Unknown Kadath*, he would externalize his greatest childhood terror, the night-gaunts, who in the novel are made allies of the protagonist Randolph Carter, Lovecraft's alter ego.

As much as the death of his grandmother Robie Phillips had shaken young Lovecraft, and taught him the meaning of mourning and loss, nothing could have prepared him for the death of his grandfather, whose passing shattered the boy's entire world into jagged shards that were destined never to be reassembled. Whipple Van Buren Phillips may have been a hard man with whom to do business, but he was an indulgent surrogate father to Lovecraft, who gave the boy the physical expressions of affection he had failed to receive from his cooler and more distant grandmother, and was receiving less often from his mother.

Whipple died on March 28, 1904, of what was then called an apoplectic stroke, otherwise known as a cerebral hemorrhage. He had been visiting at the house of a political associate on a Sunday evening when the stroke hit him. He was carried home to the Phillips mansion, where he died shortly after midnight on Monday morning. Lovecraft was only thirteen years old. Stress had been building within the old man for years, as he watched his once prosperous business empire slowly erode away, forcing him to cut back on his expenditures. In 1899 he had jumped into what he then thought was a golden investment opportunity, and in concert with a group of business partners founded the Owyhee Land and Irrigation Company. The greater bulk of his holdings went into keeping the company alive. How could he have foreseen the spring flood of 1904 that destroyed the company's only significant asset, its irrigation canal? This natural disaster wiped out the last of the Phillips fortune, and it occurred only a few weeks prior to the old man's fatal stroke.

When Whipple had been decently buried in the family plot at Swan Point Cemetery, and the proceeds of the will read, the other members of the family discovered that their once-great fortune had dwindled to a mere $25,000, of which Susie Lovecraft received $5,000 and young Howard got $1,500.[19] Lovecraft also inherited his grandfather's gun collection, though it is difficult to imagine a member of the family less suited to make use of them, since he was averse to killing any living animal. He eventually ended up giving all the guns away, apart from a flintlock musket that he kept as an ornament. The painful decision was made by the three sisters and their brother to sell the family mansion at 454 Angell Street. Susie resigned herself to moving into a five-room apartment that made up the first floor of a somewhat smaller house at 598 Angell Street, where she had the use of the attic for storage and access to the cellar.

Lovecraft's uncle Edwin had been married since July 30, 1894, and was living in his own house, so he was not directly involved with this move up the street, other than to help them carry the furniture. Susie's older sister, Lillian, had married Franklin Chase Clark, a medical doctor and amateur poet, on April 10, 1902, and was living with her husband. Her younger sister, Annie Emeline Phillips (1866–1941), had married Edward F. Gamwell on June 3, 1897, and was living in Cambridge, Massachusetts, where Edward worked as a newspaper editor. Lovecraft's mother must have felt truly alone for the first time in her life.

Lovecraft tried to continue on as though nothing had changed. He carefully rebuilt his fantasy village of New Anvik in the empty lot next to the new house, but it was not the same. Secretly, Lovecraft vowed that one day he would earn enough money to buy back the family mansion, so that it would remain in the Phillips name. This juvenile dream was destined never even to approach realization. Overnight, Lovecraft went from being very rich to being relatively poor, at least by the standards of his former lifestyle, and he grew progressively poorer for the remainder of his life, so that by the time of his death he was suffering a genuine poverty the likes of which he could not even have imagined in early boyhood.

He must have noticed an immediate change in the attitude of his neighbors and playmates, and even in the way he was treated by their servants. The whims and affectations of the grandson of a wealthy business owner may be laughed off as harmless eccentricities, particularly when the boy stands to inherit a fortune one day, but those same affectations will find a much less tolerant reception when they are exhibited by the fatherless child of a widow with a declining income and no prospects for the future. For the first time, but not the last, Lovecraft began to entertain serious thoughts of committing suicide. The notion of oblivion attracted him, but he found himself repelled by the sheer untidiness involved in the various ways he could think of to terminate his life. Drowning appealed most to him, but he finally decided against it.

The years between his grandfather's death in 1904 and his five-year-long nervous collapse beginning in 1908 must have seemed to Lovecraft like a slow descent into hell. His world had been turned upside down by the absence of Whipple Phillips' steady guidance, the loss of the family fortune, the move from the Phillips mansion—and in the fall of 1904, Lovecraft entered his first year at Hope Street High School. The ordeal of high school is difficult for anyone, but for those who are odd in their speech or behavior, who have eccentric affectations, who put on airs of superiority, and, to top it off, who suffer from bizarre facial grimaces, high school is a thousand times more painful, and usually ends up scarring the psyche for the rest of that person's life.

The other teenagers quickly adopted a nickname for Lovecraft—they took to calling him "Lovey." Lovecraft did not dwell in detail on incidents of bullying in his letters, but he did mention that he was involved in some rough fistfights during the first year of high school, most of which he lost. His tactic was to glare murderously at his opponent and scream, "By God, I'll kill you!"[20] Perhaps physical bullying was less common in Providence at the start of the twentieth century than it is in most places today. Mental and emotional bullying, however, would have been inevitable and unceasing. Lovecraft responded by adopting an attitude of indifference. He trained himself to regard the other teenagers as alien beings with whom he had nothing of importance in common, and took to observing their activities the way a scientist would observe microbes in a petri dish. This did not endear him to his schoolmates.

Given his revulsion against human sexuality, his indifference toward music, his positive dislike of dancing, his odd mannerisms, and his outsider attitude, it is more or less to be expected that he had no girlfriends. It has been suggested that he was at least latently a homosexual, but this is not supported by his lifelong hostility toward homosexuality, at least in the abstract—he knew several homosexuals during his life and does not seem to have had too much difficulty getting along with them on a personal level. Perhaps he was a suppressed homosexual, but it seems more likely that he was merely asexual—that he had so successfully turned his mind away from sexual affairs that the normal erotic impulse within him was unusually weak. This sublimated sexual energy had to go somewhere, and as we shall see in future chapters, it went into mediumistic sensitivity and artistic creativity.

The year 1904 was made more difficult by the unexplained disappearance of Lovecraft's pet black cat, Nigger-Man, which he had raised from a kitten. All his life Lovecraft had an intense love for cats. The loss of his childhood pet struck him hard. It must have seemed to him just another part of the conspiracy of the Fates to deprive him of everything he had ever loved. He withdrew from Hope Street High School at the end of the term. The usual reason was given—weakness of health—but we may suspect that Lovecraft found the necessity to interact on a social level with other teenagers taxing, particularly due to his fallen economic status, and it may have led to psychosomatic problems. There really does not seem to have been much wrong with Lovecraft's physical health when he was a young man, other than self-indulgence—he never exercised, and he enjoyed candy more than solid food. His various maladies and weaknesses arose from mental stress.

From an academic standpoint Lovecraft did not do badly during his first year of high school. He actually found himself enjoying the subjects and respecting his teachers. With an average mark of 81, his best subject was Latin, his worst algebra, although he discovered that he could handle geometry due to its visual nature. His difficulty in grasping the principles of algebra worried and vexed him, since he knew that a sound knowledge of it was required if he was to pursue his intention to become a professional astronomer. Lovecraft had grown accustomed to having academic subjects come easily. His memory was uncommonly strong, and this aided him in learning such subjects as Latin and history, subjects for which a strong memory is required, but a good memory alone is useless when it comes to solving algebraic problems. Lovecraft discovered to his dismay that he really was not mathematically minded.

Lovecraft skipped the school year that began in the fall of 1905. The usual cause was given, that his nervous condition made it impossible for him to attend classes. If adolescent social difficulties were the underlying reason, nothing was written about them by Lovecraft. When he resumed his schooling in the fall of 1906, he was nicknamed "the Professor" by his fellow students. It had become known at the school that his articles on astronomy were being published in professional newspapers. This earned him a measure of respect, or, at least, pigeonholed him as a bookworm, a stereotype comprehensible to his classmates. Again, he did well academically. His best subject this year was physics, his worst was again algebra, but even so, he passed it.

The school year beginning in the fall of 1907 was his last year of formal education. Although he would later claim to have earned his high school diploma, the reality was that he left school in the spring of 1908 with two years remaining in the usual schedule. Naturally, this meant that he was ineligible to attend Brown University, and could not train to become a professional astronomer. Lovecraft himself laid the blame on algebra. In a letter to Robert E. Howard, he wrote:

> In studies I was not bad—except for mathematics, which repelled and exhausted me. I passed in these subjects—but just about that. Or rather, it was *algebra* which formed the bugbear. Geometry was not so bad. But the whole thing disappointed me bitterly, for I was then intending to pursue *astronomy* as a career, and of course advanced astronomy is simply a mass of mathematics. That was the first major set-back I ever received—the first time I was ever brought up short against a consciousness of my own limitations. It was clear to me that I hadn't the brains enough to be an astronomer—and that was a pill I couldn't swallow with equanimity.[21]

His dropping out of high school in 1908 was precipitated by a total nervous collapse that initiated the most mysterious—indeed, it might be called the weirdest—period in Lovecraft's entire life, five full years of withdrawal from human society during which he essentially lived as a hermit, receiving no one as a visitor, talking to nobody if he could avoid it, sleeping during the daylight hours or puttering around behind drawn window blinds, and leaving the house to wander the deserted streets alone by night. A neighbor who was a little girl at the time later remembered that he would suddenly appear in the darkness on Angell Street, walking with quick steps, never looking to the side or responding to those he passed. "His appearance always frightened me. He was certainly the neighborhood mystery. He would never speak to any of us, but kept right on with his head down."[22]

Lovecraft tried to make himself invisible. No doubt his passage on the streets elicited snide remarks and insults from those he habitually ignored, which would have pained his sensitive nature no matter how much he pretended otherwise. A trolley ride downtown became a torture to him that he could barely endure. Writing about himself in the third person, he later remarked on this hiatus in his life, "In those middle years, the poor devil was such a nervous wreck that he hated to speak to any human being, or even to see or be seen by one; and every trip to town was an ordeal."[23]

The prevailing characteristic to notice about this period in Lovecraft's life is his intense sensitivity. Interactions that would seem casual to most individuals caused him mental and emotional pain that was so intense, it was almost physical. De Camp mentions several odd fears, such as a hypersensitivity to strong smells, an aversion to loud noises, and fear of being in a crowd.[24] Lovecraft once confided to Donald Wandrei that he had feared the sea from the age of two years.[25] He did the only thing he could do—he withdrew from such interactions. It seems probable to me that his suppressed sexuality heightened this sensitivity. It was also responsible, at least in part, for his increasingly strange and involved dreams, which had progressed beyond the night-gaunts to visions of dream cities that Lovecraft seemed to fly over like a bird.

It was at this time that he started to become morbidly self-conscious about his appearance. This was not solely due to his involuntary facial grimaces. His mother had taken to remarking to a neighbor, Clara L. Hess, about his facial deformity—which was a bit odd since Lovecraft did not have a facial deformity. True, he was not handsome in the usual sense of the term. His chin was too long, his mouth compressed, his ears prominent, but he was hardly deformed. He also developed the conviction that his spine had assumed a permanent curvature due to his nightly astronomy sessions at the telescope of Ladd Observatory. No such curvature is evident in photographs of him.

Lovecraft's reduced writing output during this period consisted mainly of unmemorable poetry written in the eighteenth-century style of Gray and Warton, and dry works on the sciences such as the more or less valueless 1910 text *A Brief Course in Inorganic Chemistry*. He gradually ceased his scientific studies, which were in any case going nowhere. For a time he continued playing with beakers and burners in his makeshift chemistry lab in the basement of the house at 598 Angell Street, but he was unable to focus his mind. Among his many complaints, he suffered from migraines: "I found myself so wretchedly bored that I positively could not study for more than fifteen minutes without acquiring an excruciating headache for the rest of the day."[26]

At last, in 1912, he dismantled the lab at his mother's request—she was afraid he would poison himself or blow up the house. Around the same time he stopped climbing the hill to Ladd Observatory at night to peer through the university telescope. Without the prospect of a university degree, his plan of becoming a professional astronomer was dead, and he knew it.

No biographer of Lovecraft has ever offered a convincing explanation as to why he would feel compelled to withdraw from the world so completely, for such a protracted period of time, and subsist in what he described as an almost vegetative condition. In many ways his response was similar to that of shell-shocked soldiers in the First World War, who after returning home could only tolerate dim light and quiet environments. But as to what horrific event might have provoked this vulnerable condition, there is no evidence. Lovecraft himself did not know what caused it, or if he did know he kept silent. The nervous collapse, which was no "near collapse" in this case, seems to have arisen cumulatively over the period beginning with the death of Whipple Phillips in the spring of 1904 and ending with Lovecraft's withdrawal from high school in the spring of 1908.

We may speculate that in part it was due to Lovecraft's final realization that all his dreams had turned to dust. He would not go on to become the cultured English gentleman of the Lord Dunsany mold because there was no money. He would not assume the family business because it no longer existed. He would not retire gracefully to the Phillips mansion because the mansion had been sold out from under his feet. He would not become a respected professor of astronomy at Brown University because his mind was too weak for mathematics. All those he loved most, apart from his mother, had one by one died or moved away. His few boyhood friends and acquaintances were progressing to more mature pursuits, such as competition amongst themselves for the attention of girls, while he was just beginning to come to the realization that he could no longer spend idle days playing in the dirt in his own little fantasy world in the vacant lot beside his house.

At least some of the motivation for his withdrawal from other people in his community was a burning sense of shame. He did not feel that he could hold his head up and look others in the eye with whom he had associated in more optimistic times. Some years later, he would write to a correspondent about his former schoolmates at Hope Street High School, "The only persons who could now be real friends are those who never knew me in my days of high hope and expansive ambition . . . I do not hate or envy my old acquaintances—I merely wish to sink out of their sight if I cannot shew some achievements to match theirs."[27]

Over the course of this five-year period of complete withdrawal from human society, Lovecraft's well-known eccentricities were cultivated. The list of Lovecraft's personal affectations would be a long one, but here we may take note of some of the more prominent curiosities in his behavior.

He suffered from a pervasive lethargy that made it difficult for him to move from his bed, or concentrate his mind on any work that did not awaken his imagination. As a result, he spent much of the day sleeping in bed, or lying around the house in his "dressing gown and slippers."[28] For example, in 1911 when he and his mother were invited to Thanksgiving dinner at the house of his Aunt Lillian, he left a note the night before for his mother to find in the morning instructing her to go on without him, because he wanted to sleep late. Characteristically, the note was written in verse.[29] Earlier that same year, on his twenty-first birthday, in spite of his aversion to trolley cars or perhaps because of it, he had spent the entire day riding aimlessly around Providence on the trolleys, sitting alone on the seats staring out the windows and brooding about his life.

During this reclusive period, he began to speak and write like an educated Englishman of the eighteenth century. Indeed, he became an English gentleman insofar as it was within his power. Part of this affectation was expressed in a disinclination to do any manual labor, as such labor was, in Lovecraft's opinion, beneath the dignity of a gentleman. Another aspect of this mania was his repugnance at the thought of accepting money for his writings—gentlemen did not write for money. His astronomy columns were given away for free, not sold, to the newspapers that published them. This would have been fine, had he actually been a gentleman with a gentleman's estate, but he was an increasingly impoverished New Englander with strange ideas and no prospects.

Although Lovecraft vigorously denied any belief in reincarnation, he thought of himself as displaced in time, a man born out of his natural and proper historical period, and he did his best to remedy that error of Fate by speaking and writing archaically. This affectation of style greatly hindered the acceptance of his writings later in life, and it was many years before he finally shook off the worst of it, although he never truly embraced a modern writing style. He became obsessed with old things—old buildings, old streets, old furniture, old books, old graveyards with old gravestones, genealogical records, diaries from the Colonial period.

Around this time he began to worry about madness, specifically the state of his own sanity. His father had lost his mind, and lately his mother had begun to show signs of emotional and mental instability. She would latch onto strange notions and could not be persuaded to abandon them. It was still a few years before she started to see hallucinations, as her husband had done in the Chicago hotel room in 1893, but Lovecraft must have known that her mind was not quite right. He brooded on the dangers of marriage between first cousins, as his grandparents Robie and Whipple had been, and the damage such a union might do to the minds of the progeny. If both his father and his mother suffered from madness, what did that say about his own prospects for retaining his sanity?

As we know today, Lovecraft had little to worry about from a genetic standpoint. Marriage between first cousins is unlikely to produce serious genetic defects. At the time, this was not understood, and the problems that were seen to arise from multigenerational inbreeding, a not uncommon occurrence in the rural villages of New England that would frequently be mentioned in Lovecraft's stories, were also assumed to plague, to a lesser degree, unions between first cousins.

Lovecraft was close to his mother, but it was a love-hate relationship on her part. Gone was the maternal devotion she had showered upon him as an infant, replaced by a distance and a strangeness of manner. Susie did not like human contact, particularly not from her son. There were no displays of affection between them, such as hugs or kisses on the cheek. Lovecraft referred to his mother as a "touch-me-not."[30] This distance between mother and child was not uncommon for the time—his grandmother Robie had also held him at arm's length, even when he was Little Sunshine—but his mother had begun to express distaste, even revulsion, toward him. Perhaps in part she was simply disappointed by his abnormal behavior and failure to advance in the world as he approached adulthood.

The most curious of Lovecraft's many affectations was his conviction that he was an old man in a young man's body. He took to referring to himself as "grandpa" and used similar epithets for himself signifying age. He sometimes referred to his aunts as "my darling daughter" or "my dear grandchild."[31] He adopted the mannerisms of an older man—this may be one reason his high-school nickname was changed from Lovey to the Professor. As already mentioned, he was convinced that his spine was curved and tended to walk with a stoop to his shoulders, although he could straighten up when he wished. He wore his father's old suits, ties, shirts and other apparel, and shunned modern fashions in hairstyles and clothing.

The hiatus from 1908 to 1914 is the most important period in Lovecraft's life. It served as the crucible in which Lovecraft, the creative artist, was forged. It provided him with the solitude and the distance from human society that allowed him to develop in his own unique and bizarre fashion. As I wrote at the opening of this chapter, Lovecraft was never normal. His idiosyncrasies were so deeply ingrained that he was simply incapable of abandoning them in the face of intense social pressures to do so. As a consequence, they would undoubtedly have killed him had he not been able to withdraw for these years and construct a kind of rationalization for his conflicting inclinations and beliefs that he could live with.

What Lovecraft did during these five years of solitude was erect a scaffolding that allowed the two aspects of his personality—the hard-nosed rationalist and the impressionistic visionary—to coexist without ever actually interacting. It was necessary for Lovecraft to denigrate and diminish the importance of his dream visions, if only to gain the illusion of some degree of distance from them, but at the same time it was necessary for him to write them down and dwell upon them in his fiction, in order to control them. Lovecraft was both attracted by these dreams and terrified of them. He felt that to become lost in them was to be consumed by them, but yet he could not simply ignore them because they held too much meaning, too much power.

How long his period of withdrawal might have endured, or whether it would have reached its natural termination in Lovecraft's suicide, we will never know, since it was interrupted by a discovery that gave Lovecraft the direction for his adult life. Seemingly by accident, he found that his writings could be used as a social bridge to reach out to the rest of the human race. As we shall see, while he found face-to-face interactions painful, he came to enjoy the distance and control he was able to achieve through the words flowing from his Waterman fountain pen. Phoenix-like, Lovecraft the amateur writer rose from the ashes of the dead dream of Lovecraft the professional scientist.

3.

WEIRD TALES

I t is difficult to adequately describe how antisocial Lovecraft was at this stage in his young adult life. For five years he lived in almost complete solitude with his conceits, affectations, and prejudices, allowing no outside observer to criticize his odd behavior or his often extreme opinions. When anyone tried to get through to him, he withdrew behind the drawn shades of the ground-level apartment at 598 Angell Street, aided and enabled in his misanthropy by his mentally unstable mother. In this unhealthy hothouse environment evolved a singularly bizarre and malformed blossom. He was not only convinced of his own racial and cultural superiority over most of the other citizens of Providence, and indeed of the entire human species, but he was also determined to point out this difference and correct the errors and shortcomings of mankind using witty but archaic English that had not been in fashion for two centuries.

Lovecraft found a lot wrong with the world on which he had turned his back. He despised blacks, Asians, Arabs, Jews, Mexicans, Italians, the Irish, Poles—indeed virtually everyone whose heritage was not Anglo-Saxon. He was unhappy with American immigration policies, with the ethnic groups living in Providence, and with socialist

ideology in general. He hated immigrants not only for what he perceived to be their tainted blood, but also for their evil appearance, the
harsh sound of their languages, their vulgar manner of dress, rude behavior, foul odors, discordant ethnic music, and un-English attitudes.
His first published poetry, sixty-two lines of heroic couplets titled
"Providence in 2000 AD," appeared in the March 4, 1912, issue of the
Evening Bulletin newspaper, in which he mocked the efforts of the Ital-
ian community in the Federal Hill slums to have the name of one of
the streets of his beloved Providence changed from Atwells Avenue to
Columbus Avenue. He was a strong advocate of Teutonic supremacy,
and in later years would admire Hitler and the Nazi Party. Another
of Lovecraft's less shining moments as a human being came in 1913,
when he composed a poem entitled "The Creation of Niggers," in
which he compared black people to apes.[1]

It is useful to place Lovecraft's virulent racism into the context of
his period and social class. Today it would be looked upon as deplor-
able, but at the beginning of the twentieth century it was the norm
among white New Englanders. Lovecraft may have been a bit more
vehement than his neighbors, but he wasn't saying or writing anything
about blacks, Jews, and immigrants that would have aroused wide-
spread condemnation, or even raised many eyebrows. The name he
chose for his black cat, Nigger-Man, was not in Lovecraft's mind a racist slur, but a term of affection. He loved that cat as much as he loved
any human being. Such terms were not considered highly offensive, or
even particularly derogatory, by those who used them. For example,
when Agatha Christie, the renowned English writer of mystery novels, came to title her latest novel of 1939, she called it *Ten Little Niggers*,
and it was published in November of that year under this title in the
United Kingdom.[2] The island on which Christie's story takes place was
called in the novel Nigger Island. Bear in mind, this was two years after
Lovecraft's death.

Another of Lovecraft's more bizarre antisocial affectations that matured during his five-year withdrawal from society was his frequent expression of regret to his fellow countrymen that the United States was no longer ruled by the British crown. He regarded it as a great misfortune that America had gained independence. In a letter written in 1922 he referred to "the lamented rebellion of the colonies, with the unfortunate victory of the rebels and the succession of all His Majesty's Dominions south of Canada."[3] It was his hope that in some future age England and America could once again be united under the British monarchy. Whether those who listened to this crackpot opinion were more offended or amused by it can only be conjectured. They probably regarded it as an artifact of his consuming mania for the eighteenth century.

Over the course of the five-year withdrawal into solitude that followed his nervous collapse in 1908, Lovecraft gradually came to accept that he was not destined for the life of a professor of astronomy at Brown University. He found it impossible to study science due to his growing boredom with the subject. He later confessed, "I wanted the glamour and mystery and impressiveness of the sciences without their hard work."[4] He turned his active interest away from chemistry and astronomy, instead focusing most of his mental energies on fantasy in the form of escapist reading. Lovecraft devoured voraciously all manner of literature, from the Bible and Shakespeare to what L. Sprague de Camp called the "precursors of the so-called pulp magazines" with their bright covers and lurid adventure yarns. Lovecraft bought and read *The Argosy, All-Story Magazine*, and *Cavalier*.[5] He particularly enjoyed *All-Story Magazine* because it tended to publish fantasy and horror stories.

He felt somewhat embarrassed to have developed such a liking for magazine fiction, but nonetheless he drank it in with the fervor of a man dying of thirst in the desert. In the nights his ceaseless craving for the strange and uncanny was nourished by his unnaturally vivid dreams, and during the days it was fed by the fantasy fiction of the pre-pulps. As he read the magazines, he must have thought to himself that he could write better stories than these—and indeed, he could write better stories, as he demonstrated when he finally got around to doing so. But at this early stage in his life, when he was just entering man-hood, the realization that writing weird stories was the thing he could do best in all the world had not yet dawned on him. He was more concerned with proving himself as a literary critic, a poet, and a social satirist who defended the virtues of all things English and condemned the rest of the human race in archaic rhyming couplets.

He had already produced in 1908 a passably good horror story, "The Alchemist," which ranks among his adult works, although it is not considered one of his best efforts. It was written just at the onset of his five-year retreat into himself. This story would not see first pub-lication until 1916, after his withdrawal from the world had run its course. He seems to have written it and then forgotten about it. In his isolated life, there was no one to encourage him to write more prose, no one to suggest to him that his natural genius lay in the composi-tion of weird stories. Lovecraft had to discover this for himself, and as is often the case with solitary artists, the blind spots in his own self-image for many years concealed the obvious.

In the meantime, an indolent Lovecraft amused himself by pen-ning a withering criticism of the love stories by Fred Jackson that ap-peared in *The Argosy*. The letter was published in the September 1913 issue of the magazine, and elicited an angry response from fans of Jackson. Lovecraft's main private irritation with the stories was proba-bly that they were taking up space that might better have been filled by fantasy or supernatural fiction, but he wrote in what he later termed "quaint Queen-Anne prose" and used satirical wit to attack Jackson's competence. "This letter, which was printed in the September number, aroused a veritable tempest of anger amongst the usual readers of the magazine. I was assailed and reviled by innumerable letters, which appeared in the editorial department."[6]

When a reader of *The Argosy* named John Russell responded to Lovecraft's attack on Jackson with a bit of humorous poetry, Lovecraft upped the ante by sending in "a 44-line satire in the manner of Pope's *Dunciad*."[7] This was published in the letters section of the January 1914 issue and created even more anger among readers, who howled for Lovecraft's blood. Lovecraft responded with yet another scathing attack in antique pentameter verse. This went back and forth for a year or so until the editor of *The Argosy* finally informed Lovecraft that he was not going to publish any more of their letters because readers were complaining that they took up too much space in the magazine. The two poetic pugilists got together and composed a final pair of poems for the October 1914 issue, in which they reconciled their differences and bade farewell to readers.[8]

This bit of literary foolishness might have passed unnoticed into history had one of the readers of the magazine not been Edward F. Daas, a resident of Milwaukee, Wisconsin, who happened to be president of the United Amateur Press Association and editor of its magazine, *The United Amateur*. The *Press* in the title of the organization did not refer to newspaper reporting, but to the small printing press. The UAPA was composed of amateur writers who published their own little magazines out of their private funds, and circulated them among their friends and family. Lovecraft had published his first amateur periodical, the *Scientific Gazette*, at the age of eight years using carbon copies, and later the hectograph printing process, so the concept was hardly new to him.

Daas wrote to Lovecraft asking him to join the UAPA, and while on a trip to New York even went so far as to stop and visit Lovecraft in Providence to repeat the invitation. Lovecraft, finding himself with nothing to do at that stage in his life other than think of ways to commit suicide, accepted. He joined the group on April 6, 1914. This was the key turning point of Lovecraft's life. It marked his transition from failed scientist to amateur writer, and set him on the rails of what was to be his future career. He later wrote, "With the advent of the United I obtained a renewed will to live; a renewed sense of existence as other than a superfluous weight; and found a sphere in which I could feel that my efforts were not wholly futile."[9]

Members of the UAPA paid a yearly fee. The convention was held in late July, during which various officials of the organization such as the president, treasurer, editor of the magazine, and so forth were elected. Each member was encouraged to publish his or her own periodical, and to write poems, stories and articles for the periodicals of other members. Copies of the periodicals were exchanged among members by mail. There was no minimum amount of writing or publishing required to remain a member of the UAPA—members were free to write as much or as little as they wished.[10]

Lovecraft embraced the micro-cosmos of amateur publishing in America with enthusiasm. At long last he had found his natural environment. Communicating with other amateur writers by letter correspondence freed him from the self-consciousness and nervousness he always felt when conversing with strangers face to face. The very idea of amateurism—writing not for money but solely for the love of writing—appealed strongly to him. English gentlemen were permitted to have eccentric hobbies as long as they were never profitable, or so proclaimed the stereotype, and Lovecraft was a living embodiment of the cliché of the English gentleman.

In January 1915, he had his first essay published in *The United Amateur*. In April he published the first issue of his own literary periodical to share with other members, *The Conservative*, which eventually ran to thirteen issues. He was appointed to the rather pompously titled position of chairman of the Department of Public Criticism, and was elected in July as first vice-president. It was a case of Lovecraft having an infinite amount of free time on his hands, and the UAPA needing members willing to do the necessary grunt work to keep the organization functioning. He was elected president from 1917–18, and served three terms at various times as official editor of the UAPA.

In 1917 he joined the rival writers' group, the National Amateur Press Association, not because he was defecting from the UAPA but merely in an attempt to draw the two groups more closely together. He served as interim president for the NAPA from November of 1922 until July of 1923, and became a member of the Bureau of Critics for that organization in 1931. Lovecraft contributed a copious and unceasing river of work to amateur journalism from 1914 until 1921, and indeed continued to send forth articles and critical reviews until 1936. At various times he served in an editorial capacity on six amateur periodicals other than his own journal, *The Conservative*. He eventually rose to became the most prominent exponent of amateurism in America. Throughout his life he always regarded himself as an amateur writer, never as a professional.

On April 6, 1917, America at last entered the First World War, which had been raging on in Europe for the previous three years. This precipitated a farce in Lovecraft's life of Chaplinesque proportions. Given his strong feelings about England, Lovecraft felt compelled the following month to go to the recruiting center of the Rhode Island National Guard and enlist in the army. He was worried that he would be rejected as unfit, but much to his amazement he passed the medical exam and the army doctor declared him in perfect health. The questions during the examination made no reference to past mental breakdowns, so he said nothing about them. He was not exactly an eager recruit, but he told himself that he would go to Europe at the first opportunity and that the experience of combat would either kill him or cure him of his neuroses. He fully expected that it would be the former, and regarded enlistment as a act of suicide.

All this was, of course, no more than a fantasy in Lovecraft's mind. He had no real desire or intention to go to war, he merely felt an obligation to make the gesture of enlisting before his name came up in the draft. He returned home from the recruiting office to inform his mother that he was now a soldier, and predictably she became hysterical. What else could Lovecraft have expected? He must have known what her reaction would be. She called in the family doctor, frog-marched her son back down to the recruiting office with the doctor in tow, and demanded that Lovecraft's name be stricken from their books, citing instances of his various mental breakdowns. After some reluctance, the recruiting officer agreed to de-enlist Lovecraft, although the army doctor told Lovecraft that "such an annulment was highly unusual and almost against the regulations of the service."[11]

This farcical affair of Lovecraft the soldier illustrates how completely he was still attached to the skirts of his mother. Bear in mind that he was no callow teenager—in May of 1917 Lovecraft was a man of twenty-six years of age. He could easily have overruled his mother and the family doctor—after all, he had already been enlisted into the army. Instead, he chose to allow Susie to save him from himself. By this rather convoluted and silly exercise in impotence, Lovecraft satisfied his need to at least make a display of being eager to fight for his country, without ever incurring any real risk that he would actually be compelled to follow through on it. If he felt embarrassment at being plucked out of the rough hands of the recruiters and thrust safely back into the folds of his mother's petticoats, he did not indicate it in his subsequent references to the debacle. Not too unhappy with the turn of events, Lovecraft went back to "civilian life, scribbling as of old."[12]

It was through his activities with the UAPA in 1917 that he began to correspond with Samuel Loveman, an amateur poet who worked as a bookseller in Cleveland, Ohio. Lovecraft admired Loveman's poetry. When he noticed that Loveman's membership in the UAPA was about to expire, he renewed it himself on Loveman's behalf. Loveman later became Lovecraft's closest friend in his adult life, even though he was a Jew. Lovecraft remarked at the time to his correspondent Rheinhart Kleiner, "Loveman has become reinstated in the United through me. Jew or not, I am rather proud to be his sponsor."[13] Lovecraft had lost his childhood friend, Chester Munroe, who had moved away to Asheville, North Carolina, and to some extent Loveman served as a replacement.

One of the curious dichotomies of his nature is that although his views on racial and ethnic groups other than his own were virulently bigoted, when engaging in individual human contact he was pleasant and friendly. It would be easy to dismiss this split personality as hypocrisy on Lovecraft's part, but according to those who knew him, it seems to have been sincere. His best friend as an adult, Samuel Loveman, was a Jew, and he ended up marrying a Jewish woman, Sonia H. Greene. He genuinely liked and respected those of other ethnicities when he interacted with them as friends, but at the same time he felt free to say and write the most poisonous collective criticisms of immigrants, blacks, and Jews. In the July 1917 issue of *The Conservative* he wrote, "Race prejudice is a gift of nature, intended to preserve in purity the various divisions of mankind which the ages have evolved."[14]

To the other amateur writers with whom Lovecraft began to interact at clubs and conventions, he must have seemed a queer duck indeed. One of his friends, Alfred Galpin, remarked on "the strange half dead, half arrogant cock of his head weighed down by its enormous jaw, the rather fishy eyes . . ."[15] His skin was deathly pale from his years of sleeping during the day and leaving the house mostly at night. He had the habit of sitting stiffly at meetings, staring straight ahead and only turning to look at another writer when he wished to speak to that person.

This kind of limited interaction is a symptom of Asperger's syndrome, a behavioral handicap that has been called a mild form of autism and that usually afflicts those of higher than average intelligence. It seems to me not at all unlikely that Lovecraft suffered from Asperger's, but in his day the condition would never have been recognized—the syndrome was only first diagnosed by Hans Asperger, a Viennese psychologist, in 1944. Asperger's sufferers are characterized by an inability to socialize, have extreme difficulty forming deep friendships or bonds with the opposite sex, and tend to shut down in social groups because they do not know the appropriate social responses that are expected of them.

The other amateur writers mocked Lovecraft behind his back, but found him to be on the whole harmless good fun. They even began to respect him over time, as the clarity of his intellect and his innate abilities as a writer began to become more widely known. On the personal level, once he overcame his initial self-conscious reserve, Lovecraft was an uncommonly likeable individual. He was polite, affable, self-effacing, and willing to assist anyone who needed help. His ability to socialize was limited, however, to those he perceived as kindred spirits, and of these he found precious few. He always considered himself to be an outsider. In 1926 he wrote to his elder aunt, "I am essentially a recluse who will have very little to do with people . . . I am always an outsider, to all scenes and all people . . ."[16]

What Lovecraft meant when he called himself an outsider was a sense of strangeness and not belonging. The average person feels the same thing for a few days when starting classes in a new school, or the first day of a different job, or moving into a new house, but Lovecraft felt it all the time, day after day, year after year, no matter how long he remained in a place or how often he interacted with other people. For the average person, this sense of separateness goes away fairly quickly. For Lovecraft, it never went away—the discomfort and nervousness were with him all the time.

It was Lovecraft's involvement with amateur journalism that enabled him to get his early stories published professionally. Lovecraft was hopeless at promoting his own work. He simply could not do it, and would not even try to do it. However, the contacts he made in the UAPA and NAPA served him well in later years, since some of those amateurs went on to positions in professional publishing or started their own professional magazines. In 1916 he showed his short story "The Alchemist" to four members of the UAPA. He had never even attempted to have it published. As he wrote at the beginning of that year to his correspondent Rheinhart Kleiner, "The tale was written 11 years ago, yet it is my latest attempt at fiction."[17] He seems to have confused its date of writing with his 1905 story "The Beast in the Cave"—"The Alchemist," written in 1908, was published in *The United Amateur* in November of 1916 and met with a measure of favor. He was urged by other amateurs to write more stories. In response, Lovecraft wrote during the summer of 1917 "The Tomb" and "Dagon."

The first is a horror story involving a young man's strange obsession with an old tomb and the dead that lie within it, the ghosts of whom he sees and talks to in his dreams, but the second, "Dagon," may be called the first of Lovecraft's tales dealing with the Old Ones. "Dagon" was based on a dream in which an island emerged out of the open sea due to a geological upheaval of the sea floor, an idea that he would later develop in his story "The Call of Cthulhu." In 1918 he wrote the story "Polaris," based on a dream that concerned the tormenting memories of a past life in the distant prehistory of the human race. That same year he collaborated with another amateur of the UAPA, Winifred Jackson, to write the story "The Green Meadow," which is based on a dream by Jackson. This story carried the pseudonyms of both Lovecraft (Lewis Theobald, Jun.) and Jackson (Elizabeth Neville Berkeley) as co-authors, which was rare for Lovecraft—when he collaborated with other writers in future years, it was usually in the capacity of ghostwriter, and his name did not appear on the byline.

The year 1918 was notable for another reason—Lovecraft made his first professional sale, a poem titled "The Marshes of Ipswich," to the *National Magazine*. De Camp remarked that this was the first money Lovecraft was known to have earned in his life.[18] Bear in mind that Lovecraft was nearing thirty years of age. It was not merely that Lovecraft was poor at earning money—for the first half of his life, he simply refused to do it. In his distorted view of the world, a proper English gentleman did not work for money. A gentleman was perfectly permitted to labor for his own amusement, or to help a friend, but he could not accept payment for it. This archaic and unrealistic attitude, which Lovecraft was never able to cast aside completely, prevented him from achieving commercial success, even on a small scale, with his writings during his lifetime.

For several years the mental health of Lovecraft's mother had been failing. She withdrew from society and became increasingly strange and reclusive, avoiding having anyone but members of the family visit in her flat, which acquired a stale and claustrophobic atmosphere. She began to see at twilight from the corners of her eyes strange shadow figures lurking in doorways and behind hedges, and was terrified to go out of the house. A neighbor would later write concerning Susie's visions, "I remember Mrs. Lovecraft spoke to me about weird and fantastic creatures that rushed out from behind buildings and from corners at dark, and that she shivered and looked about apprehensively as she told her story."[19]

Finally, in January of 1919, a serious nervous episode complicated with abdominal difficulties occurred that caused Susie to leave her flat at 598 Angell Street and go to stay at the home of her elder sister, Lillian, in the hope that the change of environment would have a beneficial effect. Her younger sister, Annie, took up temporary residence with Lovecraft to look after his needs in his mother's absence.

Lovecraft's life was turned upside down. It was the first time he had ever been separated from his mother. For two full months he did almost nothing. On January 18 he wrote to one of his correspondents, "I cannot eat, nor can I stay up long at a time. Pen-writing or type-writing nearly drives me insane, but my nervous system seems to find its vent in feverish and incessant scribbling with a pencil."[20] Lovecraft tried to find optimism in the diagnosis of the doctor who examined his mother that her stomach problems were not organic but were neurotic. He wrote in the same letter, "Such infirmity and absence on her part is so *unprecedented*, that it cannot but depress me, despite the brightest bulletins of her physician . . ."[21]

His mother, who had been getting progressively less rational for years, finally reached a stage where Lovecraft and his aunts Annie and Lillian could no longer take care of her. On March 13, 1919, Susie Lovecraft was committed to Butler Hospital, where her husband had died in madness twenty-one years earlier. Thus, both of Lovecraft's parents went mad. He must have wondered if there was a future padded cell waiting for him in Butler Hospital. He dreaded the place and never went inside when he visited his mother—he met with his mother only outside, in the landscaped grounds of the institution, which were like a small park.[22]

The shock of committing his mother to the insane asylum almost unhinged Lovecraft. He found the flat at 598 Angell Street "but half a home for want of its dominant figure."[23] All his life he had been tied to his mother's apron strings, and suddenly those strings were severed. He began to suffer from nervous strain that made him dizzy, gave him splitting headaches, and caused his vision to blur. Not for the first time in his life, his thoughts turned to suicide. He wrote, "Existence seems of little value, and I wish it might terminate!"[24] Similar suicidal thoughts would obsess him two years later, after the death of his mother at Butler Hospital on May 24, 1921, as a result of complications from gall-bladder surgery. He wrote at that time, "For my part, I do not think I shall wait for a natural death; since there is no longer any particular reason why I should exist."[25]

It seems to me of significance that when Susie Lovecraft experienced nerve problems at the beginning of 1919, it was found necessary that she leave her own home and visit for a time with her elder sister to recuperate, in view of the fact that her younger sister was able to come to the flat and live with Lovecraft in her absence. Why did Annie not take care of Susie in her own home? This move to Lillian's may have had nothing at its base other than practical domestic considerations, but on the other hand, it is possible that it was made on the advice of her doctor that Susie be removed from the presence of her son—or at least, removed from the environment of her flat.

I am now going to make a speculation that has never before been made in print, and which will be viewed as outlandish by those with no first-hand, practical experience in the occult. It is quite possible that Susie Lovecraft's hallucinations of shadow figures were caused by her son's troubled dreams, and by the stories he composed based on those dreams. Lovecraft had the habit of sitting up all night, brooding and meditating upon various ghastly horrors with singular mental focus and intensity while his mother slept in a room nearby. In sleep, the mind becomes receptive, and there is an inherent receptivity between members of the same family. Susie was already emotionally and mentally unstable. She may well have had the stuff of her son's nightmares impressed on her mind so deeply while she slept, that she began to see shadow creatures of nightmare while she was awake.

What she was seeing is today a recognized paranormal class of manifestation known variously as *shadow people*, *shadow men*, or *shadow beings*. They are usually glimpsed from the corner of the eye, and often

appear as an amorphous, moving black mass of shadow that sometimes has a pair of eyes and sometimes assumes a humanoid shape.
It is perhaps needless to point out that Lovecraft's night-gaunts are a
type of shadow being. They appeared to him in his dreams as black
figures with no faces. His child's mind cast them into a form he could
understand, that of a kind of devil with horns and a barbed tail, but
Susie's mature mind perceived them in a less clearly delineated state.

The emotional trauma of his mother's madness and incarceration
rendered Lovecraft's own mind open to new obsessions, and in the autumn of 1919 he discovered the short stories of Lord Dunsany in the
form of the 1910 collection *A Dreamer's Tales*. He was so enraptured
by Dunsany's short fantasy fiction that he later declared in a letter,
"The first paragraph arrested me as with an electrical shock."[26] They
were exactly the sort of stories he himself wanted to write—and little
wonder, since the fantastic scenes described by Dunsany were similar
to the visions in Lovecraft's own dreams. He read all the Dunsany he
could get his hands on. On October 20 he traveled to Boston in order
to hear Dunsany give a lecture that evening at the Copley-Plaza Hotel.
Fresh from the influence of Dunsany's lecture, Lovecraft wrote the
story "The White Ship," and in November of the following year wrote
a similar dreamer's tale, "Celephaïs."

Eventually he would grow a bit disillusioned with Dunsany, whose
later writings did not live up to Lovecraft's expectations, but at the time,
Dunsany was his ideal of what a writer and a man should be—Dunsany
was an Anglo-Irish peer schooled at Eton and Sandhurst, with a title and
lands that included Dunsany Castle in County Meath, Ireland. A true
gentleman who possessed an ample income and had no need to write
for money, he did it for his own amusement. He was a champion chess
player who invented his own variant form of chess, called Dunsany's
chess, and for a time he was the pistol-shooting champion of all Ireland.
He served as a captain in the Royal Inniskilling Fusiliers during World

War One, and was wounded in battle while Lovecraft was waiting out the war in Providence behind his mother's skirts. In short, Dunsany was everything that Lovecraft himself longed with all his heart to be, but could never hope to become. As the star-struck Lovecraft wrote in one of his letters, "Dunsany is myself."[27]

In 1919 Lovecraft had his lavishly sycophantic poem of adulation, titled "To Edward John Moreton Drax Plunkett, Eighteenth Baron Dunsany," published in the amateur periodical the *Tryout*. It was actually mailed to Lord Dunsany by Alice Hamlet, an acquaintance of Lovecraft who had attended the Dunsany lecture with him. Dunsany was kind enough to respond with the most gracious of letters thanking her for the poem, and thanking its author for his "warm and generous enthusiasm, crystallized in verse." The poem is noteworthy for only one thing, its sheer wretchedness, but I cannot resist quoting one rhyming couplet, which in my opinion must be one of the worst, if not the very worst, poetic couplets ever penned in the English language:

So now o'er realms where dark'ning dulness lies,
In solar state see shining PLUNKETT rise![28]

In 1921 a fellow amateur writer and former president of the NAPA, George Julian Houtain, who had just started his own professional magazine, *Home Brew*, made the arrangement that Lovecraft should write a series of horror stories at the payment rate of five dollars per story, his first professional prose fiction sale. These took the form of a connected serial, and may be regarded as six chapters of a single story, although each was written to stand alone and was published separately. Lovecraft titled them collectively "Herbert West—Reanimator." He began writing the series in September and finished in April or May of 1922.

He took his inspiration from the novel *Frankenstein* by Mary Shelley. In the stories, West is a medical experimenter who develops a serum that, when injected into a corpse, brings the corpse back to a horrifying semblance of life. Lovecraft wrote the stories with an attitude of distaste because he was doing it for money, a very ungentlemanly thing to do, yet they have a kind of frenzied energy and inventiveness that has made them one of Lovecraft's more memorable works. The animated corpses were the precursors of the zombies so popular and so prolific in modern cinema.

In 1922 he sold the story "The Lurking Fear" to *Home Brew*, and it was also published in parts as a serial. Lovecraft had no use for the magazine, which contained low humor and which he characterized as a "vile rag," but something more interesting loomed on the horizon. A new magazine appeared on the stands in March of 1923 that was titled *Weird Tales*. As the title implies, it was wholly devoted to weird fiction, the first such magazine of its kind. Lovecraft liked its choice of stories. In May of that year, he submitted five of his own to the editor, Edwin Baird.

The cover letter he enclosed with the stories, which Baird printed in the letter section of the September 1923 issue of *Weird Tales*, is a model of how not to write a cover letter. Lovecraft committed almost every possible mistake someone new to selling freelance fiction could make. De Camp, who possessed vast experience both as a freelance writer and as an editor, observed that in his introductory letter "Lovecraft had done everything to assure rejection of his stories: . . . He all but begged Baird to return his manuscripts."[29]

In the letter, Lovecraft talked too much about himself and his tastes, using a superior and somewhat dismissive tone. He informed Baird that he was only submitting the stories because friends had urged him to do so, and that their acceptance or rejection was a matter of no importance to him. He made a point of telling Baird that he paid no attention to the "demands of commercial writing" and instructed Baird to read only the first two stories, and if they were unsatisfactory, not bother reading the other three. He told Baird that if by some miracle the stories were considered for publication, he would only consent for them to be published if they were printed without any editorial changes "down to the very last semicolon and comma." However, the stories would probably not be found satisfactory, Lovecraft wrote, because one of them, "Dagon," had already been rejected by another magazine, to which Lovecraft had submitted it "under external compulsion." In closing, he informed Baird in a patronizing way that he liked *Weird Tales*, even though the stories in it were "more or less commercial—or should I say conventional?"[30]

Lovecraft got the miracle he was looking for. Most editors would have rejected the stories unread on the basis of this wretched cover letter alone, but Baird must have been in an uncommonly forgiving mood that day. He sent the stories back to Lovecraft with a letter instructing him to retype the stories double-spaced and resubmit them. Stories were submitted to professional magazines typed and double-spaced to make reading and editing them easier on the magazine editor's strained eyesight. Lovecraft had not known this, or had not cared. His feelings were hurt by what he regarded as a rejection. "I am not certain whether or not I shall bother. I need the money badly enough—but ugh! how I hate typing!"[31] He retyped only one story, "Dagon," and resubmitted it. Baird bought it and published it in the issue of October 1923. Subsequently, the other four stories were bought by Baird and appeared in the magazine.

Thus began an enduring and productive relationship. Over the course of Lovecraft's career, *Weird Tales* would publish more of his fiction than any other single outlet and would be responsible for a sizeable portion of the money he earned as a fiction writer. Many of these stories were published under his own name, but many others were revised or ghostwritten by Lovecraft for other writers, and his name did not appear on the byline. Some of the more canny readers were able to deduce that Lovecraft was the writer from internal evidence in the stories, but the majority of buyers remained unaware of just how much of their spooky reading pleasure was being supplied by Lovecraft.

The first editor of the magazine, Baird, liked Lovecraft's way of writing and was receptive to almost everything Lovecraft submitted. However, *Weird Tales* began to struggle for sales, went into debt, and its publisher J. C. Henneberger replaced Baird as editor after thirteen issues with a frequent contributor to the magazine, the writer Farnsworth Wright. The new editor was much more resistant to Lovecraft's prose style, preferring the more down-to-earth style of such later contributors as Robert Bloch and Robert E. Howard. As a member of the amateur journalist community, Wright had suffered criticism from Lovecraft in the past; when the opportunity arrived to turn the tables he took it, and forced Lovecraft to edit his stories in ways Lovecraft resented, or simply did the editing himself after accepting the stories without consulting Lovecraft. He rejected some of Lovecraft's greatest works, such as his short novels *At the Mountains of Madness* and *The Shadow Over Innsmouth*. Nonetheless, under Wright's heavy-handed and critical leadership, *Weird Tales* began to recover.

Lovecraft always resented criticism, although he was outwardly gracious to those who gave it. He tolerated rejection very poorly. It caused him to doubt both the value of his existing works and his ability to write new stories. This hypersensitivity is curious, in that Lovecraft always cultivated a superior detachment from the reflexive reactions of the greater mass of humanity. Lovecraft was embarrassed by this contradiction between the impassive pose he affected and his actual response to rejection, which was emotional. When one of his stories was declined, he simply stopped trying to sell it. This quixotic behavior greatly frustrated his friends. He wrote on the subject to August Derleth in 1932: "I can see why you consider my anti-rejection policy a stubbornly foolish and needlessly short-sighted one, and am not prepared to offer any defense other than the mere fact that repeated rejections *do* work in a certain way on my psychology—rationally or not—and that their effect is to cause in me a certain literary lockjaw which absolutely prevents further fictional composition despite my most arduous efforts."[32]

What modern readers today may not realize is that the majority of Lovecraft's contemporaries did not very much like his stories. They were too strange, too archaic and verbose, and lacked familiar personal and social relationships. Lovecraft had little interest in character development, and none at all in romantic interaction. Michel Houellebecq made the trenchant observation that in all of Lovecraft's work there is not a single reference to sex or money, adding, "He writes exactly as though these things did not exist."[33] This statement is a bit of Gallic hyperbole—Lovecraft does allude to both sex and money in his stories. However, he does not dwell on either sexual pleasure or the monetary value of things. His characters are not motivated to any large degree by sex or money.

This aversion to his work among readers was especially strong toward his Dunsany-influenced dreamworld tales, such as "The White Ship" and "The Quest of Iranon." When a Lovecraft story was published in *Weird Tales*, it would elicit angry letters demanding that more modern writers be given a chance to appear in the magazine. These letters were never published in the "letters" section, but they were read by Farnsworth Wright. In his reluctance to accept Lovecraft's work, Wright was only echoing this general feeling by a significant portion of readers that Lovecraft's work was not sufficiently modern or realistic.

Lovecraft's choice of story material was based on three loves, which he identified in a letter: "(a) Love of the strange and the fantastic. (b) Love of the abstract truth and of scientific logick. (c) Love of the ancient and the permanent."[34] The first love is responsible for his baroque, Oriental descriptions of cities, palaces, and temples in his dreamland stories, and for his references to magic and witchcraft. The second love caused him to support his later mythos tales with accurate scientific information, which resulted in some critics classifying them as science fiction rather than as horror. They are a blending of the two genres which at the time was unique to Lovecraft, and which might be called gothic science fiction, or science horror. We can see the descendants of these stories in such films as *Alien* and *Event Horizon*. The third love gave rise to the setting of many of his stories in old streets, ancient cities, decaying colonial houses, forgotten graveyards, moldering libraries, quaint bookshops, and haunted ruins.

These three loves were not always kept separate, but were sometimes mingled in the same story. For example, in *At the Mountains of Madness* there is an extended and rather dry scientific analysis of the crinoid race (showing his love of science) side by side with a description of the immemorial and massive ruins of their lost city in Antarctica (his love of the ancient), which is inhabited by giant subterranean albino penguins (his love of the strange). In his story "The Dreams in the Witch-House," the venerable architecture of Lovecraft's town of Arkham, which Lovecraft derived from Salem, Massachusetts (love of the ancient), is enlivened with the fantastic spectral presence of the witch Keziah Mason (love of the strange), who travels through time and space by means of a higher-dimensional alien geometry (love of science).

Lovecraft might have made a good living as a writer for *Weird Tales* and the other magazines of the burgeoning pulp fiction market (such as the science fiction magazine *Astounding Stories*, to which he eventually sold *At the Mountains of Madness*) had he been willing to compromise his artistic principles, and had he possessed a somewhat thicker hide to shield him from criticism. His literary friends did their best to steer him in this direction, but their efforts were hopeless from the start. Lovecraft could not compromise his work for money. The nearest he came to hack work was his ghostwriting efforts, and even to these writings he gave his best effort. Some of his ghostwritten stories are among his finest fiction—for example "The Mound" and "The Curse of Yig," both written for Zealia Bishop based on vague story ideas she presented to Lovecraft. For all practical purposes these two tales are entirely Lovecraft's work.

Lovecraft's most famous client as a ghostwriter was the magician and escape artist Harry Houdini (1874–1926), who went to the publisher of *Weird Tales*, J. C. Henneberger, with the idea for a supposedly true story he wished to have ghostwritten for him and published in the magazine. The story was to be based on events Houdini claimed to have experienced beneath the pyramids of Egypt. Lovecraft was not greatly impressed by Houdini. He considered Houdini's account complete balderdash. Nevertheless, he was attracted by the lure of certain money promised by Henneberger upon delivery, and composed the story with the intention of having his own name appear on the byline along with that of Houdini, until Henneberger pointed out that since the story was written in the first person as a true account of Houdini's actions, it would be more plausible if only Houdini's name appeared.

The story was originally titled by Lovecraft "Under the Pyramids." It was published in the May-June-July 1924 issue of *Weird Tales* with the title "Imprisoned with the Pharaohs," bearing only Houdini's name. Lovecraft was paid one hundred dollars for his work several weeks after the delivery of the manuscript.[35] Houdini told Henneberger that he was pleased with the result, and later paid Lovecraft seventy-five dollars to write a magazine article on astrology for him. Always happy to write for a guaranteed payment, Lovecraft subsequently planned more collaborations with Houdini as his ghostwriter, but Houdini's sudden death on Halloween of 1926 put an end to the prospect.

4

DREAM TRAVELER

Lovecraft suffered from a severe polarization of personality that he was never able to confront directly. On the one side, he was a materialist and a scientific rationalist, unwilling to credit the existence of anything that could not be observed with the senses and analyzed quantitatively. From early childhood he flatly rejected with his conscious mind all forms of religion, superstition, magic, occultism, spiritualism, and the paranormal. He wrote articles mocking astrology and astrologers, and he held an equal contempt for anyone who professed belief in an unseen world. On the other side of his personality, he was one of the most gifted astral visionaries that America has ever produced, capable of seeing and visiting in his dreams astral landscapes of astonishing complexity and beauty, and of conveying through his writings these visions so that they resonate in the collective unconscious of the human race to this day.

Lovecraft never acknowledged his mediumistic side. All his adult life he continued to dismiss his dreams as trivial, even though he spent the greater portion of his creative energies transforming them into poems and stories. He never seriously asked himself why he was devoting his life to something his conscious mind regarded as of no real value. Had he been able to confront this conundrum, he might have achieved a fusion between the two sides of his nature, the scientific with the psychic, the rational with the spiritual, but he could not conceive how two such seemingly contradictory viewpoints could coexist.

He may have been afraid to make an attempt to reconcile the dichotomy of his mind out of apprehension as to where such an experiment would lead. One of the settings in Lovecraft's fiction is the maelstrom of ultimate chaos, which is ruled by the drooling idiot god, Azathoth. It is the final end of all things, which is only to be reached when all barriers have been crossed and all doors unlocked. Azathoth represents madness, and madness arises from chaos. All his life Lovecraft feared going mad. Both his parents had gone insane. He recognized in his own strange affections for graveyards and old buildings, his aversion to other human beings, his headaches and nervous collapses, the nascent buddings of madness.

Little wonder that he steadfastly refused to grant his strange dream visions, or his repeated reincarnation dreams and sense of déjà vu, any weight or meaning. It is not that he ignored the significance of these psychic events in his personal life; it is more a case that he was constitutionally unable to bear to think of them as meaningful, even for an instant, lest that belief should grow beyond his control and sweep him from everyday material reality into a whirling vortex of chaotic madness. He dared not credit the occult with any greater significance than as a source of trivial amusement. The outré and the weird were far too real in his life for him to ever look directly at them, so he peeked at them from the corners of his eyes in the way we peek at the blinding sun, yet told himself that they were unreal. The occult fascinated him, but it also terrified him, although he never admitted as much— he could not afford to give it that much power over him.

Although he did not seek to dream strange dreams, and in his early years did everything he could to prevent it, Lovecraft's talent for dreaming was inherent in his very nature. His childhood nightmares frightened him to such an extent that he would lie awake night after night, vainly trying to elude sleep. He never quite overcame this primal terror of the things that visited him in his bed. The most horrifying were the night-gaunts, which were as I have pointed out a type of shadow people, but they were only one abomination among many. As a man, he was able to go without sleep for prolonged periods of time that astonished those who knew him—an ability perhaps nurtured by his self-imposed discipline in early childhood of staying awake past the normal hour of bedtime.

Many of Lovecraft's earlier weird stories are based on his actual dreams, either wholly or in large part, and the topic of dreams figures prominently in much of his early work. It would be fair to say that Lovecraft was obsessed and consumed with dreams. The 1917 story "The Tomb" concerns a young man, obviously patterned after Lovecraft himself, who repeatedly falls asleep in front of an ancestral mausoleum and dreams of interacting with the antique shades of the dead contained therein. It was written in June after Lovecraft went for a walk through Swan Point Cemetery, where his father, grandfather, and grandmother lay buried. In the summer of that same year he wrote "Dagon," which is based on a dream he had of an island that abruptly arose out of the midst of the ocean, covered with mud and slime.

He would later use this same dream event as the basis for the story "The Call of Cthulhu," which has other dream elements as well. In the story, an artist dreams of Cthulhu and crafts a bas-relief of his image, which he takes to an expert at Brown University to have examined. This incident is based on a dream in which Lovecraft himself fashioned a bas-relief from clay depicting Egyptian priests, and took it to a museum in Providence to be examined. In the dream, the curator of the museum remarked that the piece was not ancient but modern, just as the expert in the story remarks that the artist's bas-relief is not ancient. In the dream Lovecraft responded with these words, which he later inserted with only a few alterations into his story: "This was fashioned in my dreams; and the dreams of man are older than brooding Egypt or the contemplative Sphinx or garden-girdled Babylon."[1]

In 1918 he wrote the story "Polaris" based on a dream of a strange city between sheltering hills, and he collaborated with one of his fellow amateurs, Winifred Jackson, on the dream-based story "The Green Meadow." In 1919 he wrote "Beyond the Wall of Sleep," which concerns the reality of dreams. That same year, his discovery of Dunsany's collection of short stories, *A Dreamer's Tales*, had a profound effect in propelling him along a course he had already begun to follow independently—the composition of stories set in the land of dreams. Under this Dunsany influence he wrote in 1920 "The White Ship" and "Celephaïs," both stories set in the dreamlands.

There are probably more dream elements in his poetry and prose than have ever been recognized, but even the stories that we know to be based directly on dreams are significant for their number and importance. A partial list includes "Polaris," "Dagon," "Nyarlathotep," "The Green Meadow," "The Crawling Chaos," "Herbert West—Reanimator," "The Nameless City," "The Doom that Came to Sarnath," "The Statement of Randolph Carter," "Pickman's Model," "The Call of Cthulhu," "The Shadow Out of Time," "Azathoth" (fragment), "The Very Old Folk," "The Evil Clergyman" (fragment), "The Thing In the Moonlight," and the poem "Recapture" (sonnet 34 of *Fungi from Yuggoth*).

Some of his works that concern dreams as a central theme are "The Tomb," "Polaris," "The White Ship," "Celephaïs," "Beyond the Wall of Sleep," "The Crawling Chaos," "Ex Oblivione," "Hypnos," "The Silver Key," "Through the Gates of the Silver Key," "The Call of Cthulhu," "The Dreams in the Witch-House," "Imprisoned with the Pharaohs," and *The Dream-Quest of Unknown Kadath*.

Numerous briefer references to dreams and dreaming occur throughout the *Necronomicon* mythos. The dread tome the *Necronomicon* itself was dreamed by Lovecraft, and indeed its very name was not invented by him but was received passively in a dream, before he had any notion of its meaning. At the start of his career as a writer of cosmic horror tales, Lovecraft did little more than set his dreams and nightmares down on the page, and indeed he sometimes wondered if he could even claim credit as the author of the stories, since he was not so much composing them as narrating what he had seen in sleep.

A notable example of this verbatim transcription of a nightmare is the 1920 story "Nyarlathotep"—the title character is one of Lovecraft's Old Ones, a being of immense power and antiquity associated with the god Azathoth, who came to earth ages ago from beyond the visible stars. Over the years Nyarlathotep evolved a complex identity and took on varied masks in the *Necronomicon* mythos, but at the beginning he was only a figure in a dream. One fateful night, Lovecraft awoke out of sleep with a headache and immediately picked up his pen. He later wrote to his friend Kleiner, "I was in great pain—forehead pounding and ears ringing—but I had only one automatic impulse—to *write*, and preserve the atmosphere of unparalleled fright; and before I knew it I had pulled on the light and was scribbling desperately."[2] The first paragraph of the story was written before he had come fully awake, and the rest of the story is an almost exact description of his dream, as related in the letter to Kleiner.

For some weeks prior to receiving this momentous dream of Nyarlathotep, Lovecraft had suffered from headaches and dizziness, the result of nervous strain that manifested itself in a "curious tugging of nerves and muscles" around his eyes. This tugging made it impossible for him to read fine print. He wrote to Kleiner that it "rather startled" him while it persisted. The obvious presumption is that Lovecraft's eyes were failing and that he needed glasses, but this presumption is unfounded. The curious tugging eventually went away and left his vision as it had been before it started.

It is possible that this tugging of the muscles around his eyes was no more than a random artifact of nervous strain, but there is another speculation that we may indulge, if only as food for meditation. Lovecraft had for many years been living the life of an ascetic. He had withdrawn from society, avoided crowds, spent most of his time in solitary study, and ate only enough food to keep his body functioning. He neither smoked nor drank, and his sexual life was nonexistent. In effect, he was living the life of a virtuous medieval monk without the burden of religious dogma. It is possible that this ascetic lifestyle, coupled with sexual abstinence, awoke in Lovecraft spontaneous spiritual manifestations of the body that are recognized in various Eastern religious and philosophic disciplines.

It is the common practice in Eastern esoteric schools, such as that of Chinese tao, Tibetan bon, and Hindu tantra, to deliberately use suppressed sexual energy to provoke the awakening of magical or paranormal abilities, among them the gifts of astral vision and astral travel. In Lovecraft's case, this awakening may have occurred spontaneously, without him ever realizing what was going on, but it was no less potent for having been unsought. Suppressed sexual energy is employed by these eastern sects to arouse something known in India as kundalini, a natural fiery energy that resides at the perineum, but which when aroused ascends up the spine, bringing with it various psychic perceptions and manifestations as it passes through key occult centers of the body known as chakras.

One of the early signs of awakening kundalini energy in the body is involuntary muscular movements such as muscle jerks and twitches. They are precursors to the awakening of psychic gifts. It is worth noting that in the Spiritualism of the late nineteenth and early twentieth centuries, automatic writing or drawing was commonly preceded by involuntary movements of the medium's body.³ These involuntary movements were believed to open channels in the medium's nervous system through which the spirits were able to communicate. Having been prepared in this way, mediums became oracular instruments for spirits.

Lovecraft's activated psychic perception was accompanied by a heightened sensitivity toward other human beings that almost overwhelmed him. Coupled with his inability to relate socially to others in the usual way, due perhaps to Asperger's syndrome, he found that he was able to fend off madness only by withdrawing from the world. At first, as these latent psychic abilities awakened within him during the years 1908 to 1914, Lovecraft was compelled to seek almost complete solitude, but later as he gained some control over his extreme sensitivity, he was able to begin to interact with other human beings in a limited way, individually and in small groups. Even so, he never gained a familiar ease in social interaction.

The experiences Lovecraft went through when writing his story "The Statement of Randolph Carter" late in 1919 were similar to those that had earlier given rise to the story "Nyarlathotep." He had a vivid and detailed dream of accompanying his friend Samuel Loveman into an ancient cemetery for the purpose of descending into one of the crypts to investigate secret tunnels beneath it. Awakening with what he termed "a prize headache,"⁴ he quickly wrote the events of the dream down, changing almost nothing other than his own name and that of Loveman. He called himself Randolph Carter, a character who was to become his alter ego in the *Necronomicon* mythos. Carter moved through the world of dreams even as Lovecraft himself did during sleep, but Carter had full control, whereas Lovecraft did not.

He gradually became aware that his dreams were unlike those experienced by other human beings. This consciousness of their difference from ordinary dreams crystallized around the year 1918, with the dream vision of a city that served as the basis for his short story "Polaris," written in the first half of that year. In his dream, Lovecraft found himself observing "a city of many palaces and gilded domes, lying in a hollow betwixt ranges of grey horrible hills."[5] He realized that he had control over his movements within the dream—or, rather, that he could control the position of his point of view from which he observed the city, since at the start of the dream he possessed no body but was merely a position in space.

He experienced the strong conviction that he had once known the city well, and that if he could only remember its name and what had transpired there, he would be drawn back in time thousands of years to its physical reality. This prospect both attracted Lovecraft and terrified him, so that he retreated into wakefulness. When he came to write his story, he made his narrator dream of viewing the city as a disembodied point in space, just as Lovecraft himself had actually done, but then the unnamed narrator of the story is drawn into the body of one of the inhabitants of the ancient city, which Lovecraft called Olathoë, in the land of Lomar. Thus he achieved in his character what he had been too fearful to undertake in his own dream. As Darrell Schweitzer observed of the story "Polaris": "It is taken almost entirely from Lovecraft's dream, with only a few rationalizations added by the conscious writer."[6]

This is what we know today as lucid dreaming. This term was not widely known in Lovecraft's period, although it had been coined in 1913 by Frederik van Eeden, a Dutch psychiatrist. A lucid dream is a dream in which the dreamer becomes aware that he is dreaming, and gains a measure of control over his thoughts and actions while still within the dream. The concepts of both astral projection and reincarnation were well known to Lovecraft, having been popularized by Theosophy. The technique of astral projection described by the Theosophist Oliver Fox (real name Hugh Callaway) was to become aware during a dream by deliberately taking note of any oddity or incongruity in the dream setting. Once aware of this oddity, Fox was able to move about independently within the dream with full conscious awareness.[7]

The method used by Fox to achieve astral projection, described in his 1938 book *Astral Projection: A Record of Out-of-the-Body Experiences*, was the same method, more or less, that Lovecraft had discovered independently but hesitated to exploit out of an unconscious dread of inducing madness in himself. Fox noted that "the mental effort of prolonging the dream produced a pain in my head—dull at first but rapidly increasing in intensity—and I knew instinctively this was a warning to me to resist no longer the call of my body."[8] On several occasions Lovecraft mentioned in letters awaking from his vivid dreams with a headache.[9]

Not all of Lovecraft's dreaming astral projections were so remote in time and space. His description of a seedy section of Paris near the river Seine in the 1921 story "The Music of Erich Zann" is particularly vivid and evocative. Lovecraft had never visited Paris. According to de Camp, someone once asked Lovecraft how he had managed to capture so well the atmosphere of Paris without ever having been there, and Lovecraft replied "he had indeed been there—in a dream, in company with Poe."[10]

It was not lost on Lovecraft that many of his dreams might be interpreted as remembered past-life experiences. Again and again he alluded to reincarnation, only to dismiss it with resolute contempt. In the same dream in which he fashioned the bas-relief out of clay and showed it to the curator of a Providence museum, the curator stared at Lovecraft with awakening terror and demanded in a soft voice, "Who are you?" Lovecraft casually replied "My name is Lovecraft— H. P. Lovecraft—grandson of Whipple V. Phillips." The aged curator brushed his words aside, saying in a petulant tone, "No! No!—*before that!"* The italics are Lovecraft's. Lovecraft told the old man that he recalled "no other identity save in dreams."[11]

The character of the old museum curator, who symbolizes by his age and white hairs recondite knowledge, is telling Lovecraft in his dream that he has lived before, but Lovecraft denies the suggestion, asserting that he has only lived other lives "in dreams." Even within the dream itself Lovecraft maintained a distinction between the importance of waking life and the triviality of dream life. Yet this distinction was not so much one that he actually believed, as it was a distinction that he desperately wanted to believe for his own continuing sanity. Consciously he was able to maintain the view that dreams are trivial things, but on a deeper level he knew this was a lie. For Lovecraft, dreams were the most important things of all.

In his letters, Lovecraft made a number of references to reincarnation that indicate a fascination with the subject. In a 1933 letter to J. Vernon Shea, he talked about walking as a young boy through a historic section of Providence and feeling a strong affinity for the architecture of the old houses. He compared the feeling to what he experienced when looking at eighteenth-century engravings by William Hogarth in a picture book that was kept in the parlor in the Whipple mansion, and to images of the American Revolution that were in one of his coloring books (the following italics are Lovecraft's): "It was *familiar*—I had *always* known it—I had *seen it before*—it was *part of me* in a sense that no other scene ever was . . . and so I dreamed about it by night and visited it by day whenever I could."[12]

He referred to reincarnation in connection with the dream that gave rise to his story "Polaris," but only to dismiss it.[13] In yet another letter he asserted, "I am really a relic left over from Queen Anne's age," and made the provocative comment, "In this manner my style was formed; not as a conscious archaism, but as though I had actually been born in 1690 instead of 1890."[14] Referring to the profound impression he received from Marblehead, Massachusetts, which he first visited on December 17, 1922, Lovecraft wrote to his Aunt Lillian that although he had never lived in that place, yet it "gives me at times an intensely poignant illusory sensation of having done so in the period around 1750–1760."[15] Notice his emphasis that the impression was an illusion—he did not want his aunt to imagine that he believed in reincarnation.

Perhaps one reason Lovecraft was so attracted to the idea, if not the act, of suicide was the longing to put off his corporeal body so that he could move about freely in time and space, as he did in his dreams. He was obsessed with the eighteenth century, but he felt a vague sense that he had inhabited still more remote times and places in some other existence that he could barely sense at the limits of his awareness. Late in his life he wrote to August Derleth, "The commonest form of my imaginative aspiration—that is, the commonest definable form—is a motion backward in time, or a discovery that time is merely an illusion and that the past is simply a lost mode of vision which I have a chance of recovering."[16] He best expressed this personal longing for the past in his short story "The Silver Key," in which Randolph Carter—who always represents Lovecraft's ideal conception of himself—turns away from his present life and passes through a dimensional gate that returns him to the period of his childhood.

It is impossible to determine whether there was anything that might be classed as esoteric at the root of Lovecraft's obsession with the past and with dreams. Throughout his life he stoutly—one might almost say defensively—maintained a complete disbelief in any aspect of the supernatural, even its spiritual side. *"I never had the slightest shadow of belief in the supernatural"*[17] he asserted in a letter, underlining the words, when referring to his childhood rejection of religion, and we must take him at his word, at least on the surface. But it cannot be denied that the supernatural, in its various forms, had an interest in

Lovecraft. It harried his thoughts day and night, by turns seducing him in his musings and terrifying him in his dreams.

Writing down his dreams was Lovecraft's way of objectifying them and controlling them. In the person of his story character, Randolph Carter (and to a lesser degree other characters in his fiction), Lovecraft projected himself back into the dreams on the written page, where he could consciously and deliberately determine the outcome. His need to command and conquer his dream world finds its ultimate fulfillment in his novel *The Dream-Quest of Unknown Kadath*. It is a flawed masterpiece, but a masterpiece nonetheless. Lovecraft, as the dream adventurer Carter, strides across the map of the dreamlands heroically, mastering in succession its various terrors.

Carter makes his first appearance in the mythos as the callow accomplice of the occultist Harley Warren, in the dream-story "The Statement of Randolph Carter," written in 1919. The story is cast in the form of a statement given by Carter to the police, who are investigating the disappearance of Warren, but it is really no more than an account of Lovecraft's actual dream, in which he substituted the name Harley Warren for that of his friend Samuel Loveman, and the name Randolph Carter for his own name. In this story, Carter is very much the follower and Warren the leader. However, by the time Lovecraft came to write his story "The Unnamable" in 1923, Carter has progressed into a professional writer of horror tales and a connoisseur of the weird.

When Lovecraft wrote *The Dream-Quest of Unknown Kadath*, Carter has evolved in Lovecraft's imagination into an accomplished dreamer—someone who possesses the ability to dream lucid dreams and to move around the dreamlands with full independent awareness, conversing with the inhabitants and interacting with the places of these lands, which possess a consistency and persistence similar to the places and people of the material world. Carter is able to dream deeper and to travel further than other dreamers. He is the Odysseus of dreams, the far voyager across strange seas and distant lands. In his quest to find fabled Kadath in the Cold Waste, he confronts numerous dangers and overcomes many obstacles, including a hostile Nyarlathotep, who seeks to destroy Carter by trapping him in the vortex of ultimate chaos—for Lovecraft the chaos of Azathoth symbolized madness. Were Carter to fall into the vortex, he would never be able to return to the waking world. He avoids this snare and emerges from his dream odyssey sane and content to return to his beloved Boston, which is for Carter what Providence was for Lovecraft, the most perfect place on earth.

In the course of his travels through the dreamlands, Carter has occasion to confront and come to terms with some of the things that had frightened Lovecraft in his childhood nightmares. In this novel, Carter is able to enlist the aid of the night-gaunts to help him reach the summit of the mountain Kadath, through the mediation of the ghouls. The black, faceless creatures that had most terrified Lovecraft in childhood become not only allies in Carter's quest for Kadath, but absolutely essential to his fulfillment of that quest. It is their wings that bear Carter up to the summit. In this plot device, we see Lovecraft shaping his night terrors into his friends and allies.

The Dream-Quest of Unknown Kadath was begun in October of 1926 but not completed until the first month of the following year. At the same time Lovecraft was working on this novel, he dashed off the short story "The Silver Key," which was probably written in November 1926. The events of the story appear to take place after Randolph Carter has completed his long dream quest of Kadath. Carter has grown world-weary and cynical. The prosaic demands of everyday life have made it impossible for him to travel into his dreams, as he did in the past, and he longs for the days of his boyhood when he was happy.

The description of Carter's state of mind at the opening of the story is a biographical sketch of Lovecraft's own attitude toward life:

> They had chained him down to things that are, and had then explained the workings of those things till mystery had gone out of the world. When he complained, and longed to escape into twilight realms where magic moulded all the little vivid fragments and prized associations of his mind into vistas of breathless expectancy and unquenchable delight, they turned him instead toward the new-found prodigies of science, bidding him find wonder in the atom's vortex and mystery in the sky's dimensions. And when he had failed to find these boons in things whose laws are known and measurable, they told him he lacked imagination, and was immature because he preferred dream-illusions to the illusions of our physical creation.[18]

In Randolph Carter's revulsion against waking reality we can see Lovecraft's own often expressed tedium with the world and its trivial cares, which caused him to repeatedly consider suicide as a way to end the ennui. Carter's failure to find solace in the advances of science reflects Lovecraft's disillusionment with chemistry and astronomy. Carter is mocked for his conviction that the mental images of dreams are no different in essence from the mental images of real things, and for his preference of dreams over waking life. In the end, Carter triumphs over his prosaically minded critics by using the silver key of dreams to open a gate through time and space, allowing him to slip back into his own childhood, where he can dream unhindered by the duties and cares of adult life.

Lovecraft once expressed the sentiment in a letter that "adulthood is hell."[19] It is worth noting that he wrote these words when he was thirty years of age, and that in the story "The Silver Key," Randolph

Carter is thirty years old. It is impossible not to draw the conclusion that Carter's sentiments about reality and dreams are those of Lovecraft himself. Lovecraft could not return through time to the past when he had been happy, but he expressed the desire to do just that, and undoubtedly would have done it had he possessed the silver key of dreams that was Randolph Carter's legacy from his uncanny and somewhat sinister ancestors.

Yet despite Lovecraft's almost fatal fascination for the beauty and joys of dreaming, he was never willing to take the ultimate and irrevocable step in his philosophy, and equate dream reality with waking reality. To do so would have been to lose his final anchor to our common world and be whirled away into the vortex of ultimate chaos, never to emerge. Writing about the dream that gave rise to his story "Polaris," he noted in a letter to Maurice Moe:

. . . that dream was as real as my presence at this table, pen in hand! If the truth or falsity of our beliefs and impressions be immaterial, then I am, or was, actually and indisputably an unbodied spirit hovering over a very singular, very silent, and very ancient city somewhere between grey, dead hills. I thought I was at the time—so what else matters? Do you think that I was just as truly that spirit as I am now H. P. Lovecraft? I do not . . .

I recognize a distinction between dream life and real life, between appearance and actualities. I confess to an over-powering desire to know whether I am asleep or awake—whether the environment and laws which affect me are external and permanent, or the transitory products of my own brain.[20]

This is a fascinating passage on several levels. We see Lovecraft writing explicitly his own name, as though to reaffirm his identity. You will remember that in his dream of the clay tablet, he did the same thing when asked by the museum curator at Providence who he might be, and in that dream he went so far as to give the name of his grandfather as well. This repetition of his own name suggests an unconscious need to reaffirm to himself his own identity. In the first part of the quotation above, he plays with the view that his dream experience and his waking experience are equivalent in their degree of reality, but in the second part he shifts and argues the opposite, that there is in fact a distinction of importance to be drawn between dream life and what he chooses to call in the letter "real life."

Theosophy recognized the reality of dreams as an aspect or perception of the astral planes. Lovecraft was somewhat familiar with the ideas of Theosophy, although he dismissed them as nonsense. He understood that occultists regarded dreams as real. In his dream stories and in his novel *The Dream-Quest of Unknown Kadath*, Lovecraft presents the dreamlands as a real place—not a tangible location that can be fixed on a map, but a world in which dreaming minds can interact, learn, suffer, and even die. Those who choose to stay and live in the dreamlands, forsaking waking reality, either vanish and are never seen again, or their corpses are discovered in the waking world.

There is a parallel to be drawn between those who enter the dreamlands in Lovecraft's fiction and those who enter the land of fairy in European folklore. Time does not move at the same pace in the dreamlands as it moves in the waking world, and neither does it do so in the land of fairy, where it may pass more swiftly or more slowly than it passes in our everyday reality. Folktales relate that some of those who are taken into fairy mounds are never seen again, but it sometimes transpires that they are found lying on the grassy mounds, either dead or in a deep sleep from which they cannot be awakened. It may even happen that a man lost in the land of fairy for many years will return to his former village greatly altered by his experiences. In

Lovecraft's story "Through The Gates of the Silver Key," Randolph Carter returns to the everyday material world after having vanished without a trace many years previously through a dream gate opened by his silver key—Carter is greatly altered by his experiences.

The representation of dreams as a form of persistent reality has been called by the Lovecraft scholar Donald R. Burleson *oneiric objectivism*.[21] This is the premise that dreams are as real as, and perhaps in some respects more important than, waking reality. Lovecraft adopted this literary theme quite independently, as a result of his own vivid dream experiences and his ability to attain a degree of self-awareness and volition in his dreams, but it was greatly accelerated when others mentioned to him that his short story "Polaris" was similar to the stories of Lord Dunsany.[22] After reading Dunsany's collection *A Dreamer's Tales*, and recognizing in Dunsany's stories what he had been struggling to articulate in his own work, Lovecraft wrote a number of stories set in what he came to call the dreamlands.

These stories, which in my opinion are underrated, have an indefinable quality of poignant regret, as of a joy that has just passed but still lingers strong in the memory. Just as when writing his horror stories Lovecraft was most concerned with re-creating the cosmic horror he had felt in his nightmares, in his dream stories his primary goal was to evoke in the reader the pleasant but bittersweet melancholy and languor that he had felt in his more pastoral dreams of sun-gilded domes and abandoned temples.

It is sometimes difficult to tell whether a Lovecraft story is set in the dreamlands or in the distant past. This is the case with a number of tales, such as "The Doom that Came to Sarnath." Confusion arises when Lovecraft mentions a city, or another geographical feature such as the mountain Kadath or the Plateau of Leng, in what is presumably the ancient world, but also mentions it elsewhere as part of the dreamlands. Yet there is no reason why a place cannot exist both in the past and in dreams. We often dream of places that once existed, but have been lost to time, such as the fabled Arabian city of Irem, and in the dreams we are present in those places just as though they still existed.

Lovecraft blurred the distinction between dreams and waking by introducing the concept of alternative dimensions. This merging of dreams with higher dimensions is most evident in his story "The Dreams in the Witch-House," in which the protagonist Walter Gilman finds himself able to pass through a dimensional portal to distant worlds and strange realms not of this earth while he remains in a dreaming state. Occultists have speculated that dreams may be a kind of higher dimensional reality, and that our dreaming is a passage of our mind into that reality, during which we leave our inert flesh behind like a discarded suit of clothing to soar free and unbounded, following the dictates of our fancy.

The writing of the novel *The Dream-Quest of Unknown Kadath*, which is Lovecraft's longest work of fiction, served to purge Lovecraft of the need to focus his primary creative interests in the dreamlands. He did not abandon the theme of dreams, but thereafter it became less dominant in his writings. At the end of "Through the Gates of the Silver Key," Lovecraft's alter ego Randolph Carter, whose mind inhabits the body of an alien being, is abducted through a dimensional portal, never to be seen again by his friends on this planet. In bidding a final farewell to Carter, Lovecraft indicated that his long battle of wills with the horrors of his childhood nightmares was at last resolved—if not with victory, then in uneasy truce.

5

LITTLE BOTTLE
OF POISON

The death of his mother at Butler Hospital on May 24, 1921, due to complications arising from gall-bladder surgery, shook Lovecraft to the core. Although he had been living apart from her at 598 Angell Street for more than two years, ever since she had been committed to Butler for insanity on March 13, 1919, he had never really managed to emerge from behind her skirts. Even delusional and locked away in a secure facility, Susie had continued to cast her shadow over his life. He idealized her both alive and in death, writing in a letter shortly after her passing, "My mother was, in all probability, the only person who thoroughly understood me . . . I shall not again be likely to meet with a mind so thoroughly admirable."[1]

Following his mother's commitment to Butler Hospital, Lovecraft had considered suicide. An excuse that he gave himself for not ending his life at this time was that it would have caused his mother distress. Her death removed the impediment. He now contemplated killing himself almost with eagerness: "During my mother's lifetime I was aware that voluntary euthanasia on my part would cause her distress, but it is now possible for me to regulate the term of my existence with the assurance that my end would cause no one more than a passing annoyance."[2]

For a time he became listless, aimless, drifting. He wrote to his friend Kleiner, "This bereavement decentralizes existence—my sphere no longer possesses a nucleus, since there is now no one person especially interested in what I do or whether I be alive or dead."[3]

It is an observable reality of life that those obsessed with suicide fall into two readily distinguishable groups—those who talk ceaselessly about ending their lives, and those who actually do it. There is little overlap. Lovecraft belonged to the former group, just as his fellow *Weird Tales* writer and correspondent, Robert E. Howard, belonged to the latter. Despite the numerous times Lovecraft contemplated suicide, brooded on it, mulled over the methods, and predicted death by his own hand in his letters, he never actually made the attempt.

Once he recovered from his initial sense of rootlessness following his mother's death, his spirits began to improve. For the first time in his life he found himself his own man, able to make his own decisions without the emotional burden of satisfying the expectations or obtaining the approval of another human being. His aunts did not inhibit him—Lovecraft had never regarded them as authority figures. Released from his mother's shadow, his spirits expanded like the blossom of a flower at last able to find its way to the sun. He began to travel around New England, visiting fellow amateur writers, doing some sightseeing, and attending amateur writing conventions.

Some of those he visited at this period were single women. Whether or not Lovecraft was consciously aware of his search to replace his mother with a similarly intelligent, dominant female presence in his life via the bonds of holy matrimony, it is noteworthy that immediately after his mother's death he began to think of women. In the same letter to Kleiner in which he bemoaned his aimlessness and bereavement at his mother's loss, written only nineteen days after her death, he casually mentioned before closing that he really should pay a visit to "an exceedingly learned and brilliant new United member—

Miss M. A. Little, A.B., A.M., a former college professor now starting as a professional author . . ."[4] The learned lady had written to Lovecraft inviting him to drop by her home in Hampstead, New Hampshire, and Lovecraft's two aunts, perhaps endeavoring to play the part of matchmakers, had urged him to accept her offer.

This particular meeting with Myrta Alice Little, who was only two years older than Lovecraft, took place on June 8, and although it involved a distance of less than one hundred miles, it was the longest journey undertaken by Lovecraft thus far in his life.[5] It was followed by a second get-together in New Hampshire on August 25. Both came to nothing, but they show that Lovecraft's heart was open to matrimonial possibilities.

At the National Amateur Press Association's yearly convention at Boston, which was held that year on July 4, Rheinhart Kleiner introduced Lovecraft to a forceful and vivacious contributor, a widow from New York named Sonia Haft Greene (1883–1972). Sonia was a well-paid executive in the retail clothing trade, but she had developed an interest in creative writing. Her interest soon shifted its main focus to Lovecraft. Not long after their meeting, she made the generous contribution of fifty dollars to the rival UAPA, an act of largess that no doubt inclined Lovecraft more favorably toward her.

She could afford it—at the time when most single women would not have dared to consider attempting to work for a living, she was making a salary of ten thousand dollars a year. She was ahead of her era—the Roaring Twenties had not yet really begun to roar, nor the flappers to flap. The commencement of the decade of the 1920s marked the early beginnings of a new period of social freedom for women. The Nineteenth Amendment to the U.S. Constitution, which for the first time guaranteed women the right to vote in all state and federal elections, had been ratified only a year prior to Lovecraft's meeting with Sonia. Change was in the air.

In some ways, Sonia was an unlikely woman to interest Lovecraft on the personal level. She was a Jew who had been born Sonia Haft Shafirkin in a small town near Kiev, in the Ukraine. She emigrated to Liverpool, England, with her mother and brother sometime around 1890, and followed her mother to New York in 1892. In 1899 she married Samuel Seckendorff, and a year later gave birth to a son. The boy died after only three months, a not-uncommon event for infants in those times of unsanitary living conditions and rampant disease, but in the spring of 1902 Sonia gave birth to a daughter, Florence Carol.

Samuel Seckendorff changed his last name to Greene for social reasons, and his wife also adopted the name. It was not a particularly happy marriage. Sam Greene committed suicide in 1916. Forced to make her own way in the world, Sonia went into business. She quickly gained an executive position at the upscale Manhattan clothing store Ferle Heller's.[6] It was in 1917 that she first became interested in the world of amateur writing and publishing, which for her must have been an intellectually stimulating diversion from the garment trade. Her financial independence ensured her a warm welcome at the NAPA—the organization was always short on funds.

In addition to being a Jew, Sonia was older by half a dozen years than Lovecraft, a single mother with an adult child, and a businesswoman. By the New England conventions of the time, any one of these conditions would have made her an unsuitable match for the pampered son of an old Baptist family of Providence. Nonetheless, there were several factors in her nature that Lovecraft found immensely attractive. It must be borne in mind that he was unconsciously searching for a woman to replace his mother.[7] Consequently, her age may actually have been more of a positive than a negative factor. He liked her intelligence, her social graces, her independent manner and strong will, all of which reminded him of his idealized mental memory of Susie Lovecraft before her madness. Her obvious wealth would not have alienated him. She spent her money lavishly, and was not stingy about buying fine dinners and taxi rides for her amateur literary friends.

Her Jewishness was less insurmountable an impediment than might be supposed from Lovecraft's virulent anti-Semitic opinions. Lovecraft was always more general than specific in his expressions of racial intolerance. He hated Jews collectively, but when interacting with them individually, as he did with his friend Samuel Loveman, he found little to criticize. In his own mind, he rationalized this incongruity by telling himself that the Jews he liked were likeable precisely because they transcended the worst aspects of their Jewishness. And although it would never have been expressed in words, the fact that Sonia was a modestly rich Jew rather than a poor Jew did not hurt her prospects.

If Lovecraft was attracted to Sonia on a crass and unspoken level by her wealth, it must also be said that Sonia was attracted to Lovecraft because of his respectable New England heritage. He was of a "good" Christian family of Providence that could trace its bloodline back to Plymouth Rock. She sought respectability and acceptance beyond her immediate ethnic circle in New York. It must have passed through her mind more than a few times that to be married into the venerable Phillips family of Rhode Island would not hurt her efforts to raise her social status.

The rumor has arisen on the fringes of Lovecraft scholarship that Sonia was in some manner connected with the infamous magician Aleister Crowley. It was promoted by Colin Low in his infamous *Necronomicon Anti-FAQ*, an Internet document that puts forth the specific information that Sonia met Crowley in 1918 in New York at the curiously named Walker's Sunrise Club, a dinner club at which lectures were given on various topics of art and literature. Low stated that Sonia encountered Crowley at this club when he was delivering a talk on modern poetry. Crowley is supposed to have quickly seduced her and made her his lover. Low suggests that it was Sonia, drawing upon ideas she had received from Crowley, who inspired Lovecraft to write about the *Necronomicon*.

Colin Low has admitted that the entire Greene-Crowley interlude was his own invention.[8] There is no evidence at all that Sonia met Crowley or had any serious interest in occult matters. Even so, the legend has received an enthusiastic reception among occultists who are anxious to connect Lovecraft with the prevailing esoteric currents of his time. It is beyond question that Sonia would have heard about Crowley. He was in all the more sensational newspapers, and was demonized by the London press as the "wickedest man in the world." In 1918 he published his Gnostic Mass in the March issue of the New York periodical *The International*.[9]

It is not beyond possibility that Sonia could have met Crowley. He spent the summer of 1918 in what he termed a "magical retreat" on Oesopus Island in the Hudson River.[10] Some of his time was muscularly engaged in painting on the cliff faces of the island in large red letters the motto of his self-created religion of Thelema, "Do what thou wilt." It is surely one of the most prominent early examples of graffiti vandalism in America, and must have aroused a certain amount of talk in New York City. If Sonia ever did encounter Crowley during his New York sojourn from 1914 to 1918—and there is not a shred of a document to suggest that she did—it would have consisted of no more than a brief social brush with greatness signifying nothing in either of their lives.

Sonia and Howard seem to have found a common understanding almost immediately, although most of Lovecraft's initial enthusiasm focused on her deep purse. She used her money to finance the publication of two issues of the amateur periodical *The Rainbow*, in both of which Lovecraft's writings were featured. In the October 1921 issue, his "Nietzscheism and Realism" appeared, a set of aphorisms extracted from two of his early letters to Sonia. Lovecraft also revised a poem she had composed, and this was published along with his aphorisms. The May 1922 issue of the periodical contained Lovecraft's dream-world story "Celephaïs," written in November of 1920 when Lovecraft was still deeply under the influence of Lord Dunsany.

In August 1921, she sent Lovecraft a copy of George Bernard Shaw's latest play *Back to Methuselah* as a gift, and wrote to tell him that she intended to pay him a visit in Providence during the following month. Lovecraft's letters covering this period are euphoric, so evident is his personal happiness. He positively gushes to Rheinhart Kleiner about Sonia's pending visit, writing: "Surely Mrs. G. is the find of the present year amateurically . . ."[11] Indeed, his letters sparkle with such good humor and effusiveness of high spirits that he sounds inebriated. It must be concluded that Lovecraft was falling in love for the first time in his life.

On the afternoon of September 4, 1921, Sonia Greene arrived in Providence for a two-day visit. She took a room at the opulent Crown Hotel and held court, as it were, in the lobby and the dining room, where she receiving Lovecraft and his literary friends. Immediately following her arrival, Lovecraft escorted her on a walking tour of the College Hill district. Sonia made appreciative noises at the right times when Lovecraft pointed out the architectural beauties of the Colonial houses along Angell Street, but Lovecraft noted that her enthusiasm was more muted than his own. This is scarcely to be wondered at since Lovecraft was a fanatic on the subject.

Lovecraft introduced Sonia to his Aunt Lillian, who was favorably impressed by Sonia's manner, and no doubt also by her expensive and stylish Manhattan clothing—his aunt was accustomed to enduring all manner of assorted riffraff among Lovecraft's amateur-writer friends at 598 Angell Street. Sonia stood out from the rest. Lovecraft wrote two weeks after the visit that "my aunt has ever since been eloquent in her praise of Mme. G., whose ideas, speech, manner, aspect, and even attire impressed her with the greatest of favorableness."[12] After returning to the hotel for a meal paid for by Sonia, Lovecraft escorted her to a free open-air band concert at Roger Williams Park. He was impressed that Sonia was so extravagant with her money that she hired a taxi to get the amateur writing group there, but he would not let her repeat this Croesian madness, and prevailed on her to take the tramline back from the park to the hotel. Before leaving the next day, Sonia asked Lovecraft to visit her in New York.

A number of meetings took place between Greene and Lovecraft over the next eighteen months. Lovecraft fulfilled his promise to visit with Sonia on April 6, 1922. He stayed for six nights at her flat at 259 Parkside Avenue, in a fashionable section of Flatbush, Brooklyn, while Sonia slept at the house of a neighbor in order to preserve the proprieties. Lovecraft met Sonia's teenage daughter, Florence—his own future daughter-in-law—and was not overly impressed, to judge by his comments in a letter to Maurice Moe, in which he described her as "a pert, spoiled, and ultra-independent infant rather more hard-boiled of visage then her benignant mater."[13] The distaste was mutual. Florence avoided Lovecraft as much as possible, though what she held against him is not immediately clear. She may have disliked the way Lovecraft and his amateur literary cronies were sponging off her mother's pocketbook.

Sonia wanted to get Lovecraft to herself at the seaside resort town of Magnolia, Massachusetts. While visiting Providence on a rainy Sunday in June, she had repeatedly offered to pay for Lovecraft's entire trip out of her own funds, and Lovecraft at last accepted. He wrote to Maurice Moe: "I declined as many times as courtesy permitted—but if she is determined to blow de coin, it ain't no business of mine to stop her!"[14] Lovecraft seems to have had few ethical scruples about allowing a woman to pay his way. This is surprising in view of his pretension of being an English gentleman.

He arrived at Magnolia on June 26 and stayed with Sonia until July 5. It was the first romantic liaison of his life, and there can be little doubt that romance was its prime purpose, the previous meetings between them having at least the superficial veneer of social visits. One memorable moonlit night, Sonia kissed him on the lips. Sonia later wrote that Lovecraft went as white in the face as a sheet. When she asked him what was wrong, he informed her that it was the first time he had been kissed since infancy.

Sonia admitted that upon first setting eyes on Lovecraft at the Boston NAPA convention, she had not been favorably impressed by his physical appearance, although she grew reconciled to his looks over time. She wrote, "I admired his personality but, frankly, at first not his person."[15] As for Lovecraft, he expected nothing other than expressions of revulsion and rejection from women, where intimate relations were concerned. Once, he asked Sonia quite seriously, "How can any woman love a face like mine?"[16] He must have been astonished and deeply moved when Sonia pressed her lips to his.

During this tryst he helped Sonia compose a short horror story that came to be published the following year, in the November 1923 issue of *Weird Tales*, under the title "The Invisible Monster." Lovecraft had titled it "The Horror at Martin's Beach," the title by which it is known today. Sonia later claimed to have originated the idea for the story, but Lovecraft reworked it extensively, and as is true with so many of his collaborative efforts, it is obviously more his story than hers.

Other visits between them followed, but it was at Magnolia that Lovecraft took the bait and Sonia set the hook. She had determined in her own mind to have him, and after that, Lovecraft had very little control over the matter. He was simply overwhelmed on the emotional level by her generosity, her praise, and her attentions, all of which he had never experienced from any woman other than his mother. The sexual aspect did not appear to play a significant part in their growing closeness. There is no way to know if Lovecraft had intercourse with Sonia during that vacation at Magnolia, but it seems unlikely, based upon his disdainful attitude toward sexuality and his complete lack of prior experience with women.

In early August of 1922 Lovecraft traveled to Cleveland, Ohio, to visit with his correspondent Alfred Galpin. He stayed for two weeks at the Galpin family house at 9231 Birchdale. He also spent time with his friend Samuel Loveman, whose flat was located just around the corner at the Lenore Apartments building. Here he saw for the first time some of the artwork of Clark Ashton Smith, who was one of Loveman's friends. Lovecraft was impressed with the "hideous drawings," which he described as "grotesque, unutterable things."[17] On the way to Cleveland he had stopped briefly in New York to visit Sonia, but on the return leg of the trip he again dropped in to see Sonia and stayed with her in Flatbush from the middle of August to the middle of October. He would later write to his Aunt Lillian about this extended period together with Sonia that "congeniality was tested and found perfect in an infinity of ways."[18]

The romantic relationship continued to flourish in this manner throughout the winter and into the following year. It was a productive time for Lovecraft, and a supremely joyous time. Indeed, we are able to fix not only the year, or the day, but the very hour and almost the minute of the greatest happiness in his entire life. It was not, as might be supposed, the hour of his marriage to Sonia, but rather his first glimpse of the town of Marblehead, Massachusetts, the snow-covered antique roofs of which Lovecraft saw illuminated by the rays of the setting sun. Years later Lovecraft would write, "I account that instant—about 4:05 to 4:10 p. m., Dec. 17, 1922—the most powerful single emotional climax experienced during my nearly forty years of existence. . . . That was the high tide of my life."[19]

Poor Sonia! Not the first glimpse of her face when they met in Boston, not the first sight of her nakedness on their wedding night, but the rooftops of a quaint old New England town excited Lovecraft's supreme, lifelong emotional climax. What chance of success did their union have? Even so, a proposal of marriage was finally made, and accepted. We do not know who proposed, but the assumption is that Sonia took the initiative, as she would later do in all their sexual unions as man and wife. Without informing his two aunts of his intention, on the Sunday of March 2, 1924, Lovecraft departed Providence on the 11:09 a.m. train and arrived at Grand Central Station in the afternoon, where he was met by his fiancée. He married Sonia Greene the following day at Saint Paul's Chapel, an Episcopal church at the corner of Broadway and Vesey Street, very close to the future site of the World Trade Center. It appealed to Lovecraft because it is the oldest church in New York City.

Prior to the ceremony, the happy couple obtained the marriage license, and Sonia bought her own wedding ring from a Jewish dealer. She started to buy a modest white-gold band, but Lovecraft induced her to select a more expensive platinum model surrounded by twenty-four diamond chips for eighty-five dollars, assuring her that he would give her back the money out of the first check he received from his next *Weird Tales* sale. He had in mind the sale of the story he had ghostwritten for Harry Houdini, which he had titled "Under the Pyramids." The publisher of the magazine, J. C. Henneberger, was to pay one hundred dollars for it upon receipt rather than upon publication. It seems sadly appropriate, indeed almost fated, that Sonia should be forced to buy her own ring.

On March 4 the happy couple traveled by train to Philadelphia for their honeymoon. It his confusion and the emotional excitement of his impending marriage, Lovecraft had left his typed final draft of "Under the Pyramids" at the Providence train station. In Philadelphia he rented a Royal typewriter for a dollar, and while Sonia dictated his story from the pen-written manuscript, Lovecraft painfully pecked out the double-spaced text a second time. Sonia told Lovecraft that she enjoyed helping him with his work, and for a time he entertained the fantasy that she might become his literary secretary.

After the honeymoon, they returned to live in Sonia's Flatbush apartment. Florence, Sonia's daughter, moved out of the apartment when Lovecraft moved in. It was just prior to her twenty-second birthday. She seems to have had scant use for Lovecraft, and little inclination to think of him as her stepfather. Lovecraft was initially optimistic about his life as a New Yorker. He received several hints about possible jobs in publishing, and it was suggested to him that his stories might be published as a book. Alas, all these tantalizing lures were no more than sparkles on distant waters.

Things went well enough for several months. Lovecraft pretended to look for work, and wandered around New York with his literary friends, coming home at all hours of the night, while Sonia paid the bills without complaint. The writers gathered weekly in a convivial association that they called the Kalem Club, after the last names of its founding members, all of which began with K, L, or M. The club did not receive its name until February of 1925, but existed for some time prior to this in an informal way. Lovecraft appears to have been the cohesive center of the group, which did not thrive after his departure from the city. Any day or night of the week, Lovecraft could be found socializing with one or more members.

He quickly grew fat on Sonia's excellent cooking, going from a lean 145 pounds to a plump 200 pounds. His pencil-thin neck expanded to a number 16 collar. Sonia declared that he looked much more handsome with some flesh on his bones, but to Lovecraft his body felt bloated and unnatural. His entire married life had an unnatural alienness about it. He could scarcely believe that he was living in the great metropolis, a married man. It was almost dreamlike.

The marriage started to sour when Sonia lost her job at Ferle Heller's. She decided to open her own hat shop in Manhattan and poured her savings into it. The hat shop was a dismal failure, and when she at last closed its doors in July, she had gone from being a relatively well-to-do woman to being only a step removed from poverty. The strain took its toll on her health. In October 1924, she was hospitalized for nervous-stomach problems—probably an ulcer aggravated by her financial worries. No work presented itself in New York. She had to take what she could get, and toward the end of December found a job with the Cincinnati department store Mabley & Carew. She left Lovecraft behind and went west by train on December 31.

All this time, Lovecraft had contributed little or nothing toward their financial expenses. It had been his intention to "contribute to the common fund as much as he safely could,"[20] but it is doubtful whether he remained faithful to this initial resolve. He lived as a kept man, playing the part of the literary lion to his admiring circle of amateur writing cronies in the Kalem Club, wandering around New York sightseeing and socializing. He had begun to seriously look for a job in the latter half of 1924, any kind of a job. Before this, he had made a few discreet inquires at publishers, magazine offices, literary agencies, and newspapers about writing positions, always without success, but now he swallowed his pride and resigned himself to take whatever he could get.

To his great shame and embarrassment, he discovered that no one would hire him to do anything. His skills were worthless in New York. All prospective employers wanted someone with job experience, and since Lovecraft had never held a job of any kind, he had none to offer. The nearest he came to employment was in late July 1924, when he accepted a position as a canvassing salesman for the Creditors' National

Clearing House, a collection agency. The job entailed going from business to business trying to interest owners in contracting with the agency. It was work on commission—it paid no salary of any kind. Lovecraft lasted less than a week, earned not a single dime, and was relieved to offer his resignation.

It was obvious to both of them that Sonia could no longer afford to maintain the expensive Flatbush apartment for Lovecraft after she moved to Cincinnati. She urged Lovecraft to come with her. Lovecraft stubbornly refused to give up New York. During the autumn of 1924 he kept his eye open for a single room not more expensive than five dollars per week, which was about half what he might expect to pay for a comfortable room in a decent building. On January 1, 1925, the day after Sonia left for Cincinnati, Lovecraft moved his precious furniture and other belongings into a room in the northwest corner of a decaying brownstone located at 169 Clinton Street, near the edge of the seedy waterfront neighborhood of Red Hook, in Brooklyn.

Lovecraft took the room, which boasted a small entrance alcove that was almost a second room, in the belief that even though that part of Brooklyn might be rough-and-tumble, the building itself was respectable. It soon became apparent that its days of respectability, at least by Lovecraft's standards of propriety, were fading memories. Many of the boarders were of ethnicities abhorrent to Lovecraft. The sight of them in the hallway, the sounds of their alien music and foreign languages through the walls, the smells of their cooking, all revolted his senses and sickened him. The Irish landlady, Mrs. Burns, who had impressed Lovecraft on first meeting by her perfect, cultured English accent, proved to be less charming as their acquaintance lengthened. "Only later was I to learn of her shrewish tongue, desperate household negligence, miserly watchfulness of lights and unwatchfulness of repairs, and reckless indifference to the class of lodger she admitted!"[21]

Lovecraft discovered that, horror of horrors, he had a Syrian living in the room next to his, who played "eldritch and whining monotones on a strange bagpipe which made me dream ghoulish and incredible things of crypts under Bagdad . . ."[22] To the modern reader, this reaction may seems extreme to the point of hysteria, but Lovecraft had a visceral revulsion toward foreigners that he could not control. Sonia would relate after the failure of their marriage that when she and Lovecraft were walking the streets of New York and encountered a group of immigrants, Lovecraft would become so animated and enraged that she feared for his sanity.[23]

While living in Sonia's fashionable apartment in Flatbush, Lovecraft had spent most of his time exploring the shining, freshly scrubbed Anglo-Saxon face of New York, but after his move to his room on Clinton Street, he found himself unable to block out the sights, sounds, and odors of its ethnic underbelly. In one of his letters to his Aunt Lillian, he called New York "a hell to a sensitive Nordic."[24] The shock to his sensibilities was extreme. Almost overnight, he went from relative contentment to abject, unabated misery. He simply could not endure the environment near Red Hook, yet he did not have the money to leave it. He procured a little bottle of deadly poison and took to carrying it around with him in his pocket everywhere he went, so that at any instant when the horror of his life became too intense to bear, he could swallow the poison and end it.

Life had not even begun to humiliate Lovecraft. In May of 1925 the outer alcove of his room was robbed while he lay asleep in his bed in the inner room. There was no sign of a break-in. Lovecraft deduced that the thief or thieves must have had a key either to the outer door, or more likely to the door that connected his room with the adjoining room. He suspected two young Syrian men of the crime, the faces of whom Lovecraft had never actually looked upon. Stolen were all his suits save for one not worth stealing, his newer "Flatbush" overcoat, Sonia's wicker suitcase, and various electronic parts for a radio worth around one hundred dollars and belonging to Samuel Loveman, who was storing them in Lovecraft's room. Loveman had bought the radio parts on credit and had not yet even finished paying for them.

In his fevered imagination, the rooming house took on the qualities of a nightmare and became almost a living entity. "I conceived the idea that the great brownstone house was a malignly sentient thing—a dead, vampire creature which sucked something out of those within it and implanted in them the seeds of some horrible and immaterial psychic growth."[25] The violation of his room inspired him to write "The Horror at Red Hook" in one continuous burst that began on August 1 and concluded the following day. In this story, Lovecraft poured out his revulsion toward immigrants and the neighborhood of Red Hook itself, making it the scene of a debased cult of Yezidi devil-worshippers who kidnapped and sacrificed children to the demon goddess Lilith in the tunnels under the streets.

Meanwhile, in Cincinnati, Sonia's nervous stomach problems had continued. She was forced to enter a hospital, and as a result lost her job at the department store. In late February 1925 she returned to New York, bruised by life but not defeated in spirit. She spent the spring of that year apart from Lovecraft, living at the house of a female doctor in Saratoga Springs while she tried to cure her gastric problems. She reunited with Lovecraft during June and July, but also in the summer she found a job at Halle's, the most prestigious department store in Cleveland, Ohio, that was too good to pass up, and again left Lovecraft to his own devices.

He escaped from the horror of Red Hook and his depressing room on Clinton Street by exploring New York City and its surrounding environs. While visiting Elizabeth, New Jersey (which Lovecraft referred to by its older name of Elizabethtown), on August 11, he bought a dime composition book and wrote in pencil the story "He," about a visitor to New York who becomes lost in the twisted streets of Greenwich Village and slips back in time to Colonial New York. Elizabethtown had in October of the previous year inspired the story "The Shunned House." The resemblance of the town to the New England with which Lovecraft was familiar, and for which he longed with all his heart, opened the creative floodgate of his soul.

He was able to distract his mind from the misery and horror of his living conditions near Red Hook by composing an extended critical essay on the progress of supernatural horror fiction, which he titled "Supernatural Horror in Literature." This was written at the urging of W. Paul Cook, who wanted it for an amateur magazine he intended to publish called *The Recluse*. Lovecraft began this book-length essay in November 1925 but did not manage to finish it until May of 1927. It goes without saying that he was never paid for this considerable effort. It is a major piece of work, and has been widely regarded as one of the best essays of its kind. It is without doubt the best nonfiction writing he ever did.

During his dreary grind on the outskirts of Red Hook, Lovecraft continued to meet with his circle of literary friends in the Kalem Club. They met on Wednesdays at the rooms of various members, but most frequently in Lovecraft's Clinton Street room. He was able to play the part of genial host, having nothing else to occupy his time and energies, although his entertainment budget was limited—his aunts were supposed to send him fifteen dollars per week from his investments, but they only sent five, and that at irregular intervals.[26] Lovecraft traveled with his fellow amateurs on various local sightseeing junkets in an attempt to get away from Red Hook, and relieve some of his mounting hopelessness. He was rapidly sliding into a state of morbid depression.

Lovecraft's repeated references to suicide were not lost on his friends. Frank Belknap Long wrote to his aunts to advise them about the situation. In December of 1925, his Aunt Lillian wrote to Lovecraft suggesting that he should consider moving back to Providence. She dangled the lure of a possible job offer, which like so many others was no more than a mirage. Lovecraft resisted admitting defeat in New York. He responded to her letter by writing that were he to move back to New England, he could never think of leaving it again. He and Sonia had talked about the possibility of her getting a department store job in Boston, a city Lovecraft believed he could endure, but at that particular time her Cleveland job hinted at the prospect for advancement and was too good to cast away.

Lovecraft had only praise for his wife's patience and support during this period when he was unable to find work in New York, or to earn anything substantial from his writings. He called her willingness to accept without complaint his "combination of incompetence and aesthetic selfishness"[27] a quality of saintliness that was uncommonly rare. We see in these remarks a degree of self-disgust, and even self-hatred. Lovecraft had no illusions—he regarded himself as an abject failure, both as a writer and as a husband. Only the mirage of a job prospect as assistant to his friend James Ferdinand Morton, a former president of the NAPA and Kalem Club member, who was to become the curator of the Paterson Museum in New Jersey, kept Lovecraft in New York. It came to nothing, as did so many of his hopes.

The sole paying position Lovecraft managed to obtain during his entire period of living in New York City was a temporary job hand-addressing envelopes for advertising catalogues in the back of the Dauber and Pine book store at Fifth Avenue and 12th Street, where Samuel Loveman worked. Needless to say, Lovecraft did not get the job himself—it was obtained on his behalf by his friend. In March of 1926 he began addressing ten thousand envelopes, a task that took him six weeks and paid the princely sum of $17.50 per week. Still, it was a good deal more money than he was accustomed to earning, and he welcomed it.

It was while Lovecraft was engaged addressing envelopes that the plans of his aunts to get him back to Providence before he committed suicide came to fruition. They arranged for Lovecraft to rent a room in the lower level of a rooming house at 10 Barnes Street in Providence, to the north of Brown University, and for his Aunt Lillian to rent a room in the same house on the upper level, so that she would be close enough to take care of him, as she had done while he was still living at 598 Angell Street. His aunts even sent Lovecraft the train ticket to come home.

Lovecraft was jubilant at the prospect of getting out from under the shadow of Red Hook. It was akin to release from a prison. He had not been in such good spirits since the period just prior to his marriage. Indeed, apart from his orgasmic first vision of Marblehead, which was the undisputed high point of his existence, the two happiest events of his life were his arrival in New York and his departure from New York, and of the two, the leaving was undoubtedly the more joyful. He later called his two-year-long nightmare in New York his "queer dream about being away from home."[28]

Sonia did not object to the move. She must have realized that her husband was dying inside by slow degrees in New York. She had just prior to his departure given up her job in Cleveland, the hoped-for promotion having come to nothing, and she helped him move his belongings to Providence on April 17, staying with him for a week until he was settled.[29]

The house at 10 Barnes Street was a brown Victorian structure built around 1880 by friends of the Phillips family, all of whom were long dead. Lovecraft's room was a former dining room with a fireplace, and it boasted a kitchenette alcove. So great an improvement was it over his room on Clinton Street that it seemed like heaven to Lovecraft. He approved of his fellow boarders, and he approved of the neighborhood the house occupied. Most of all, he approved of the view from his window, which gave a pleasant prospect of stately trees, antique houses, and an old-fashioned garden. It was a place in which he could feel that his spirit was at peace, a place where he could write. The wonder is that he had been able to write anything during his nightmare in New York, so intense had been his unhappiness. He gushed in a letter to Frank Belknap Long and the other members of the Kalem Club, "Contented? Why, gentlemen, I am *home!*"[30]

Sonia talked with her husband and his aunts about the prospect of her opening her own hat shop in Providence. Lovecraft's aunts told her calmly but in no uncertain terms that it was impossible to even think that the wife of a member of the respected Phillips family should ever work for a living. Really, it was too vulgar even to consider for a moment. Lovecraft concurred with their decision. This was Sonia's last, desperate attempt to find a way to save their marriage. She must have known that it was already over, but she made this final gesture to remain close to her husband, who could not hope to support her in his single boarding-house room with no significant income and no future prospect for any improvement in his finances. She returned to Brooklyn to look for work.

Over the next two years, Sonia and Lovecraft saw little of one another. They corresponded by letter. She induced him to come back to New York to visit with her for a week in the middle of September 1926, while she was in the city on a business trip, and in 1928 Lovecraft came to Brooklyn to help her open yet another hat shop. He stayed at her apartment at 395 East 16th Street from April 24 to June 7.[31] It must have been an ordeal, and did not lead to a renewed closeness.

Their divorce took place in the spring of 1929. The final decree was granted under the liberal divorce laws of Rhode Island, on the spurious pretext that Sonia had been unfaithful to Lovecraft. Yet again, as so often in his life, Lovecraft played the passive part and allowed a woman to take the initiative. Initially, Lovecraft was against the divorce on the ground that it was unseemly for a Providence man of good family, but his wife at last convinced him that it would be the best for both of them. For some unknown reason, Lovecraft never got around to actually signing the divorce papers, so it was not technically finalized. This was a matter of no moment to either party.

Lovecraft was philosophical about the dissolution of his marriage. He wrote that he and Sonia were simply unsuited for union in their basic natures, he with an "Apollonian aesthetic" and she with a "Dionysian aesthetic."[32] By this he meant, in part, that she enjoyed sex and he did not. Sonia would later confide to August Derleth that she had been forced to take the initiative in all their lovemaking, but that once he was set into motion Lovecraft was "an adequately excellent lover."[33] However, he did not care for physical contact; in place of a kiss or an embrace, Lovecraft was in the habit of linking his little finger with hers—a habit, perhaps, that he had picked up from his mother. That was his comfort level of physical intimacy, two fingers touching. In view of his neurotic fixations and general aversion to physical contact, it is something of a miracle that he was able to perform in bed at all.

Lovecraft summed up the marriage problem in a revealing letter to Maurice W. Moe, in which he wrote: "With a wife of the same temperament as my mother and aunts, I would probably have been able to reconstruct a type of domestic life not unlike that of Angell St. days, even though I would have had a different status in the household hierarchy."[34] He was looking for a mother substitute, a woman to take care of him as his mother had done, and as his aunts were still doing. He wanted a way to slip back into the lifestyle he had enjoyed while his mother was performing all of the domestic duties and responsibilities, leaving him free to do nothing but read, write, and dream away his days. Sonia had been unable to grant him this childlike freedom from care due to money constraints.

The last meeting between Sonia and Lovecraft took place in March 1933, in Hartford, Connecticut. Perhaps Sonia was attempting one final time to discover if there was any flickering spark remaining of their lost love. If so, she was disappointed. She left for California later that year, after tearing up all of Lovecraft's letters to her and ceremonially burning them in the middle of an open field.[35] In 1936 she married a Jewish man, Dr. Nathaniel Davis, and took his name. Lovecraft was completely out of her life—she only learned about his death in 1945, some eight years after the fact.

6

YOG-SOTHOTHERY

Many of Lovecraft's horror stories concern godlike beings he called the Old Ones—a general term for both alien races and individual entities of great knowledge and vast power. They descended to our world long before the arising of the human species, and established themselves on its lands and in its seas. For various reasons, the Old Ones withdrew themselves prior to the beginnings of human history, but they did not go far. They watch and wait at the boundaries of our world for the opportunity to regain their former mastery over its lands and over its current dominant species—us.

It is difficult to discuss the Old Ones because this term was not applied by Lovecraft to a single alien species or to only a single hierarchy of beings. Lovecraft used it as the descriptive title for half a dozen different alien races. Members of any intelligent alien race that had existed in the dim pre-history of the earth were referred to as "the Old Ones" in ancient occult records such as the *Necronomicon*, and by the members of surviving human cults dedicated to their worship, simply because such beings were so ancient. They are the "Old Ones" because they are the ones from the old times of long ago. The various species of Old Ones differ greatly in their natures, but they are all alien to this planet and they all predate the human race.

Indeed, a crinoid race sometimes called the Elder Things, to differentiate them from other races of "Old Ones," is said to have used genetic science to create the human species as a food source, and also as a kind of cosmic joke. In the short novel *At the Mountains of Madness*, human explorers in the abandoned city of the Elder Things find sculptures depicting these primitive proto-humans: "It interested us to see in some of the very last and most decadent sculptures a shambling primitive mammal, used sometimes for food and sometimes as an amusing buffoon by the land dwellers, whose vaguely simian and human foreshadowings were unmistakable."

Lovecraft referred to his mythos stories in a self-deprecating way as his *Yog-Sothothery*, a reference to Yog-Sothoth, the cosmic gatekeeper who has the power to open dimensional portals that permit the Old Ones to enter our earthly reality. He obviously considered Yog-Sothoth the key figure in his alien mythology, or he would not have named it in this way. After Lovecraft's death, the writer August Derleth, who through various wheelings and dealings managed to gain control over Lovecraft's literary works, began to refer to Lovecraft's mythology as the Cthulhu mythos. It is known by this misleading title even to the present—misleading, because it wrongly suggests that Cthulhu is the central figure of the mythos.

In my own writings I prefer to call Lovecraft's mythology the *Necronomicon* mythos, since that dreaded occult text, scried by Lovecraft in his dreams, seems to me even more central to his mythic vision than Yog-Sothoth. It is generally agreed by Lovecraft scholars that the term "Cthulhu mythos" coined by Derleth is an unfortunate mistake. Cthulhu is undoubtedly the most popular of the Great Old Ones with the general public, but he is not the most important. That honor should go either to Yog-Sothoth or to Nyarlathotep. However, the enormous size of Cthulhu, coupled with his strange appearance and dramatic entrance in the key mythos story "The Call of Cthulhu," have conspired to make him the fan favorite.

Derleth first mentioned the "Cthulhu mythology" in the essay "H. P. Lovecraft: Outsider," which he published in June 1937 to honor Lovecraft shortly after Lovecraft's death. Concerning his choice of the term, Derleth wrote in this essay that over time it was noticed that Lovecraft's stories began to exhibit a coherent myth-pattern that was so convincing, readers searched for references to it in museums and libraries. It came to be called the "Cthulhu mythology" because this myth-pattern first revealed itself in Lovecraft's story "The Call of Cthulhu." However, around 1931 Derleth had suggested to Lovecraft that his mythology be named the "The Mythology of Hastur,"[1] so Derleth may have had misgivings about the term "Cthulhu mythos" himself.

In the initial phase of his writing career, Lovecraft did not set out to create a connected and internally consistent mythology. It arose piecemeal from his nightmares. He copied down his eerie dreams and made them into stories, or incorporated parts of his dreams into his tales, and at some point he became aware that he was building a fictional mythos. Rather than fight against this tendency, he embraced it. What began unconsciously was carried forward with deliberate intent. When his literary correspondents referred to various parts of his evolving mythos in their own stories, Lovecraft encouraged them, and in return he took bits and pieces of their work and incorporated them into his Yog-Sothothery stew.

After Lovecraft's death, correspondents such as August Derleth continued to write stories that incorporated aspects of his mythological world. In this way, the *Necronomicon* mythos expanded beyond Lovecraft and became a living literary entity that continues to thrive to this day. The mythos has evolved in ways Lovecraft would never have approved. For example, Derleth introduced a dichotomy of good against evil between the alien races, and tried to associate the leading figures of the Old Ones with the four ancient elements: fire, water, air, and earth. Neither of these innovations bears any trace of Lovecraft's concept of the mythos. Lovecraft rejected the existence of absolute good and evil, and never grouped his Great Old Ones into any formal hierarchy, most certainly not a hierarchy of elementals.

Numerous literary scholars and fans of the mythos such as Derleth and the writer Lin Carter attempted to pin down what defines a mythos story. Some bracketed the mythos quite narrowly and restricted the number of stories to around a dozen, while others favored a broader definition. I am one of the latter group. I place a story into what I term the *Necronomicon* mythos if it makes reference to the *Necronomicon* or to any of the Great Old Ones—the named godlike beings from beyond the stars. The mythos is an interconnected web of references. When a story uses an element of that mythic web, it becomes a part of the web. On the question of what makes a mythos tale, Joshi and Schultz wrote that "most critics failed to note that HPL scattered references to his pseudo-mythology, his imaginary topography, and his mythical books across many stories, making the exercise of segregating them into mutually exclusive categories a futile endeavor."[2]

For example, some authorities might not classify Lovecraft's dreamlands novel *The Dream-Quest of Unknown Kadath* as a mythos tale, but I place it within the mythos because it features Nyarlathotep, the active, intelligent agent of the demon-sultan of chaos, Azathoth, who is also referred to in the novel. These links, and other mentions of mythic aspects such as the Plateau of Leng, move the entire dream-lands cycle into the mythos—since, if the *Dream-Quest* is part of the mythos, it follows that any story set in the dreamlands defined in this novel must also be part of the mythos universe.

By a similar process of adhesive inclusion, I class the stories that take place in Lovecraft's mythological New England settings, which Lovecraft referred to as his Arkham cycle, as part of the mythos as a whole. These tales concerning the fictional towns of Arkham, Dunwich, Kingsport, and Innsmouth, the Miskatonic Valley and the river of the same name winding through it, and venerable Miskatonic University, make numerous mentions of the *Necronomicon* and the Old Ones. Lovecraft's fictional New England settings are thus part of the mythos universe, and it follows that any event set in these unique localities must also be a part of it.

Lovecraft's mythos stories are bound together by a set of startlingly modern presumptions. In 1927 he wrote to Farnsworth Wright, editor of *Weird Tales*: "Now all my tales are based on the fundamental premise that common human laws and interests and emotions have no validity or significance in the vast cosmos-at-large."[3] In the universe in which these stories occur, there is no supreme God and no demonic anti-force, no Adversary such as exists in Christianity. Some, though not all, of the beings that were called gods or devils by past human civilizations were alien entities. They are not merely removed from us in distance through normal space, but occupy dimensions so strange that their very substance can scarcely exist in our reality. For example, Cthulhu's gelatinous body needs no food to sustain it, and when broken apart, reforms itself. The race of "Old Ones" known as the Mi-go are so alien that when they die, their bodies evaporate to nothingness rather than decay. The Old Ones of "The Dunwich Horror" are so alien that the human eye refuses to see them, and they pass invisible.

These aliens possess sciences so strange and yet so potent, they appear to men to be magical in nature. The science fiction writer Arthur C. Clarke may have been thinking of the Old Ones when he wrote his famous maxim, "Any sufficiently advanced technology is indistinguishable from magic."[4] Remnants of their wisdom, such as the manner of opening dimensional portals, have been preserved in the *Necronomicon* and similar occult texts in the form of magic rituals, and at times have been employed by imprudent human beings, usually to their sorrow. These aliens are still worshipped as gods by degenerate cults, and are sometimes summoned into our world through opened portals using what the cultists think of as the black arts. However, there is no magic in the usual sense in Lovecraft's mythos; there is only higher alien science and mathematics, which are mistaken for magic by those human beings who use them without ever truly understanding them.

Throughout his life, Lovecraft remained an avowed agnostic, but toward his death he tended to hold a more overtly atheistic view. Even as a very young child he had rejected belief in the supernatural, denying the existence of God and the angels in his Sunday school classes. For Lovecraft, the supernatural embraced not only all forms of magic, but all forms of religion and spiritual belief as well. He rejected the idea of an afterlife and scoffed at reincarnation. He thought astrology, Theosophy, and other aspects of the occult were bunkum. He was in general agreement with Harry Houdini, who spent considerable time and effort exposing fraudulent spirit mediums, in the opinion that all spiritualists were frauds.

Lovecraft's cynical philosophy arose directly out of his personal sense of alienation from the rest of the human race, and from his intellectual conviction that there is no higher purpose to human existence. Forever the outsider, he regarded the mass of other people as no more than details of the background through which he moved. He wrote to his Aunt Lillian, "The people of a place matter absolutely nothing to me except as components of the general landscape and scenery."[5] This detachment from the usual emotional dependencies allowed him to place the human race, and indeed the entire planet upon which we dwell, in accurate perspective when compared with the rest of the universe.

Very few individuals are able to comprehend just how insignificant we are in the greater scheme of things. Even those who presume to know the scale of the universe in an abstract sense are incapable of appreciating it viscerally. Lovecraft was one of those few exceptions. His study of astronomy had taught him the vastness of space, and his study of geology and history had given him a similar grasp of the vastness of time. He resolutely refused to retreat from these chilling realities into the comforting cocoon of religious dogmatism. He could scarcely bear to contemplate the sheer inconsequence of human existence in a random and pitiless universe, but he was unable to turn his mind away, and the vision of emptiness that forever confronted him seared into his imagination like a white-hot poker.

Not only are space and time vast beyond the capacity of the human mind to comprehend, but they are voids. Only a few tiny flecks of light called stars swirl in little eddies called galaxies that are lost in the unending darkness, and if any other forms of life inhabit planets around any of those tiny flecks, that life must be so alien that we might very well be unable to recognize it as alive. It would certainly feel less kinship for us then we feel for the insects that share our DNA heritage. There is every prospect that such alien life, were it to exist, would be vastly more ancient than humanity. In the duration of the universe, stars have been born and have died, and new stars such as our own sun have arisen in their places—our sun is composed of the matter of dead stars, as are our own bodies. In this inconceivable stretch of aeons, our species has only existed for the blink of an eye.

What fearful sciences and arts must such ancient, alien beings have created in their vast span of existence? Modern human science has been around for five hundred years—what must the science of a race that has existed five hundred million years look like? Questions such as these occupied the mind of Lovecraft while he gazed through the telescope of

Brown University at the Ladd Observatory during the nights of his boyhood, and they shaped his strange dreams.

In his mythos, Lovecraft postulated that the earth has been visited many times during its ancient history by alien races with the capacity to leap the distance between the stars, and even the barriers of time and the dimensions of reality. These races came from beyond the stars—or, as Lovecraft put it in his letter to Farnsworth Wright, from "nameless vortices of never-dreamed-of strangeness, where form and symmetry, light and heat, even matter and energy themselves, may be unthinkably metamorphosed or totally wanting."[6]

The assumption at the root of this musing that the earth has been visited in its past by aliens is the same that supposes that, given enough time, a dozen monkeys banging away randomly on typewriters will produce the complete works of Shakespeare. If there are ancient alien races dwelling among the stars and lurking between the dimensions, races possessed of advanced technology that to us would seem magical, eventually they must find the earth if they have all eternity in which to search. Since the modern human species has existed only for an instant in the cosmic scale of events, visitations of aliens to this planet almost surely took place in our past, or will occur in our future. It is less likely that such visits would chance to happen during the brief period of our recorded history.

Lovecraft further postulated in his mythos that the aliens who visited our world in the past did not depart, but remain here on the margins of our reality, unseen and usually unsuspected, waiting for a more congenial set of conditions to develop that will allow them to emerge from their places of repose and rule our world, as they ruled it in past ages and will rule it in the ages to come. If indeed they are still here, it follows that they must lie hidden in some way, or we would already be overtly aware of them. The human race as a whole remains ignorant of their presence at the edges of our reality—it is only a few sensitive individuals who have managed to glean hints of their imminence from ancient occult records or from psychic whispers. How is this blindness to be explained?

The explanation is one of self-preservation. The mass of human-kind deliberately disregards the existing fragmentary hints about the Old Ones. Our continuing ignorance is the result of an unconscious determination to deny their reality. Even when the facts of their existence are correlated and presented, as at odd times they have been in the press or in published papers and books, we refuse to recognize them. This willful blindness is our defense against madness, for were we to be made fully cognizant of the Old Ones and their natures, the human mind would spin off its axis and be lost in chaos. Only the strongest of our species are capable of confronting even a part of the truth about the Old Ones without immediately going insane. Thus, Lovecraft wrote at the beginning of his most famous short story, "The Call of Cthulhu":

> The most merciful thing in the world, I think, is the inability of the human mind to correlate all its contents. We live on a placid island of ignorance in the midst of black seas of infinity, and it was not meant that we should voyage far. The sciences, each straining in its own direction, have hitherto harmed us little; but some day the piecing together of dissociated knowledge will open up such terrifying vistas of reality, and of our frightful position therein, that we shall either go mad from the revelation or flee from the light into the peace and safety of a new dark age.

Lovecraft intimated in his brief history of the *Necronomicon* that its author, Abdul Alhazred, had gone mad after learning the truth about the Old Ones while wandering in the great Arabian desert known as the Empty Space. Throughout the history of the book, those who have chanced to read it have lost their reason, killed themselves, or met with mysterious and unfortunate endings. It is not the book itself that is the danger; it is the knowledge contained on its pages. Madness arises from too much reality. Lovecraft echoed the sentiment of the eighteenth-century English poet Thomas Gray: "When ignorance is bliss, 'tis folly to be wise."[7] In the mythos, ignorance is the only thing that preserves us from chaos.

The frail human mind wraps the Old Ones in familiar shapes with which we are able to cope—we can see only those things for which we possess some frame of reference. These guises reduce the Old Ones to the level of archetypal patterns. Nyarlathotep, who is faceless, has countless avatars that he uses to communicate with humans without instantly driving them insane: the form of a young pharaoh of ancient Egypt, that of a traveling stage performer, that of the fabled Black Man of the witches' sabbat, that of a veiled priest robed in yellow silks.

Yog-Sothoth has no face, but appears to men most commonly as a bewildering conglutination of iridescent, interpenetrating spheres that floats on the air. Shub-Niggurath sometimes comes as the black goat of the witches' sabbat, but she has no inherent face or form that would be comprehensible to human consciousness. Azathoth, even though he is referred to as the "demon-sultan," is neither a demon nor a sultan, but can most nearly be described as a vortex of negative energy.

Cthulhu, who is said in a quotation from the *Necronomicon* that occurs in "The Dunwich Horror" to be cousin to the Old Ones, and far enough removed from them that he can "spy them only dimly," has a somewhat more tangible form—yet when men landed by ship on risen R'lyeh and inadvertently opened his tomb, all who looked on his translucent body perished in raving madness save one, and that man eventually took his own life. The serpent god Yig, worshipped by the Plains Indians, is able to change his shape at will, sometimes appearing as a serpent and sometimes as a man with the head of a snake. He brings madness or death to those who meet him.

The alien entity Tsathoggua, first conceived by the writer Clark Ashton Smith in 1929 as a sleeping, obese toad-god, but who made his first appearance in the August 1930 issue of *Weird Tales* in the Lovecraft story "The Whisperer in Darkness," was transformed by Lovecraft into a being without a fixed form. For Lovecraft, the shape of a toad-like creature was merely one of the shapes Tsathoggua chose to adopt. The true nature of Tsathoggua is that of a viscous black liquid that can flow and transmute itself. In Lovecraft's story "The Whisperer in Darkness," Tsathoggua is described as "amorphous," and in his story "The Horror in the Museum," published in the July 1933 issue of *Weird Tales*, Tsathoggua transforms himself from his black toad-like shape into "a long, sinuous line with hundreds of rudimentary feet."

The thread running through Lovecraft's descriptions of his Great Old Ones is the inability of human sight to fix their shapes, or of the human mind to conceive their true natures. This is not the result of any cloaking magic or invisibility science, but is due to the strange composition of the Old Ones. Our visual perception is inadequate to convey them other than in the masks of archetypical figures with which we are somewhat familiar from our dreams and myths, and our mental processes revolt and run mad when confronted with their essential otherness. Those who worship them transform them into gods and those who loathe and fear them revile them as devils, but they are merely alien to a degree beyond our capacity to even imagine.

Lovecraft never asserted that the Old Ones are real, and he gently mocked those who made this suggestion to him in letters, but he did put forth in a serious way the premise that alien races such as the Old Ones could be real and might very well have visited the ancient earth during her long and unknown history. Below the level of his cynical scoffing at all forms of spirituality and the supernatural was the nagging awareness that the Old Ones arose from his dreams, and that his dreams came from some unknown place beyond his control and beyond his conception.

One of the more modern aspects of Lovecraft's Yog-Sothothery is its atheism. Lovecraft's mythical universe has no God—or, at least, no God that would be recognized as such by any conventional religion. Lovecraft's God is a mockery of the Christian deity. His name among men is Azathoth. Whereas the God of Christians sits enthroned in light at the apex of the orderly cosmos, Azathoth sits on a black throne at the center of the swirling vortex of chaos. Whereas the Christian deity is omniscient, Azathoth is a mindless idiot. Whereas the Christian God notices and grieves for the fall of the least sparrow, Azathoth neither knows nor cares about any suffering in the universe. He is the God of randomness, the God of chance, the God of meaninglessness.

Lovecraft read the German philosopher Friedrich Nietzsche around the same time he came to know his future wife, Sonia Greene. In Nietzschean terms, the Old Ones are beyond good or evil. They have been worshipped as gods and reviled as devils, but it is the limitation of the human imagination that casts the Old Ones in these supernatural roles. Lovecraft was careful to make the distinction between what the Old Ones actually are, and what they are perceived to be by human beings. After his death, August Derleth added to the mythos and introduced alien forces of goodness and light to counterbalance what he regarded as the evil and darkness of Lovecraft's Old Ones. Derleth called his benign aliens the Elder Gods, a term never used by Lovecraft.[8] The "Elder Ones" are mentioned by Lovecraft in an enigmatic way in his story "The Strange, High House in the Mist," but there is no indication that he intended them to be viewed as the ultimate source of goodness and order in the universe.

One man's god is another man's devil. Who can know the thoughts of the gods? In a practical sense, the Old Ones are gods. They are not supernatural, but their natures are so alien, and their achievements so far in advance of those of humanity, that they appear as gods to men, and in Lovecraft's mythos, they are worshipped as gods by ancient human cults, some of which have survived to the present in obscure backwaters of the world. The same alien beings regarded as gods by their cults of human worshippers are looked upon as demons by the faithful followers of conventional religions. It has always been so, and if Lovecraft's Old Ones do exist on some level of reality, it is inevitable that they be worshipped, and yet also inevitable that they be reviled.

Lovecraft wrote about the more conventional gods of human history, but he set them in the dreamlands, and made them the creations of human beings. In the mythos, the gods of the Greeks, Celts, and of other ancient pantheons did not fashion men after their image, but rather, men made the gods by dreaming them into existence. It was the repeated dreams of their worshippers that gave these "gods of earth" a kind of permanence. They exist still in our dreams, all the gods of our mythologies with recognizable names, faces, and forms.

Those gods who are best remembered, and hence dreamed about most often, are larger in size than those who have been forgotten. Yet even the greatest of them is weak in comparison with the Old Ones. As Lovecraft informed us in *The Dream-Quest of Unknown Kadath*, all these pale gods of earth that were fashioned over the millennia by the dreams of humanity have been gathered together and are at present being held prisoner by Nyarlathotep within a great palace atop Mount Kadath in the Cold Waste. He keeps them at his beck and call and forces them to dance for his amusement.

Lovecraft's concept that advanced alien beings visited the earth in the distant past and interacted with the ancient human race was used, in a watered-down form, by Erich von Däniken as the basis for his theory of ancient astronauts, expressed in his 1968 book *Chariots of the Gods?* and in numerous later works. Von Däniken sought to explain spiritual visitations of gods and angels in strictly material terms, as actual meetings with aliens. If we are to believe the advocates of the UFO phenomenon, such visitations are not confined to the past but still occur today. Lovecraft died a decade before the modern UFO craze began in 1947, and we can only conjecture what he might have thought about it. He would probably have dismissed it due to the lack of physical evidence to support it. He would have found the gray UFO aliens far too familiar, too humanoid, to be taken seriously, and the motives of the grays would have struck him as trite.

Lovecraft did not regard his mythos as possessing any great importance in the scheme of things. He wrote to his friend Frank Belknap Long, Jr., "I really agree that Yog-Sothoth is a basically immature conception and unfitted for really serious literature."[9] In the same letter, he added the thoughtful comment that the only way his Yog-Sothothery might have permanent artistic value is as a vehicle by which "fixed dream-patterns of the natural organism are given an embodiment and crystallization."[10] This, of course, is exactly what Lovecraft was doing—crystallizing his recurring personal dreams into universal mythic archetypes. His Yog-Sothothery, which he spoke about in so slighting a manner, was nothing less than the creation of an entirely new mythology for the modern age.

With the exception of the Oxford don and fantasist J. R. R. Tolkien, no other writer of popular fiction in the twentieth century was able to set forth such a cohesive and compelling mythology for the modern West. In Tolkien's case, it was a deliberate act. He wrote his *Lord of the Rings* and other related works with the explicit purpose of creating a completely new myth cycle that would serve the needs and interests of Westerners. By contrast, Lovecraft's mythos grew spontaneously over a period of many years, and it was only after it had come into being that he recognized it for what it was—yet of the two mythological creations, Lovecraft's is much more compelling to the modern mind. Tolkien drew upon his expertise in ancient languages and medieval manuscripts, but Lovecraft drew upon his knowledge of science. His atheistic, outsider philosophy is becoming more relevant with each passing year, as belief in formal religion falters and traditional mores and conventions come under social assault.

Lovecraft held the view that all forms of human religion were equally absurd, but he also took the position that if any of them were to be taken seriously, they all must be accepted, since they all arose in the same way from the dreams of men and rested on the same tenuous foundation of faith. He maintained that the solemn and stately rituals of Christianity are no more valid than the religious practices of the Yezidi devil-worshippers—both are expressions of the cultures that gave them birth. In a 1930 letter to fellow *Weird Tales* author Frank Belknap Long, he wrote, "If the theism of Christus is true because our ancestors believed it, why is not the devil worship of the Yezidis equally true because they and their ancestors have believed it?"[11]

He carried this line of thought still further, and arrived at an extraordinary and daring conclusion—that all imaginary systems of cosmology must be equally valid. He wrote to Long that "although each of the conflicting orthodoxies of the past, founded on known fallacies among primitive and ignorant races, certainly has an equal theoretical chance with any other orthodoxy or with any theory of science of being true, it most positively has no greater chance than has any random theory of fiction . . ."[12] The cosmic framework of his horror stories, and indeed the cosmologies of his fellow *Weird Tales* writers, must be taken just as seriously, or just as slightingly, as those of any major world theology.

> Let us grant that in theory the doctrine of Buddha, or of Mohammed, or of Lao-Tse, or of Christus, or of Zoroaster, or of some Congo witch-doctor, or of T. S. Eliot, or of Mary Baker Eddy, or of Dionysus, or of Plato, or of Ralph Waldo Emerson,

has just as much or as little positive evidence for it as has any other attempted explanation of the cosmos. So far, so good. But this concession cannot possibly be made without extending equal theoretical authority to Chamber's Yellow Sign, Dunsany's Pegana, your Tindalos, Klarkash-Ton's Tsathoggua, my Cthulhu, or any other fantastic concoction anybody may choose to invent. Who can disprove any such concoction, or say that it is not "esoterically true" even if its creator did think he invented it in jest or fiction?[13]

Lovecraft intended to make the point that all the world's religions are no more true than the idle speculations of magazine fiction writers, and that all of them should be regarded as mere fantasies; however, we may turn his conclusion around and observe that, in his opinion, his Old Ones are no less real than the angels described in the Torah, the New Testament, and the Koran. Lovecraft was a declared agnostic only one small step removed from total atheism, and rejected all spiritual and esoteric things—but those of us who are not atheistic may find matter for reflection in his view that his Yog-Sothothery is every bit as valid a system of belief as the dogma of Christianity.

In the mythos stories, the "Old Ones" of various races are forever trying to break into our world so that they may remake it into their world. In "The Dunwich Horror," the race of monstrous invisible beings that are usually assigned the specific designation of Old Ones by mythos writers (although also called the Elder Things in the story) rely on the magic of wizards to breed with mortal women and produce hybrid offspring who will aid them in their purposes. One such hybrid is Wilbur Whateley, who may be the son of Yog-Sothoth and who seeks to employ the "long chant" in the *Necronomicon* to open the gate of Yog-Sothoth and let the Old Ones issue forth into our world.

Once they have emerged through the gate into our reality, the Old Ones will wipe the entire surface of our planet clean of all forms of biological life, in preparation for restoring the earth to a higher dimension from which it has fallen. Their purpose is to remove the entire planet from its orbit around the sun after sterilizing it. Only the hybrid offspring of human-alien couplings such as Wilbur and his invisible twin brother will remain unharmed during this cleansing of life from the earth. Dr. Henry Armitage, head librarian of Miskatonic University, learns the truth of the Old Ones' intention, and it almost unhinges his reason: "He would shout that the world was in danger, since the Elder Things wished to strip it and drag it away from the solar system and cosmos of matter into some other plane or phase of entity from which it had once fallen, vigintillions of aeons ago."

In this purpose of the Old Ones we find many echoes of the prophetic apocalyptic literature of Judeo-Christianity and Gnosticism. The earth has fallen into a degraded state, represented by its infestation with biological life. The Old Ones act the part of the vengeful angels of the book of Revelation, but they do not punish mankind for our sins—the Old Ones care nothing for our sins. It is our very nature, our very existence, that is abhorrent to them and inimical to their higher purpose. Our flesh, and indeed the flesh of all other living things, offends them, and is an obstruction to the restoration of the earth to its original perfect place. Normal flesh cannot ascend through the gate of Yog-Sothoth that will translate our planet to a higher reality.

The hybrid offspring of the Old Ones are not of normal flesh, and some of them at least will be able to make the ascent—those that more nearly resemble the Old Ones themselves. Wilbur is unsure whether his own body, strange and malformed though it is, will be alien enough to endure the transition to higher space, but he knows that his brother will have no difficulty. However, he is willing to make the attempt even though it may kill him, because he accepts it as his destiny. He intends to retreat to a city in the interior of the earth, the shielding crust of which will give him some protection. He writes in his diary, "I wonder how I shall look when the earth is cleared and there are no earth beings on it. He that came with the Aklo Sabaoth said I may be transfigured there being much of outside to work on." In the Whateley twins we can catch an echo of the one hundred and forty-four thousand virgins of Christian myth who bear the Tetragrammaton in their foreheads, and who will be the first to ascend to heaven during the Apocalyptic scouring of the earth (see Revelation 14:1–5).

The inherent power of Lovecraft's modern myth of alien-human hybrids cannot be doubted when we see it arise spontaneously in the form of UFO abduction accounts. One of the central themes of the modern UFO mythology is that the aliens who visit our planet are breeding hybrids with the human species. Women abducted by aliens are sometimes impregnated by them, and men abducted sometimes have their sperm extracted. Abductees are allowed from time to time to see the hybrid babies of this alien breeding program. There are half a dozen speculations by UFO experts as to why these hybrids may be being bred, but the most interesting with respect to Lovecraft's story "The Dunwich Horror" is that the aliens know of some future event or condition that we humans in our present natures could not survive, and they are breeding the more hearty hybrids to withstand and survive this future ordeal.

In the cleansing of the earth of all common flesh and its redemption from its fallen state, we cannot help but bring to mind the Gnostic myth of the descent of the goddess Sophia into the fleshly body of a human prostitute, to wander the world in forgetful ignorance of her former heavenly glory until at last she is redeemed, stripped of her corrupt shell of flesh, and raised once again to her throne among the stars. The earth was often treated as a goddess in Greek mythology. In modern science the theory of Gaia has generally been accepted—that the entire planet is covered with a connected web of life that has, over the aeons, transformed the planetary environment to be more amenable to living things.

The Old Ones of "The Dunwich Horror" appear to be very similar, if not identical, with the Old Ones of "The Shadow Out of Time." In this story, the Old Ones are conquered by the time-jumping Great Race of Yith and are imprisoned in caverns and passages deep underground, held there by an alien science which to men would appear to be a kind of magic. They remained imprisoned long after the Yithians had fled from their threat into the distant future, and they are still beneath the ground to this day, waiting their opportunity to break free and reconquer the world.

Another imprisoned alien race that awaits its first opportunity to reconquer this world is the spawn of mighty Cthulhu, which may be offspring of Cthulhu in the form of off-buddings from his gelatinous body that resemble miniature versions of him. They once served Cthulhu as soldiers in his conquering army. The spawn lie sleeping in stone houses that surround the palace of Cthulhu himself in the sunken city of R'lyeh, on the continent they ruled so long ago, before it descended beneath the waves of the Pacific Ocean. Cthulhu and his spawn were forced to withdraw into their stone houses when the stars went wrong in the heavens, and then the unforeseen sinking of their entire island continent cut them off from psychic communication with their servants, trapping them in their crypts on the floor of the ocean. When R'lyeh rises, Cthulhu will call his human cultists, and they will release him along with his spawn to raven the earth for his delight.

If Cthulhu and his spawn are to reconquer the world, they will have to get there before several other races of "Old Ones" who threaten our annihilation. In *The Shadow Over Innsmouth*, a deep-sea dwelling race of intelligent, humanoid amphibians is said by Lovecraft to have the power to wage war against the human race and easily defeat us, at any time they choose to emerge from the oceans. These Deep Ones worship a gigantic sea creature much like them in shape that is identified by their human worshippers as Dagon. It is not clear whether Dagon and his Deep Ones are extraterrestrial, but this possibility is not excluded by Lovecraft.

Another race of "Old Ones" with the power to wage war against humanity and utterly destroy us are the Mi-go, an alien species of fungous crustaceans described in "The Whisperer in Darkness." They came in large numbers to our planet to mine it of metals they could not find on Yuggoth, their outpost in our solar system, which we know by the name Pluto. Yuggoth is not their original home. They crossed the void between the stars from a place so distant that the very laws of matter and energy differ from ours. When one of the Mi-go dies, its corpse simply evaporates into nothingness. They have largely left the earth, but a few outposts of their kind remain in sparsely populated regions of the earth, and the small numbers of Mi-go remaining on our planet conceal themselves from our knowledge. Just as well for us, since they could, if they wished, exterminate us with ease.

Yet another race of humanoids very similar to us in appearance, who may indeed be genetically related to humans, dwells in a vast cavern beneath the Indian mounds on the plains of Oklahoma. This cavern, which Lovecraft describes in his story "The Mound," is illuminated with a natural blue radiance, and is called K'n-yan. The race of K'n-yan use human beings as a food source for themselves and their riding mounts, breeding our species in pens for this purpose. At one time they ruled the surface of our world, but hostile conditions drove them deep underground for self-preservation, and they learned to think of K'n-yan as their home. They worship Yig and Cthulhu, and at one time also worshipped the dreaming toad-god Tsathoggua. Although they have degenerated greatly from the heights achieved by their science in the distant past, they still possess technology capable of destroying humanity, should they ever choose to reemerge from their subterranean realm and claim the surface for their own.

The world of Lovecraft's *Necronomicon* mythos may be summarized as one in which humanity has no hope and no purpose, where good and evil are illusions in an incomprehensible universe ruled by chaos. There is no God and no Devil. All the ideals and principles we hold dear are merely fictions created to fend off the encircling darkness for a brief time, but that darkness must ultimately prevail. We are threatened on all sides by ancient alien races of unimaginable power who may at any instant burst forth into our reality to claim this planet as their own, and when they do so, our species will be at best a source of slave labor or meat, at worst merely an annoyance to be exterminated.

Only ignorance about our true condition prevents us from going insane. Those few individuals who learn these truths destroy the evidence of their existence, or take great care to conceal them from the mass of humanity who could never bear their revelation. Yet they continue to survive in fragments in ancient texts such as the *Necronomicon* for the diligent scholar to discover and assemble into a cohesive whole. Very soon, advancements in human sciences will make apparent our perilous situation in this pitiless universe, and the resulting madness and chaos will plunge our world into a new dark age from which we may never emerge.

Lovecraft would always look back on his time in New York City and its environs, particularly the period from January 1, 1925, until April 17, 1926, during which he lived alone in his cheap room in 169 Clinton Street at the edge of Red Hook, as an extended nightmare from which he could not wake up. It is hardly to be wondered at that his black depression and the loathing he felt toward his surroundings inhibited his output of stories. What is amazing is that he was able to write creatively at all.

The story "He" was written on August 11, 1925, during a day trip away from his Clinton Street room, and expresses his desperate longing for another place and another time, as well as his sense of alienation from New York. It was only by leaving the metropolis and traveling to Elizabethtown in New Jersey that he was able to compose the story. He wrote to fellow author Donald Wandrei, "If you want to know what I think of New York, read 'He'," and then went on to describe a modern New York that "lies stark and horrible and ghoul-gnawed today beneath the foul claws of the mongrel and misshapen foreign colossus that gibbers and howls vulgarly and dreamlessly on its site." He added "New York is dead" and called it a "maggoty corpse."[1]

The use, in the midst of this irrational tirade of revulsion, of the adverb *dreamlessly* is important, because it emphasizes that Lovecraft could not dream, in his usual way, while his mind was oppressed by the sights and sounds and smells of New York. It was for him a city without dreams, but, more importantly, a city that stole away his dreams—not only the fantastical night dreams he so often drew upon for the characters and settings of his stories, and his faculty of creative daydreaming and imagining, but also his dream of a future happy personal life with Sonia. All these dreams were taken from him while he lived in the city.

"The Horror at Red Hook" is one of the few significant pieces of fiction he wrote under the roof of the rooming house on Clinton Street. It is a poisonous outpouring of revulsion against the Syrians, Turks, and other ethnic groups he was forced to rub shoulders with every day on the sidewalks and in the shops. It concerns a cult of degenerate Yezidi devil-worshippers who sacrifice children to the demon-goddess Lilith beneath the streets of Red Hook. He began it on August 1, writing at a furious pace, and completed it the following day. It is never ranked among his best work—there is too much venom in it. Lovecraft himself always regarded this story as second-rate. The desire, indeed the emotional necessity, to vent his revulsion against Red Hook overpowered his artistic judgment during its composition.

On September 18, 1925, he wrote "In the Vault," a straight horror story based on a plot suggestion by Charles W. Smith, the editor of the *Tryout* magazine.[2] It is about an undertaker trapped in the storage vault of a cemetery along with numerous corpses in their coffins awaiting burial after the spring thaw. There are no mythos elements in the story, which is not viewed as one of Lovecraft's better efforts. He tried to sell it to Farnsworth Wright, but when the *Weird Tales* editor rejected it as too gruesome, he sent it to Smith to publish in the *Tryout* without compensation. Amateur magazines seldom, if ever, paid a dime to their contributors. The story was eventually published, for money, in the April 1932 issue of *Weird Tales*.

He was able to write just one first-rate story while living in his hated Clinton Street room. In March of 1926, shortly before his return to Providence, he penned "Cool Air," his best effort from his Red Hook period. The story concerns an alchemist who is able to maintain a semblance of life only for as long as he can keep his reanimated corpse preserved from decay by artificial refrigeration. Here, we see the mingling of science with the occult that was to become the trademark of Lovecraft's later fiction. The plot may have been partially inspired, in an inverse way, by Lovecraft's ordeal over the winter, when he had been forced to buy a small oil stove to keep himself from freezing—his landlady, Mrs. Burns, refused to turn up the heat. Lovecraft was unnaturally sensitive to the cold, perhaps in part because his usual daily intake of calories was barely at the subsistence level, and there was, for most of his adult life, no insulating cushion of fat over his skeletal frame. He was correspondingly immune to heat, and did not perspire even in the dog days of August.[3]

Only familiar furniture from the former Phillips mansion at 454 Angell Street, with which he surrounded himself on all sides in his hated room, kept him from going insane. He pretended that he was still in Providence. In this way he managed to drag himself from one day to the next. He would later refer to both 1924 and 1925 as the years that never were. He wrote jubilantly to Frank Belknap Long after his return to Providence: "Two years to the bad, but who the hell gives a damn? 1923 ends—1926 begins!" A bit further on in the same letter he remarked, "I have lost 1924 and 1925."[4]

In many respects, the year following Lovecraft's return to Providence was his most contented and productive. In a brilliant explosion of creativity extending from the summer of 1926 into the spring of 1927 he wrote "The Call of Cthulhu," "Pickman's Model," "The Strange, High

House in the Mist," "The Silver Key," *The Dream-Quest of Unknown Kadath*, *The Case of Charles Dexter Ward*, and "The Colour out of Space." This is a prodigious output of first-rate writings. *The Case of Charles Dexter Ward* and *The Dream-Quest of Unknown Kadath* are both short novels. He also found time during May of 1927 to complete his book-length essay "Supernatural Horror in Literature," his finest nonfiction work.

While languishing creatively in New York, Lovecraft had enjoyed what was for him an unusual frequency of social interaction, and it eventually took its toll on his nerves. Toward the end of his durance vile, he began to grow weary of socializing, and he avoided friends when they came to knock at his Clinton Street door by pretending that he was out. As he wrote in a letter to his Aunt Lillian, "I am essentially a recluse who will have very little to do with people wherever he may be."[5] It was not so much his choice but more the accident of his circumstances that threw him into the company of literary friends so often during his enforced stay in the city. There is no doubt that Lovecraft enjoyed long, rambling discussions with the other members of the Kalem Club during their regular weekly meetings, and exploratory excursions around New York with like-minded members of the group, but they sapped his energies. He wrote to Aunt Lillian that "most people only make me nervous. . . . It makes no difference how well they mean or how cordial they are, they simply get on my nerves . . ."[6]

An exception was the brilliant young writer Frank Belknap Long, Jr. (1901–94), a native of New York who had grown up in Manhattan. The son of a prosperous dentist, he became interested in writing while at university and made the decision to forego an academic degree in favor of a career as a professional freelance writer. His company suited Lovecraft because their interests and ideals dovetailed so harmoniously. He is best known for two weird stories, "The Space-Eaters" and "The Hounds of Tindalos." Both were published in *Weird Tales*, and both are classics. Lovecraft first met Long in April of 1922, but they had corresponded by letters for two years prior to this meeting. Long was already a member of the United Amateur Press Association, which he had joined late in 1919. The first short story he wrote was published in *The United Amateur*, official organ of the UAPA, in March of 1920. Lovecraft referred to him in a condescending but very affectionate way as "my kid protégé Frank Belknap Long Jr."[7] and as "little Belknap."[8]

Lovecraft's influence over Long's development as a writer was considerable. He took the young New Yorker under his patriarchal wing, affecting the part of the grand old man of letters and referring to himself by such terms as *grandpa* and *the old man*. Long accepted this bizarre pose, as did the other members of the Kalem Club. At the time, Lovecraft was in his early thirties and only eleven years older than "little Belknap." However, his obsessive conviction that he was an old man was already well established at the time of their meeting.

Long was the first of Lovecraft's close friends who earned a significant name for himself as a professional pulp writer, so it is fitting that he was the first writer to make fictional reference to Lovecraft's *Necronomicon*, in his story "The Space Eaters," which he wrote in 1927. The two main characters in the story, named Howard and Frank, are patterned after none other than Lovecraft and Long himself. Attached to the original version of the story was a quotation from the John Dee English translation of the *Necronomicon*—this apocryphal quotation was omitted when the story was published in *Weird Tales* the following year, but it inspired Lovecraft to include mention of the Dee translation in the brief "History of the *Necronomicon*" he composed in the autumn of 1927. Lovecraft wrote, "An English translation made by Dr. Dee was never printed, and exists only in fragments recovered from the original manuscript."

The hounds of Tindalos, from the story of the same name written in 1928, is a brilliant concept that served as the basis for many subsequent mythos stories by later writers. These alien creatures, who do not really resemble dogs at all, live outside our normal reality, but have the ability to manifest themselves in our world through any angle that is more acute than 120 degrees of arc—for example, the corner of a room. They pursue and destroy human beings who inadvertently attract their attention. Once the hounds catch the astral scent of their prey, they never relinquish the chase until they bring down their quarry.

Lovecraft liked the concept of the hounds so much, he incorporated them into his *Necronomicon* mythos by mentioning them in his story "The Whisperer in Darkness," written in the fall of 1930. They thus became a legitimate part of the original mythos, in the same way the sleeping toad-god, Tsathoggua, conceived by Clark Ashton Smith, became a part of the mythos when referred to by Lovecraft in this story, and also in "The Mound."

After Lovecraft escaped from New York back to the tranquility of Providence, he continued to maintain his close friendship with Long via letters and occasional visits. In one letter, Lovecraft related a particularly vivid dream he had on the night of Halloween, 1927. The dream took place during the first century BC, shortly prior to the period of the Roman emperors, and was set in a region of Spain that was under the rule of Rome.

In the dream, Lovecraft is the Roman provincial quæstor L. Caelius Rufus, who has been summoned to consult with other Roman leaders of the province of Hispania Citerior concerning an ongoing problem around the town of Pompelo. A primordial tribe of hill-dwellers called by the local people the Very Old Folk, who are not completely human, have been kidnapping individuals from the town to use as sacrifices in their rites on May Eve and Halloween. The gathered Roman officials,

Lovecraft among them, decide on the Kalends of November (Hallow-een night) to dispatch the fifth cohort of the Twelfth Legion to exterminate the hill tribe. As the Roman legionnaires ride up into the hills, the stars are blotted out in the night sky and their horses scream with terror. A chill wind rises, carrying with it an oppressive sense of doom. The aged proconsul of the region, P. Scribonius Libo, intones in Latin in a hollow voice, "The old evil . . . it is the old evil . . . it comes . . . it comes at last." Here, the dream ends.

Lovecraft always intended to use this uncommonly detailed dream as the basis for a story, but never got around to it. In 1929 he gave written permission to Long to use the dream as part of Long's novel, *The Horror From the Hills*, which was published in *Weird Tales* in 1931.[9]

The two men tried to establish a mail-order business together, revising the manuscripts of would-be writers. Lovecraft had been doing this revision work for some time, and must have convinced Long that there was money to be made from it. They advertised their services in the August 1928 issue of *Weird Tales*, but do not seem to have enjoyed great success with the venture. In the same year, Long wrote the preface for a projected booklet edition of Lovecraft's story "The Shunned House," which was printed but not bound between covers or distributed. When he visited New York, Lovecraft usually stayed at the apartment of Long's parents, at 230 West 97th Street. They must have found Lovecraft agreeable company, since they invited him to go with them on various road trips around New England. Lovecraft spent his Christmases at New York with the Longs for four years, from 1932 to 1935.[10]

Lovecraft and Long, in company with other *Weird Tales* writers C. L. Moore, A. A. Merritt, and Robert E. Howard, worked together in 1935 on parts of a single extraordinary story, "The Challenge From Beyond," a collaboration dreamed up by editor Julius Schwartz as a kind of tour de force of weird fiction for the third-anniversary issue of *Fantasy Magazine*. Each writer was to build on what the previous writer had written. Lovecraft wrote the central section of the story, and Long wrote the conclusion. These are the best parts of the story, a patchwork Frankenstein's monster that probably had no business achieving life.

For the heart of the story, Lovecraft used a concept that had always fascinated him—the transference of a mind over distance into another body. This concept in one form or another figured prominently in several of his most important works. He used it in "Beyond the Wall of Sleep," "The Shadow Out of Time," "The Thing on the Doorstep," and "Through the Gates of the Silver Key," and made allusion to it in other stories in the variant forms of reincarnation and possession.

Some critics might argue that after his return to Providence, Lovecraft wasted too much of his creative energy on what he called revisions—in most cases, ghostwriting for others using their story concepts or outlines as the basis. Yet many of these revised works, published without his name on the byline, are of excellent quality. The best among them are the three stories he ghosted for Zealia Bishop (1897–1968), the longest of which, titled "The Mound," is an integral part of the *Necronomicon* mythos. It was based on only two brief sentences from Bishop in which she mentioned an Indian mound that is haunted by a headless ghost. Over the Christmas season of 1929, Lovecraft turned this into a novella of just under 30,000 words that describes the mysteries of the great cavern-world hidden beneath the Indian mounds on the plains of Oklahoma and the advanced race of copper-skinned men, brought from the stars by Cthulhu, that inhabits it.

"The Curse of Yig," written a year earlier than "The Mound," is also all Lovecraft in its pitiless unfolding, although he pretended to work from a story synopsis supplied by Bishop. It is a fiendishly horrifying tale that introduces Yig, the shape-changing snake god of the

Oklahoma Indian tribes who exacts vengeance on all those who dare to kill his serpent-children. It is one of Lovecraft's best stories—the ending is still shocking, even today. The final Bishop revision, "Medusa's Coil," was written in May of 1930 and concerns the reincarnation as a mortal woman of the ancient demoness who gave rise to the Greek myth of Medusa. It is also quite good, but not as powerful as the other two.

Another revision client who did little more than supply Lovecraft with plot ideas was Hazel Heald (1896–1961), a resident of Providence whom Lovecraft came to know through his friends the Eddys. After his return to Providence from his two-year-long nightmare in New York, Lovecraft resumed his friendship with Muriel Eddy and her husband, the writer Clifford Martin Eddy Jr. (1896–1971), with whom Lovecraft had collaborated in October 1923 on the infamous story of necrophilia, "The Loved Dead," the notoriety of which is reputed to have saved the fledgling *Weird Tales* from bankruptcy. He fell into the habit of visiting them, usually in the middle of the night—he might come to their house at eleven o'clock and stay until two in the morning. He and C. M. Eddy sometimes took night walks through Providence. Lovecraft was particularly fond of strolling through Swan Point Cemetery.

In 1932 Muriel Eddy founded a small amateur writer's club. One of the members was Hazel Heald, a divorcée living in Somerville, Massachusetts, close to Cambridge, who sent Muriel a weird story, "The Man of Stone." When Lovecraft came on his customary nocturnal visit, Muriel let him read the story, and he remarked that it "did have possibilities."[11] Muriel Eddy decided to play the part of matchmaker and wrote to Heald, describing Lovecraft and saying that he was interested in her story. She gave Lovecraft a note of introduction for Heald, and Heald invited him to her home in Somerville for a Sunday supper.

Lovecraft discovered that the house was empty save for Heald, and that she had laid the table with all his favorite foods and illuminated it by candlelight. Despite this obvious romantic invitation, Lovecraft spent the evening discussing her literary gifts. They entered into a collaboration on Heald's stories, and began to correspond by mail—Lovecraft's favorite way of carrying on a relationship. Those times he visited her in Somerville, he always remained "a real gentleman in every sense of the word,"[12] as she confided to Muriel Eddy. Heald began to grow a little desperate at Lovecraft's lack of initiative. She asked Muriel to "drop a hint" that her interest in Lovecraft could be more than literary, if he were so inclined.

Lovecraft was not so inclined. Despite the broad hints, he failed to take the hook, having too recent a memory of the barb. Their platonic union was not entirely unproductive, however. Lovecraft wrote five stories based on story ideas or rough drafts from Heald. Two of them, "The Horror in the Museum," written in October 1932, and "Out of the Aeons," written in August 1933, are almost all Lovecraft's own conception and may be considered a solid part of the mythos. The first of the tales, "The Man of Stone," which Lovecraft reworked for Heald in the summer of 1932, was based on an outline by Heald and enters the mythos through references to the mythos text *The Book of Eibon*.

Of the other two stories that Lovecraft ghosted for the lovelorn Heald, the more interesting is "Winged Death," probably written by Lovecraft in the summer of 1932, about which Lovecraft declared in a letter "my share in it is 90 to 95%."[13] It concerns a man whose consciousness is transferred into the body of an insect, from which uncommon vantage place he seeks revenge on his murderer. The final product of their collaboration, "The Horror in the Burying-Ground," is a much less worthy effort. It concerns an injected substance that simulates death, and results in premature burial. Lovecraft never mentioned this story in any of his surviving letters,[14] but it was probably revised by him in 1934.

Not long after his return to Providence from New York, Lovecraft had introduced C. M. Eddy to Harry Houdini, who was performing in Providence. Houdini needed a writer to ghostwrite his projects, and Lovecraft had more revision work than he could handle. Eddy tried a short story based on an idea by Houdini titled "Thoughts and Feelings of a Head Cut Off," but Houdini did not like it well enough to have it published.[15] Eddy did research into spiritualism at Lake Pleasant, Massachusetts, for Houdini's planned book-length exposure of fraudulent spiritualists, *The Cancer of Superstition*, which was to have been written jointly by Lovecraft and Eddy, but the project was terminated by Houdini's wife after her husband's death on Halloween, 1926.

Lovecraft's most unusual literary friendship during the final decade of his life was with Robert Hayward Barlow (1918–51), a native of DeLand, Florida, who first wrote to Lovecraft in 1931, at the tender age of thirteen years. Barlow's letters brimmed over with enthusiasm for amateur journalism and for weird fiction. He kept Lovecraft in the dark about his age. Lovecraft naturally assumed from the maturity of his correspondence that Barlow was an adult. At Barlow's invitation, Lovecraft traveled to Florida to visit his friend in the summer of 1934. He was astonished to discover that the mature and educated mind with which he had been corresponding was in the body of a teenager.

Lovecraft received a warm welcome from Barlow's parents, and stayed at their house in DeLand from May 2 until June 21. The next year he repeated his visit, and remained at the house of Barlow's parents from June 9 to August 18, thoroughly enjoying the intense Florida heat. Again, Barlow's parents received him warmly and urged him to visit again. This is somewhat surprising, not only in view of Barlow's young age, but because their son was a homosexual. Today, if a forty-four-year-old man went to vacation for more than six weeks at the house of a seventeen-year-old teenager, with whom he had only communicated by letter, he might be accused of sexual predation. It seems likely that Lovecraft remained unaware of Barlow's sexual orientation.

Barlow's parents exhibited no unease over the visits. They genuinely liked Lovecraft, who could be quite charming on the personal level when he chose to exert himself. While in New York he had worked much the same magic over the minds of Frank Belknap Long's parents. Perhaps it was his neurotic self-image as a grandfatherly mentor that removed any suspicion as to his motives for associating with bright young men. At any rate, Barlow's parents approved of the relationship.

As to whether there was any reason to be suspicious, it is impossible to know. None of his contemporaries ever accused Lovecraft of homosexual inclinations, and Lovecraft himself expressed a distaste for homosexuality in some of his writings. His marriage to Sonia Greene would seem to argue against any erotic interest in young men—yet there are certain small things that raise the question. Lovecraft had no experience with women before meeting Sonia—all his friendships as a boy and as a young man had been with other males. During his marriage, he performed in a lackluster way in bed, and was never the instigator of sex with his wife. He did not show any deep regret at their separation or subsequent divorce. He made no effort to establish a romantic relationship with any other woman.

It is certainly possible to assume that Lovecraft's sex drive was uncommonly weak, or that he had so completely suppressed it as a boy that it scarcely notified him of its existence. However, it is also possible to speculate that his lack of interest in girls during his youth, and his tepid performance in bed with his wife, show a latent homosexuality. Whether this buried impulse ever awoke to express itself in an overt way is impossible to know, because there is not a shred of evidence to indicate that Lovecraft had sex with a man on any occasion during his lifetime. If such an urge existed in Lovecraft, the most likely opportunity for it to have shown itself was during his two extended summer vacations in Florida with Barlow.

Unlike so many of the enthusiasts associated with the amateur press movement, Barlow had real talent as a writer. His short story "The Night Ocean," published in the Winter 1936 issue of *Californian*, was a collaborative effort with Lovecraft that was written in Providence in the summer of 1936 while Barlow was visiting Lovecraft, but it is almost entirely Barlow's own work. It is a hauntingly moody tale of a man vacationing alone on an unpopulated stretch of beach. There are a few Lovecraftian touches in it—for example, while walking on the sand the man finds a curious large metal bead carved with the image of "a fishy thing." This seems very much like one of Lovecraft's touches, whether inserted by Lovecraft during his revision or suggested to Barlow during the initial writing of the original draft.

Most of Barlow's enthusiastic plans for publishing Lovecraft's work and the works of other *Weird Tales* writers never came to fruition. He had his own printing press, and wanted to do such projects as a collection of stories by C. L. Moore and a collection of Clark Ashton Smith's poetry. These ambitions came to nothing. He divided his energies too widely, and lacked the focus of will necessary to carry through on a difficult book project. For the 1935 Christmas season, he published Lovecraft's story "The Cats of Ulthar" in a very limited edition of forty-two copies. It was Barlow who suggested to Lovecraft in 1936 that he add the poem "Recapture" to his sonnet cycle *Fungi from Yuggoth*, thereby completing the cycle.

Some of Lovecraft's most enduring friendships were with writers he never actually met, but only corresponded with by mail. These friendships lasted for many years and involved the exchange of creative ideas, and even the circulation of finished stories and poems. Lovecraft's distant friends usually read his works long before they were ever published. They were passed from one person to another by mail, and each sent back letters containing impressions and criticism to Lovecraft. This circle of correspondents, often referred to as the Lovecraft circle, was of immense value to Lovecraft. Not only did their suggestions help him to improve his fiction, but they sometimes took an active part in finding publishers for his stories.

Among the most important of these epistolary friendships was with the Californian poet, artist, and writer of weird tales Clark Ashton Smith (1893–1961). While visiting Cleveland at the beginning of August 1922, Lovecraft saw a collection of drawings and watercolors by Smith in the apartment of Samuel Loveman, who carried on a letter correspondence with Smith and owned a private art collection. Lovecraft was profoundly impressed, and wrote to his Aunt Lillian, "Did you ever see anything more ghoulish? Smith is a genius, beyond a doubt."[16] It was only eight days later that he wrote his first letter to Smith, praising him for his poetry.[17]

C. A. Smith was a strange bird, in some ways as odd as Lovecraft. When he was born, both his parents were middle-aged. He spent much of his adult life caring for them in their dilapidated cabin near Auburn, California. Emotional problems prevented him from finishing school, but he possessed an almost photographic memory and read voraciously. In this way he gave himself an education in the liberal arts. In 1911 his poetry was noticed by the prominent West Coast poet George Sterling, who helped him find a publisher the following year for his first collection of poetry, *The Star Treader and Other Poems*. Smith was hailed by the literary intelligentsia as another Keats at the tender age of nineteen. Unfortunately, poets cannot earn a living writing poetry, as Smith discovered. Lovecraft induced Farnsworth Wright to buy some of Smith's poetry for publication in *Weird Tales*, but it was not enough. It was probably Lovecraft who turned Smith's interest to the writing of weird fiction.

Although Smith was not a drug addict, his stories have the ethereal strangeness and dreamlike qualities of an opium vision. This strongly attracted Lovecraft. He saw in Smith's fiction some of the effects he was trying to achieve in his own stories, particularly those of his dream cycle. In such tales as "The Vaults of Yob-Vombis" and "The Dweller in the Gulf," Smith achieved horror of a level that matched or surpassed the best efforts of his distant friend. In the late 1930s, Smith became frustrated by the way his fiction was being censored and butchered by ham-fisted editors in the pulps, and turned his creative energies to weird sculpture, perhaps on the reflection that no one could "edit" it once it had been made. Upon learning of Lovecraft's death, he composed the elegy "To Howard Phillips Lovecraft," which was published in *Weird Tales* in July 1937.

Another of the contributors to *Weird Tales* with whom Lovecraft formed a close and enduring friendship via letter writing, but never actually met face to face, was the creator of Conan the Barbarian, Robert Ervin Howard (1906–36). Howard was a self-educated writer who lived with his parents in Cross Plains, a small town in central Texas. His father was a country doctor. Howard wrote to *Weird Tales* editor Farnsworth Wright, in August 1930, to praise Lovecraft's story "The Rats in the Walls," which had been reprinted in the June 1930 issue of the magazine (the story had first appeared in the March 1924 issue). Wright sent the letter to Lovecraft, who responded directly to Howard. Their correspondence continued until Howard's death.

On the surface, Howard appears to have been more stable than Lovecraft or Smith, but he too had his share of emotional problems, and he was the only one of the three who ended up actually killing himself, at the youthful age of thirty years. Like Lovecraft, Howard adored his mother, who suffered from the then-incurable disease of consumption—what we now call tuberculosis. Her decline obsessed him. He spent many years helping his father care for her, while he watched the disease slowly destroy her. At around eight o'clock on the morning of June 11, 1936, while his mother lay in bed dying, Howard shot himself through the head with a .380 caliber semi-automatic handgun. He was not killed outright, but lingered into the afternoon before finally expiring. His mother died the following day.

Lovecraft was badly shaken by the untimely and unexpected suicide of his friend. After learning of the news, he wrote, "Damnation, what a loss! That bird had gifts of an order even higher than the readers of his published work could suspect, and in time would have made his mark in real literature with some folk-epic of his beloved southwest."[18] In the last year of his life, Howard had moved toward Western fiction. It is quite possible that had he lived for another three or four decades, he might have rivaled Louis L'Amour in the writing of Western novels. Even though Howard had often expressed in his letters to Lovecraft his unhappiness and his pessimism about the future of human civilization, Lovecraft had always assumed that it was merely an intellectual exercise similar to his own nihilistic ruminations.[19] Howard's suicide both shocked and saddened him. In celebration of Howard's life, Lovecraft wrote "In Memoriam: Robert Ervin Howard," which was published in the September 1936 issue of *Fantasy Magazine*.

The writing styles of Howard and Lovecraft could not have been more dissimilar. Whereas Lovecraft regarded people as mere fixtures of the landscape, and focused his efforts on building cosmic fear through plausible yet detached descriptions of scenes and events having little to do with character development and interaction, Howard's fiction was pure human action and interaction, much of it written in the first person. In Lovecraft, the mind confronts the horror and is overwhelmed by it, but in Howard, it is the flesh that strives against the horror and prevails. In spite of this difference in the style and philosophy of their fiction, each man admired the work of the other on its own merits.

They also shared in common a virulent racial intolerance toward blacks, Jews, and immigrants of various shades. Howard's tales are replete with unflattering descriptions of blacks and of fictional racial types that can easily be identified with Arabs and Asians. He regarded northern Europeans as the natural supermen, superior in every way to the lesser races and destined always to prevail over them when equally matched. His character Conan the Barbarian is the archetype of this superior Nordic strain—he is taller, stronger, quicker, more deadly, yet also more intelligent, than those he battles, and he raises himself from the status of a penniless wanderer to the throne of a great kingdom using only his quick wits, courage, and the power of his sword arm. Lovecraft found everything he admired in his own English heritage magnified and exalted in Howard's characters, particularly Conan.

He and Howard shared something else in common: a pessimistic view as to the final fate of humanity. Lovecraft conceived of mankind as ultimately trivial, a doomed species with no special importance in the cosmos, all its achievements in science and the arts destined to pass into dust unregarded and unvalued along with the species that made them. It was Howard's belief that humanity must soon enter a new dark age of brutality and ignorance, in which the higher achievements of man would be forgotten while the race of mankind yet existed. His most famous saying, "Barbarism is the natural state of mankind," occurs at the end of his 1935 story "Beyond the Black River," and is spoken by a character who confronts the inevitability that the colonial outposts of his civilized kingdom will soon be overrun by savage hordes. Had he lived, the atrocities of the Second World War and the invention of atomic weapons would only have confirmed Howard in this opinion.

Whereas Howard welcomed the return of barbarism as a fitting end to the decadence and effeminization of the modern Western culture he loathed, Lovecraft did not. Lovecraft considered the eventual collapse of human civilization inevitable, but cherished its customs and traditions, its art and architecture, its history and folklore, as the only things that made life bearable. Without them, the naked human mind confronted by the vast and pitiless greater universe would be compelled to retreat either into madness or a new dark age of ignorance. Lovecraft never regarded this coming dark age as good, but merely as an inescapable consequence of the inability of our limited mental processes to cope with our growing awareness of the reality of our place in the universe.

In Howard's story "The Children of the Night," published in the April-May 1931 issue of *Weird Tales*, Cthulhu, Yog-Sothoth, and Tsathoggua are mentioned along with the *Necronomicon*. The story concerns the awakened racial memory in a man of Anglo-Saxon descent of a snake-like race of primitive human beings regarded by the ancient Aryan tribes as vermin to be hunted down and exterminated. These Children of the Night, as the Aryans called them, had in the distant past been driven underground by the Picts, but continued to survive in small pockets. In the story, the Anglo-Saxon who has experienced the racial flashback recognizes the genetic traits of the degenerate serpent folk in the face of one of his companions, and attempts to murder him.

Howard's conception is similar to Lovecraft's Very Old Folk, a hill-dwelling tribe in Spain, the last remnant of an ancient and evil race that practices degenerate rites of worship to forgotten gods on May Eve and Halloween. The complex dream in which Lovecraft saw this race begs to be interpreted as an astral vision of a past life—but Lovecraft stoutly refused to interpret any of his dreams in this manner. Even though Lovecraft never published this dream-story, it circulated by letter among his correspondents before being incorporated into a novel by Frank Belknap Long, and may perhaps have supplied inspiration, either directly or indirectly, for Howard's ancient and evil Children of the Night.

Both Smith and Howard echoed various aspects of Lovecraft's mythos in their own bodies of work. For example, both made reference in their stories to Lovecraft's *Necronomicon*. Both referred to non-existent esoteric texts of their own devising that contain dark occult secrets dangerous for human beings to learn. These invented texts were homages to Lovecraft's *Necronomicon*, and were used by their authors in the same way Lovecraft employed Alhazred's more celebrated book—to provide necessary plot elements where required, and to impart a general air of occult mystery to the tales.

The best-known occult text invented by Smith is called *The Book of Eibon*, or in French *Livre d'Eibon*, or in Latin *Liber Ivonis*. Smith first quoted from its pages in his story "Ubbo-Sathla," which was published in the July 1933 issue of *Weird Tales*. In this story Smith mentions Tsathoggua, Yog-Sothoth, and Cthulhu, using slight variants in the spelling of their names, and makes reference to Lovecraft's *Necronomicon*. Smith also created *The Testament of Carnamagos* for his 1934 short story "Xeethra." This unholy book is a Greek text written by the necromancer Carnamagos that was discovered and recopied around the year 1000 AD by an apostate monk. It contains "chronicles of great sorcerers of old, and the histories of demons earthly and ultra-cosmic, and the veritable spells by which the demons could be called up and controlled and dismissed."[20]

Howard's apocryphal evil book is titled *Unaussprechlichen Kulten*, or in its English edition *Nameless Cults*, and was written by the German mystic Friedrich von Junzt, who never existed outside of Howard's imagination. Howard introduced his dread tome in his story "The Children of the Night." In 1932 Lovecraft attempted to give the book a German title, on the presumption that it would originally have been written in German. He came up with *Ungenennte Heidenthume*, but Lovecraft's friends criticized the translation, so Howard never used it. It was August Derleth who titled the original German edition of the book *Unaussprechlichen Kulten*, and this was adopted as the German name of the work.

The creation of a fictional book filled with mind-destroying occult secrets seems to have been almost a requirement for membership in Lovecraft's inner circle of literary friends. Young *Weird Tales* writer Robert Bloch (1917–94), who is best known today as the author of the novel *Psycho*, came up with *Mysteries of the Worm* by Ludvig Prinn for his May 1935 *Weird Tales* short story "The Secret in the Tomb." Prinn was described by Bloch as an alchemist and necromancer burned to death at Brussels during the European witch-craze. Lovecraft suggested that Bloch use the Latin form of the title *De Vermis Mysteriis* and later referred to it in this way in his own works "The Haunter of the Dark" and "The Shadow Out of Time." Bloch also invented *Cultes des Goules* by the Comte d'Erlette, a play on the last name of August Derleth. This latter mysterious volume is often incorrectly attributed to Derleth,[21] who claimed to be its inventor, but Lovecraft denied this claim and attributed it to Bloch.[22]

Derleth is, however, credited with the creation of the *Celaeno Fragments*, a collection of esoteric gleanings from the great library on the alien planet Celaeno, written by university professor Laban Shrewsbury, who had visited the planet and translated some of the books in its library. Derleth made reference to this arcane text in his story "The Trail of Cthulhu," first published in 1944.

The writer Henry Kuttner (1915–58), another member of Lovecraft's *Weird Tales* literary circle of correspondents when he was in his early twenties, created *On the Sending Out of the Soul*, an eight-page-long pamphlet supposed to have been printed at Salem, Massachusetts, in 1783. It concerns a ritual formula for bringing about astral projection, which also invokes an otherdimensional being known as the

Hydra that feeds on the minds of human beings. The pamphlet was referred to in Kuttner's short story "Hydra," published in the April 1939 issue of *Weird Tales*, after Lovecraft's death. Kuttner also created the *Book of Iod*, an evil text in the "ancient tongue," of which only a single copy survives. It appeared in his 1939 story "Bells of Horror," and was thus unknown to Lovecraft.

Lovecraft's return to Providence from New York had been a double liberation for him—freedom from the slums near Red Hook and freedom from the well-meaning but smothering attentions of his wife. Even though the divorce did not come for several years after his return to Providence, Lovecraft was effectively a bachelor once again immediately following his return. He took full advantage of his freedom to travel.

One of the misconceptions about Lovecraft is that he was always a recluse. This was certainly true of the period of his life as a young man following his major breakdown in 1908, but it ceased to be so in 1914 when he joined the United Amateur Press Association. Lovecraft asserted in his letters that he was a hermit by nature, always alone even while in the midst of crowds—but this is to be a hermit by philosophical inclination, not by physical isolation. In the years following his escape from New York, Lovecraft rubbed shoulders with hundreds of literary friends and acquaintances in the course of his frequent and extensive travels. He may have always felt himself to be the outsider, but he was not always alone.

Lovecraft saved whatever small amounts of money he was able to save after meeting his meager living expenses for the purpose of buying train and bus tickets. His enthusiasm for travel quickened after his mother was locked away in Butler Hospital, and it only grew more intense throughout the remainder of his life. For a professed hermit, he saw a remarkable amount of the eastern United States between the spring of 1926, when he was liberated from the hell of New York, and his death in the spring of 1937.

Most of his travels were confined to New England and neighboring states, but in 1930 he visited Quebec City, Canada, for the first time, and in 1931 he vacationed in Key West, Florida. These were the extremes of his northerly and southerly excursions. It would have seemed natural for him to seek out the house of his friend Clark Ashton Smith in California, but Lovecraft never ventured across the Continental Divide. While in Key West he wanted to take the boat to Cuba, but lack of funds to buy the ticket prevented him. The hot climate agreed with him. While en route he stopped off at Miami, but the architecture was too modern for his tastes and the city failed to impress him.

He made two more trips by train to Quebec City, early in September of 1932 and again around the same time of year in 1933, when he spent four days in the old city, during which he saw what resembled the black funnel cloud of a tornado, streaked with lightning, followed by a rainbow.[23] The architecture of the old stone city fascinated him. Following his first visit he wrote, "It hardly belongs to the world of prosaic reality at all—it is a dream city of walls, fortress-crowned cliffs, silver spires, narrow, winding, perpendicular streets, magnificent vistas, and the mellow, leisurely civilization of an elder world."[24] The charm of the city did not wear thin with time. After his final visit he wrote, "What a town! Old grey walls, majestic citadel, dizzying cliffs, silver spires, ancient red roofs, mazes of winding ways . . ."[25]

These visits north of the border resulted in his longest literary composition, a history and travelogue to Old Quebec titled *A Description of the Town of Quebeck*. Note the spelling of the name of the city. It was written from September 1930 through the first half of January 1931, in Lovecraft's archaic style, which he had long before abandoned for his fiction, and takes the point of view of an eighteenth-century

Englishman visiting the city. The manuscript is filled with architectural drawings by Lovecraft. The work is so tedious as to generally be considered unreadable. Lovecraft made no attempt to have it published, nor even to get it typed. He must have realized that no one would ever buy it. It was purely a labor of love on his part, a homage to the City of Quebec.

In the decade that followed his return to his beloved Providence, Lovecraft came as near to a genuine and sustained happiness as he had ever enjoyed since the days of his boyhood, prior to the death of his grandfather. He was content to enjoy from his room near Brown University his numerous literary correspondences with like-minded writers, enlivened with occasional trips to visit a select few close friends and to explore parts of New England. He ventured further afield when his straitened finances allowed it. In general, it was a productive period, during which he perfected his unique blend of science fiction with horror and produced his greatest works, such as *At the Mountains of Madness* and "The Whisperer in Darkness." Had he lived, he would undoubtedly have progressed to writing more novels, and seen some of them published. Alas! All golden times come to an end. In the midst of his contentment, Lovecraft's body was already harboring the cancer that would kill him.

8

THEMES IN LOVECRAFT

The *Necronomicon* mythos may be divided into mythos elements that occur in Lovecraft's own stories, whether created by him or merely modified and incorporated by him into his work, and mythos elements that were created by later writers but never used by Lovecraft himself. In my view, the first category represents the essential *Necronomicon* mythos, and is the more important of the two, esoterically. It is the conceptual child of Lovecraft's personal dream visions and astral projections. While not all aspects of the stories that form the essential mythos arose from Lovecraft's dreams, his dreams gave the mythos its overall shape and impetus.

This essential mythos that resulted from the discernment of a single mind was not a deliberate, preconceived creation. The mythos emerged from Lovecraft's imagination via his dreams over a period of many years in bits and pieces that are scattered across numerous stories. Only when it began to assume an obvious cohesion that was remarked upon by his friends did Lovecraft himself recognize it as an integrated vision of the universe. This unconscious process of creative evolution may be called organic, in that the mythos grew from the depths of Lovecraft's unconscious mind spontaneously, its structure unimposed.

Lovecraft himself recognized three cycles in his fiction—his dream cycle, his Yog-Sothothery, and his Arkham cycle. They may be loosely associated with the three great loves of his life, which he enumerated in a letter to his friend Rheinhart Kleiner: "(a) Love of the strange and the fantastic. (b) Love of the abstract truth and of scientific logick. (c) Love of the ancient and the permanent."[1] His dream cycle is composed of fantasy stories set in the dreamlands. His Yog-Sothothery tales involve alien races from beyond the stars and are a kind of science fiction. His Arkham cycle, which was never fully developed and which overlaps his Yog-Sothothery, is concerned with historical secrets, genetic decay, and black magic in Lovecraft's fictional city of Arkham and surrounding New England sites, and may be classed as horror fiction. In my opinion, all three cycles are linked together by references to the Great Old Ones and to the *Necronomicon*, and form what I have called his *Necronomicon* mythos.

The stories that make up this mythos have as their unifying principle Lovecraft's philosophy of life. Not that Lovecraft used his articulated philosophical views as a template for his fiction—but the stories that arose spontaneously from his dreaming mind could hardly escape the influence of his philosophical convictions, which had their roots in the same deep and mysterious place that gave rise to his dreams. His fiction and his philosophy resonate, each illuminating the other. Central to his philosophy of life was the intuited conviction that there is no God—or, at least, no God that would be recognized as God in any conventional terms familiar to the greater mass of humanity.

Lovecraft was a self-declared agnostic from a very early age, and his agnosticism had an aggressively cynical cast. As a young boy in Sunday school he outraged his teachers by challenging them on the rationality of various points of Christian dogma—so much so that he was regarded as a disruptive influence on the class.[2] It is difficult to judge whether it should be called agnosticism at all, or whether a better term would be atheism. As he grew older he became increasingly convinced, at least on the intellectual level, that there was no God and no higher spiritual meaning to existence, so it may be said that he tended ever more toward outright atheism. In 1932 he wrote to Robert E. Howard, "In theory I am an agnostic, but pending the appearance of radical evidence I must be classed, practically and provisionally, as an atheist."[3] However, Lovecraft usually referred to himself as an agnostic, so it is by this term that his views will be considered.

He may have derived the initial impulse for his agnosticism from his mother, who had a profound and dominating influence over his mind in his childhood. In a letter written shortly after her death, he asserted that Susie Lovecraft shared his opinions about the absurdity of an afterlife. "Like me, she was an agnostic with no belief in immortality, and wished for death all the more because it meant peace and not an eternity of boresome consciousness."[4] Perhaps he was projecting his own views onto his dead mother, whose agnosticism may not have been as decided as that of her son. It is virtually impossible to weigh in a balance how much Susie's agnosticism as a young woman was responsible for that of her son in his early years, against how much the adult Lovecraft's vehement and often declared agnosticism shaped his mother's spiritual views before her death. What can be said is that both mother and son shared a cynical skepticism of conventional religious beliefs.

A consequence of Lovecraft's deeply held conviction that there is no God in the usual religious sense was his belief that life holds no transcendent meaning. Lovecraft maintained that good and evil are human concepts that have no function outside the bounds of human society, but are based on personal expediency.[5] He also believed that no individual life held a higher purpose or destiny. Meaning was something we ourselves imposed on life, as a way of dealing with our existence and making it marginally bearable. On the intellectual level, at least, he denied all aspects of spirituality and the soul, and indeed the very existence of anything other than the physical realm of matter and energy. He was both a nihilist and a materialist.

When the teachings of Albert Einstein about the relativity of time and space began to gain popular currency, Spiritualists, Theosophists, and the devoutly religious used Einstein's ideas to argue that behind the veil of the material world there existed a more basic reality of the intangible. Lovecraft utterly rejected this argument. He interpreted Einstein's theories concerning the essential oneness of matter and energy, and the interconnectedness of time and space, as evidence that all aspects of reality, even the most attenuated and subtle, are at root material. He wrote to his friend Frank Belknap Long, "What these feeble-minded theists are howling about as a sudden victory for themselves is *really the materialist's trump card*. . . . the *materialist*, now using that title in a historical sense only, emerges strengthened in his position as *an atheistical (or agnostic) monist.*"[6]

Lovecraft did not allow his atheistical monism to curtail his flights of imagination, but his conviction that nothing other than the physical existed gave the expressions of his creative imagination a peculiar cast. He postulated that realms exist in the universe that are so strange and so remote from our conventional universe of time and space that we would be incapable of comprehending them, or even perceiving them. Yet these strange and incomprehensible realms are parts of the greater universe that contains us. They do not transcend the universe in some supernatural manner.

He speculated in his stories about the existence of beings so ancient, so powerful, and so utterly alien in nature that they would invariably be worshipped as gods by humanity. Yet these potent and knowledgeable beings are not gods, but are creatures of matter, even though the nature of that matter may be beyond our limited experience. The science of these alien races would appear to us to be a kind of magic due to its sophistication, but it cannot truly be magic—Lovecraft rejected the existence of magic. The magic described in the mythos as recorded in ancient grimoires is a higher science of geometry and mathematics that appears magical to us only because it is beyond our comprehension. We look upon it in the same way that an African tribesman in the nineteenth century might assume that there were demons in the boiler of a steam locomotive.

Despite Lovecraft's conviction that religion and occultism are equal superstitions—relics of a long, dark age of ignorance from which we are only now emerging—he saw no triumph of science in our future. By the tender age of seventeen years, he had already formulated his cosmic pessimism: "The futility of all existence began to impress and oppress me; and my references to human progress, formerly hopeful, began to decline in enthusiasm."[7] He tried to distance himself from this sense of futility by adopting an attitude of indifference toward not only the events in his personal life, and in human history, but also toward the ultimate fate of the human species.

Lovecraft came to hold the opinion that knowledge will never liberate us from our servitude to false beliefs, or make us into godlike beings of infinite wisdom and perfection. Just the opposite—science must prove our undoing. The greater its advancements and the more closely it seems to approach an understanding of the basic laws of the universe, the nearer it pushes us to the brink of oblivion. A retreat back into darkness is inevitable because the human species lacks the courage to bear an awareness of the awful truth of our situation—that we can never control our destiny, that we have no value and no importance in the greater scheme of things, that there is no hope and no escape, that regardless of what any of us do with our lives it will be absolutely without purpose.

The notion that our advancing sciences can ever provide meaning in our lives is a mirage that we chase across the desert of dreams, falling further behind it the faster we run. We cannot understand the origins of the universe. If there is a reason for its existence, that reason is forever beyond our capacity to comprehend. All that can be achieved through our sciences is the destruction of our comforting illusions, one after another, until we have nothing to support us in a black void of despair through which we must fall for eternity.

In Lovecraft's view, stability of the mind, even sanity itself, may only be secured through ignorance. Knowledge invariably leads to chaos. Our species must comfort itself with its traditions, its customs, its mythologies, in the same way primitive man turned his back upon the cold and darkness of the night to huddle around a flickering campfire, putting behind him the fearsome creatures lurking outside the circle of warmth. These human customs and mythologies are meaningless in the larger scheme of things, but they are all we possess to give our lives order and keep ourselves sane. Lovecraft wrote, "A great part of religion is merely a childish and diluted pseudo-gratification of this perpetual gnawing toward the ultimate illimitable void."[8]

It is the tragedy of our species that we cannot resist seeking ever greater knowledge. Even though Lovecraft had embraced in his early life the wonderment and delight that comes from penetrating the secrets of nature, in later years he warned that the ultimate consequence of this addiction to knowledge will be madness. This is the central statement of his *Necronomicon* mythos—*knowledge is madness*. We are tempted against our better judgment and recognized self-interest to learn forbidden matters, but in so doing we condemn ourselves to sorrow and dread. The more we learn, and the greater our wisdom and power grows, the closer we approach the edge of an abyss from which there is no return.

The sole possible chance we have for contentment, as individuals or as a species, lies in the blissful incomprehension of childhood. He wrote to Rheinhart Kleiner, "Faugh! what a nasty lot of brutes we are! The only true happiness lies in the partial ignorance of childhood; either of the individual or of the race."[9] This view that childhood offered the only escape from sorrow arose as a direct consequence of Lovecraft's personal life experience. As a young child he had been able to know happiness while constructing his model railroad and building the play village of New Anvik, but never thereafter. He spent the rest of his life longing for those golden years prior to the death of his grandfather and his forced removal from the family mansion at 454 Angell Street. Lovecraft projected this personal need to return to childhood upon the human species as a whole.

The biblical overtones of his conclusion have a certain irony, given Lovecraft's rejection of all religion. In Genesis, humanity is cast out of Eden for the sin of knowledge.[10] Our acquisition of greater knowledge damns us and condemns us to endless suffering and death. We are forever barred from the gates of the Garden by a flaming sword, and so cannot return to our former state of happy ignorance. However, elsewhere in the Bible, Jesus said, "Suffer little children, and forbid them not, to come unto me: for of such is the kingdom of heaven."[11]

Lovecraft's idealization of childhood is slightly different from that of modern Western culture. There is a popular belief that children are somehow more innocent and pure than adults, and therefore are in some unspecified theological manner exempt from the full burden of original sin—that they are more like the angels, and nearer to the throne of God. Their happiness is perceived as a kind of divine reward for this state of purity. Lovecraft would have rejected this argument outright. For him, the bliss of childhood was wholly a function of ignorance. Not that knowledge in itself was an evil in his philosophy— he did not accept the conventional concept of evil. For Lovecraft, knowledge was merely a burden on the mind that grew ever heavier as more was acquired, until a point was reached when no happiness was possible, and indeed when life itself became unendurable.

It is possible for humanity to build structures and to seek order in the universe, but only if we do so with the mental outlook of children, building patterns for our own diversion and pleasure that are unrelated to the essential reality underlying our existence that will burn out our minds, should we ever come to understand it. Madness is chaos. Madness is the primal state that lies beneath the cultured levels of belief and folklore and history that we usually conceive as knowledge. For Lovecraft, human customs and arts are merely ways of insulating ourselves from that reality which in the mythos bears the name Azathoth, the god of chaos who sits on his black throne at the central vortex of all time and space.

In the *Necronomicon* mythos, there are four avenues by which a knowledge of objective reality can reach us and destroy our carefully constructed play-world that alone keeps us sane: dreams, the past, the hidden, and the outside. Each of these potential dangers forms a broad category in Lovecraft's weird fiction. Expressing the danger posed by dreams, we have the stories centered on dreaming and the dreamlands. The risk of revelations from the past gives rise to the tales of lost cities, forgotten tombs, reincarnation, and the awakened shades of the dead. The risk posed by secret and forbidden knowledge yields stories that concern forbidden grimoires and the misuse of the arcane arts of magic. The threat from outside is expressed in stories that concern outer space, other dimensions, the depths of the oceans and the caves of the earth.

These four general threats to the blissful ignorance of humanity mingle in pairs and groups in the stories, and are seldom to be found treated separately. For example, in "The Dunwich Horror" it is the knowledge contained in the *Necronomicon* (the hidden) by which Wilbur Whateley intends to open the gate of Yog-Sothoth and evoke the Old Ones (the outside). However, for the purposes of analysis it is useful to consider each threat separately.

In Lovecraft's mythos, much of the objective knowledge of the universe that has been lost in the waking world is still available through dreams. It is preserved in the form of books, manuscripts, inscriptions, carvings, and the living wisdom of the inhabitants of the timeless dreamlands, where the past may be just as easily accessed as the present. The dreamlands thus represent a danger to the sanity of individual dreamers, and also to the very survival of humanity. Those who venture too far into its fantastic kingdoms risk losing themselves forever—or they may come back to the waking world bearing dangerous knowledge.

Fortunately for the human race, only a few individuals are gifted with the power of dreaming deeply while retaining full consciousness. One of the greatest dreamers is Randolph Carter, who is none other than Lovecraft himself projected into his own fictional universe. Lovecraft could dream deeply and had the power of lucid dreaming. He was thus at risk from his excursions into what he called the dreamlands, and this danger terrified him. By assuming the identity of Randolph Carter in his fiction, he was able to meet the dangers of the dreamlands and triumph over them.

In *The Dream-Quest of Unknown Kadath*, Nyarlathotep, who is known as the "crawling chaos," attempts to trick Carter into the chaotic maelstrom that lies beyond the ultimate gateway of dreams. This maelstrom is personified in the mythos by the blind idiot-god, Azathoth. To fall into this vortex is to be lost forever. Carter saves himself by concentrating on the mundane streets and buildings of his native city of Boston. The familiarity and orderliness of the human architecture shield Carter from the vortex of chaos, and he is able to regain waking consciousness—which is to say, his full sanity, for part of the danger posed by dreams is that we lose our ability to reason while in the irrational world of the dreamlands.

However, in another tale, "Through the Gates of the Silver Key," Carter is lost beyond the ultimate gate, his mind separated from his body, his attempts to regain his normal existence frustrated, perhaps for eternity. The loss of Carter, Lovecraft's alter ego, after he ventures through the gates of the silver key, suggests that Lovecraft worried, whether consciously or unconsciously, about a similar fate—that what he saw in his dreams might eventually unhinge his reason. In several other dream stories, such as "The Quest of Iranon" and "Celephaïs," protagonists are lost from the waking world in the land of dreams. This is usually voluntary—they forsake the tawdry poverty and vulgarity of waking life for the enchantment of the dreamlands. They are lured like moths to flame, and participate willingly in the end of their common reality.

The second avenue of knowledge, the past, holds secrets so terrible that they can destroy the security and sanity of individuals and families, or even threaten the very survival of humanity. One of the ways these secrets come to be revealed in the mythos is through the dead. The dead and the past have always been closely linked. Necromancy, the magic of communication with the spirits of the dead, was predominantly concerned with finding out the hiding places of lost treasures. It was this lure of buried loot that made it such a popular branch of the arcane arts from the age of ancient Greece down to the Renaissance. The dead were presumed to know many secrets not directly accessible to the living. Their spirits were summoned by various means so that they could be compelled under threat of torture to reveal their secrets.

Scientifically minded Lovecraft put a new twist on the old art of necromancy in his novel *The Case of Charles Dexter Ward*. He made the necromancy alchemical, dependent not only on the arcane lore of the Old Ones but also on the use of various extracted salts and chemical preparations. By rendering an ancient corpse down to its essential salts, it was possible to resurrect the living person as he had been in life, merely by reciting a brief invocation to the power of Yog-Sothoth, the gatekeeper of the Old Ones who can open all dimensional doorways. Death is considered an exit from this life to an existence beyond, so it is hardly surprising that Yog-Sothoth should possess the ability to open and shut the gates of death as well.

Those who dabble in alchemical necromancy are warned not to call up that which cannot easily be put down, lest they be destroyed by what they raise from its essential salts. The past is dangerous to the living because of the knowledge it contains. In the novel, the evil alchemist Joseph Curwen is destroyed by the wisdom of an ancient sorcerer called up by one of Curwen's enemies. The sorcerer does not kill Curwen directly, but it is the reawakening of the sorcerer that eventually leads to Curwen's death. Curwen is killed as a result of his imprudent delving into the past.

The past can also reveal its secrets in the forms of old journals, paintings, inscriptions, and ancient ruins. In the short novel *At the Mountains of Madness*, the secrets of the past are uncovered beneath the ice of Antarctica in the form of wall carvings that illustrate the history of the city and its alien inhabitants. In "The Nameless City," they are depicted beneath ancient ruins in the Arabian desert as colorful frescos. In "The Mound," a manuscript written by a long-lost Spanish conquistador reveals the secrets of an ancient and alien underground civilization.

Lovecraft's fear that science threatens to give us a more realistic and objective understanding of hidden realities that we will simply be incapable of accepting is represented in the third avenue of knowledge, black books such as the *Necronomicon*, *Unspeakable Cults*, the *Mysteries of the Worm*, the *Eltdown Shards*, the *Pnakotic Manuscripts*, and so on. In the mythos, the knowledge contained on the pages of these dangerous texts is the true science, beside which the science of mankind is but a plaything. This knowledge is called "occult" only because the human mind refuses to deal with it. The forgotten languages, ciphers, and magical alphabets beneath which it is sometimes supposed to lie hidden in these infamous books are metaphors for its denial and rejection by those exposed to it. As the hand drops hot iron the instant it touches it, so does the human mind flinch away from objective reality. Those who make the error of forcing a prolonged contact with that reality are burned, and those who survive carry the scars to their graves.

Although Lovecraft never stated it explicitly, it is reasonable to presume that Abdul Alhazred, the author of the blackest book of secrets, the *Necronomicon*, is known as the "mad Arab" because his mind was broken by the secrets he learned in the great Arabian desert sometimes called the Empty Space. Only a madman could accurately convey those secrets in a written document—a sane mind would reject them. All of the authors of the various black books of occult secrets mentioned in the mythos are tainted or cursed in some manner. A healthy mind could never bear to set down the information they contain, and the mere touch of that knowledge has a corrupting influence on sanity.

The last of the four avenues by which naked reality intrudes upon the carefully maintained social and philosophical fictions of humanity is from the outside—when something monstrous thrusts itself into conscious awareness, or is inadvertently awakened or revealed by the imprudent probing of curious human beings. An example of both cases is found in "The Call of Cthulhu," in which the natural rising of the lost continent of R'lyeh from the floor of the Pacific Ocean first permits Cthulhu to call his cultists to him, and in which Cthulhu is later inadvertently released from his stone house by the curious explorations of the crew of the ill-fated schooner *Emma*.

The horrifying reality too terrible to endure is not something new but has always existed, hidden just out of sight, waiting for humanity to find it in our restless explorations. We are in the position of a goat that wanders around in a minefield, browsing on the greenery, blissfully unaware of the danger that lurks unseen on all sides. One false step brings catastrophic destruction, and that false step can occur at any moment because the goat has no way of knowing where the safe path lies. In *The Shadow Over Innsmouth*, the hapless goat is the visitor to Innsmouth who will not take the hints that he is unwelcomed in the town, until it is too late—the horror that comes from beneath the sea is revealed and once known, cannot be unknown.

Sometimes the horror from outside comes completely unbidden, and is not the result of any meddling or error by the human beings who find themselves consumed by it. "The Colour Out of Space" concerns the fall of a meteorite onto a small farm not far from the fictional Massachusetts town of Arkham. From the meteor spreads a kind of alien blight that poisons all living things with which it has contact. The family that runs the farm have done nothing to deserve a visitation from outside, but by the time they begin to realize their situation, it is too late, and they are all doomed.

Throughout his life, Lovecraft was troubled by various obsessions, and these found their way into his fiction in the form of various themes—preoccupations to which he returned again and again. In his essay "On Lovecraft's Themes: Touching the Glass," Donald R. Burleson enumerated five major themes in Lovecraft fiction,[12] which I will briefly list here for the purpose of discussion:

1. denied primacy—that mankind is not the summit of life on the earth

2. forbidden knowledge—that some knowledge is too dangerous to be known

3. illusory appearances—that things are not as they seem

4. unwholesome survival—that things survive that should have perished

5. oneiric objectivism—that dreams are as real as waking reality

The first of Burleson's themes forms the basis for all of the alien species and beings that populate Lovecraft's mythos. In Lovecraft, the aliens are not somewhere else in a distant star system—they live, or once lived, right here on Mother Earth, and many of them remain here, almost near enough to touch.

The second theme is, in my opinion, the heart of the *Necronomicon* mythos, and the most important, which is why I have devoted so much of this chapter to its examination.

The third is simply that beneath the mask of the everyday and commonplace there may lurk horrors too potent to endure.

The fourth concerns Lovecraft's fascination with decay and degeneration, with things that should not be living in a sane universe but nonetheless continue to survive.

The fifth is the basis for the entire dream cycle of stories. Lovecraft stoutly rejected the premise that dreams are real with his waking consciousness, but while he lay asleep his extraordinarily detailed and unnaturally vivid dreams argued for the opposite conclusion.

As useful as Burleson's five general categories are, I would like to touch upon a few narrower themes that recur in the *Necronomicon* mythos, for the insights they offer into Lovecraft's mind.

Graveyards seem to have preoccupied Lovecraft. He enjoyed walking through Swan Point Cemetery, where his parents and grandparents lay buried. He was particularly attracted to older cemeteries and tombs. The dates on old New England tombstones transported him back to the eighteenth century, his favorite historical period. The story "The Tomb," which was inspired by an old grave marker he saw in Swan Point Cemetery while walking there one fine day in June of

1917 with one of his aunts,[13] describes a young man who likes to sleep on the ground next to an old family burial crypt and dream about the ghosts of its tenants. It is not difficult to imagine Lovecraft himself doing something similar. The story "In the Vault" was also inspired by Swan Point.[14] In "The Unnamable," Lovecraft projected himself into the story in the character of Randolph Carter, who spends time with his friend Joel Manton lounging around the Old Burying Ground at Arkham, discussing philosophy.

Lovecraft's fascination with the tomb is tied in with his interest in genealogy. He researched his own forefathers diligently, as shown by the extensive knowledge he displayed of his ancestors, particularly his maternal line.[15] Genealogy appears in a number of the mythos tales, where the doings of ancestors have a crucial bearing on the well-being of the characters. In the mythos, history haunts the present. The dead do not lie peacefully, but intrude on the lives of the living, often with fatal results. For Lovecraft, loitering in ancient cemeteries was a way to get close to the past, and to the dead. He loved the past more than the present, particularly the eighteenth century, which was for him his natural historical period—he believed himself born out of his natural time into a rude and barbarous age.

Another ancient cemetery visited by Randolph Carter in company with a friend, this time the impetuous and half-mad Harley Warren, was located in the depths of Big Cypress Swamp in Florida. The story, titled "The Statement of Randolph Carter," concerns another preoccupation of Lovecraft that formed a major theme—that of hidden gateways. Warren goes to the cemetery to explore the passageways and chambers that lie hidden below its graves. He gains access to this secret subterranean labyrinth through one of the tombs, which the two men open by shifting a heavy stone slab that covers it. The tomb becomes a door, and the grave a tunnel. Lovecraft also used this symbolism in his novel *The Dream-Quest of Unknown Kadath*, in which the ghouls have a door leading from the lower to the upper dreamworld in the form of a grave, through which they ascend.

Gateways to other worlds may be physical portals that have been concealed or forgotten, or they may be merely mathematical apertures made through normal space-time by means of what would generally be regarded as occult rituals. For example, in "The Dunwich Horror" old Wizard Whateley used magic to open a portal of Yog-Sothoth on Sentinel Hill the night his daughter, Lavinia, was impregnated with the seed of the Old Ones. The witch Keziah Mason of Arkham opens portals using an alien geometry of lines and curves drawn in blood in the story "The Dreams in the Witch-House."

Gateways provide a means of getting from our common world to other realities such as the dreamworlds, or to distant planets far removed through space. In the story "The Silver Key," Randolph Carter opens such a gate in the cave known as the Snake Den using a large silver key, a hereditary talisman passed down through his family line of wizards. In the sequel story, "Through the Gates of the Silver Key," Carter, whose intelligence is now present in an alien body, is carried through space back to the alien planet from which he escaped, by means of a dimensional portal in a strange coffin-shaped grandfather clock having four hands (to symbolize the fourth dimension). The coffin shape of the clock is a reference to the grave as a gateway.

The Snake Den, which was based on a cave Lovecraft knew in his childhood called the Bear Den, is only one of many caves and caverns that occur throughout the mythos stories. Lovecraft's caverns are often of titanic dimensions, and some of his caves have no fathomable end. There are caves beyond caves that have never been plumbed. They allure the reader with the mystery of their unexplored depths, which hold both wonders and horrors.

To mention just a few such subterranean gulfs, in "The Mound" the cavern known as blue-litten K'n-yan is massive enough to hold an entire civilization, and beneath it is another vast cavern world, red-litten Yoth, and beneath that lies still another cavern world, lightless N'kai. In *At the Mountains of Madness*, two intrepid explorers from the Miskatonic expedition to Antarctica find a vast underground sea while wandering through subterranean passages beneath the frozen city of the Elder Race. There is a rat warren of passages beneath the slums of Red Hook in "The Horror at Red Hook," and the genetically degenerate, cannibal Martense clan in the story "The Lurking Fear" have honeycombed the entire countryside with underground passages through which they can go and come unobserved. Caves extend for unknown distances that are only hinted at in "The Rats in the Walls" and "Under the Pyramids." In *The Case of Charles Dexter Ward*, the bewildering maze of passages and caverns beneath the Curwen farmhouse entraps Doctor Willett and almost entombs him. The ultimate cavern is the hollow Earth hinted at by Wilbur Whateley in "The Dunwich Horror."

Lovecraft was always fascinated by vast and endless caves. One of his first serious attempts at horror fiction was "The Beast in the Cave," about a man lost in the darkness in Mammoth Cave. Lovecraft wrote the initial draft of the story in the spring of 1904, when he was only thirteen years old, finalized it on April 21, 1905, and later revised it for publication in 1918. What was his fascination with endless caves and vast caverns all about? Part of it was fear. The idea of being lost in darkness in a underground cavern terrified him. He externalized his phobia in his stories as a way of controlling it, and thereby transcended the terror, in the same way he made the night-gaunts and the ghouls into the allies of his alter ego, Randolph Carter, in *The Dream-Quest of Unknown Kadath*.

But there was more to Lovecraft's obsession with caves and tunnels and caverns than his irrational fear of them. The possibilities hidden in the depths of secret caves represent the treasures hidden in Lovecraft's dreams, waiting to be unearthed and brought forth into the light of consciousness. The exploration of caves in mythos fiction is really Love-craft's exploration of the dark reaches of his own unconscious mind. He had no way of knowing what he might find in the depths and in the shadows, and the uncertainty both frightened and attracted him.

Another metaphor for the unconscious mind in the *Necronomicon* mythos is the sea. Lovecraft feared the sea and loathed the things that dwelt beneath its waves. Muriel Eddy told the story of opening a can of salmon to give to her cat while Lovecraft was visiting the Eddy house toward the end of 1922—Lovecraft saw the salmon and recoiled in horror. She later learned that fish and shellfish made him physi-cally nauseous, and she noted that even the sight of fish "distressed him beyond description."[16] The surface of the sea is another gateway between our common waking world and the unexplored worlds of dreams. What lies beneath the surface remains unknown, but periodi-cally things are thrust up into our consciousness that were better left hidden in the depths.

In the story "Dagon," an island rises with a strange carved mono-lith that is worshipped by a gigantic amphibious creature. A similar up-thrusting occurs in "The Call of Cthulhu," when just the tip of the highest mountaintop of the sunken continent of R'lyeh rises for a brief time above the waves of the Pacific Ocean, allowing Cthulhu to step out of his stone house. In *The Shadow Over Innsmouth*, the hor-ror from the sea is not the rising of an island, but the emergence of the Deep Ones, a race of amphibious beings that inhabit vast cities on the floor of the world's oceans, and worship a great and powerful being identified by the townsfolk of Innsmouth as the god Dagon. A German submarine explores the ruins of an underwater city that may still be inhabited in "The Temple," and in the story "What the Moon Brings" a man is strangely drawn to an underwater city of the dead, which he sees while walking along the shore at low tide. In "The Hor-ror at Martin's Beach," a line of men attempting to drag an unseen sea monster out of the ocean on the end of a rope find that they cannot release the rope and are themselves submerged beneath the waves by the rising tide.

Another important theme in Lovecraft's work is that of human degeneration through incest, or interbreeding with what is inhuman. Fear that his own genetic flaw would eventually result in his madness caused Lovecraft to write about villages of New England where generations of inbreeding had led to idiocy, deformity, and insanity, such as the village of Chorazin in "The Diary of Alonzo Typer." It worried Lovecraft that both his parents died insane, and that his grandfather Whipple Phillips had married his own cousin. His repeated nervous breakdowns (in a letter he enumerated his "near-breakdowns" as "1898, 1900, 1906, 1908, 1912, and 1919"[17]) must have given Lovecraft the daily expectation that he would lose his own mind, that it was not a question of if he would become insane but only of when. He attributed this weakness to his bloodline.

The horrors of incest and inbreeding, when carried to their nethermost extreme, are the basis for his story "The Lurking Fear," in which the reclusive Martense clan gradually severs all ties with the outside world and over the generations becomes a race of naked, animalistic monsters who shun the light of day and live underground like rats in a network of tunnels, emerging at night to seek human flesh for their food. Somewhat less extreme but still repellent is the degeneration of the families around the village of Dunwich, chief among them that of the "decayed Whateleys" who seek to revitalize their genetics by interbreeding with the Old Ones in "The Dunwich Horror."

Interspecies breeding of a less cosmic variety occurs in "Facts Concerning the Late Arthur Jermyn and His Family," in which the titular character discovers to his utmost horror that one of his ancestors had not been entirely human, but was partially simian. The shock of discovering his own less than human blood proves too much to bear, and Jermyn commits suicide by burning himself alive. Nothing but fire can cleanse the taint from his blood. His agony is penance for the sins of his grandfather, who brought the ape blood into the Jermyn family line.

The ape blood, which is picked up by Jermyn's grandfather during his explorations of Africa, is a thinly veiled reference to the blood of blacks, which Lovecraft regarded as inferior to that of the Anglo-Saxon settlers of New England. Had Lovecraft discovered during his genealogical research that one of his own ancestry had been black, his own horror would scarcely have been less than that of his character, Arthur Jermyn, although he would have comported himself in a more philosophical manner. The opening sentences of the story express Lovecraft's essential philosophy:

> Life is a hideous thing, and from the background behind what we know of it peer daemoniacal hints of truth which make it sometimes a thousandfold more hideous. Science, already oppressive with its shocking revelations, will perhaps be the ultimate exterminator of our human species—if separate species we be—for its reserve of unguessed horrors could never be borne by mortal brains if loosed upon the world.

In the story "The Unnamable," Randolph Carter relates the history of a house that stands next to the Old Burying Ground in Arkham, where he likes to lounge in the afternoons with his friend. A young unmarried girl in the house gave birth to a monster with horns on his head. She was put to death for this indiscretion, and the monster was cared for by her father until his death, after which it appears to have starved. Carter is never explicit in the tale about the father of the bastard offspring—that is the "unnamable" aspect of the story—but he alludes to a slaughterhouse. One supposition is that the girl had sex with a horned beast at the slaughterhouse, and give birth to a monster similar to the Minotaur of ancient Greek mythology.

References to secret cults form another theme of the mythos. Lovecraft's fictional Miskatonic Valley, and indeed the entire world of the mythos, contain numerous secret cults of degenerate inbred locals, or foreigners who in Lovecraft's mind are inherently degenerate, devoted to the worship and service of the Great Old Ones. They meet in out-of-the-way localities ånd perform hideous rites that would blast the sanity of a normal, healthy brain.

In "The Call of Cthulhu," a cult devoted to the worship of Cthulhu that meets in the Louisiana swamp is broken up by the police. Another cult of Cthulhu exists among degenerate tribes of Inuit in northern Greenland. In "The Whisperer in Darkness," the Mi-go preside as priests over a human cult devoted to the worship of Shub-Niggurath. "The Horror at Red Hook" has a secret cult of immigrant Yezidi devil-worshippers sacrificing children to the demon goddess Lilith under the streets of the slums. Innsmouth is dominated in *The Shadow Over Innsmouth* by the Esoteric Order of Dagon, a human cult that worships the Deep Ones and their god in the ruin of a Masonic meeting house. Members cohabit with the Deep Ones, and many of their offspring bear inhuman racial traits. In "The Haunter of the Dark," the Cult of the Starry Wisdom meets in secret in an old church in Providence, and devotes itself to interaction with a thing from outside through an alien talisman known as the shining trapezohedron.

The final minor theme that I will mention that provides insight into Lovecraft's philosophy and beliefs is that of reanimation—the revitalization of the dead. It is really a scientific-sounding form of necromancy, that most ancient kind of magic. Lovecraft was fascinated with the dead past, which he wished to bring back to life. In some of his tales this is done literally, by reviving corpses.

In the novel *The Case of Charles Dexter Ward*, the alchemist Joseph Curwen is reanimated by his descendant Ward and then proceeds, after murdering Ward and assuming his identity, to take up the work of reanimating the ancient dead that was interrupted by his own death. We see here one of the ancient dead actually displacing and re-placing one of the living. Charles Ward, through the imprudence of his research into alchemy and the necromantic methods of his ances-tor, is wholly taken over, body and soul, so that nothing of him re-mains but his image. The past consumes him utterly.

In the series of stories collectively known as "Herbert West—Re-animator," the danger inherent in reviving and restoring the dead to life is more visceral. It is not the animators who go mad, but the reani-mated corpses that run amuck and murder the living. What they have glimpsed beyond the veil of death is too horrible to bear. The sheer unveiled reality of it unhinges their reason. Herbert West himself is at least half-mad with the passion of scientific discovery, and cares noth-ing for the carnage his research brings about.

Reanimation of the dead forms a minor plot device in the story "The Mound," where it is achieved by the alien science of the de-generated red-skinned race dwelling in blue-litten K'n-yan, who use reanimated corpses for servants. It also occurs in "The Thing on the Doorstep," when the discarnate consciousness of Edward Derby is forced into the decaying corpse of his ex-wife, and animates the corpse through the power of his will in order to convey the details of her crimes to a friend—a novel form of necromancy, in which one of the dead revives himself to reveal secrets to the living. A similar example of self-reanimation occurs in "The Outsider."

For Lovecraft, reanimation was a way to carry the horror of knowl-edge from the past or from the outside to ordinary waking conscious-ness. All those reanimated in Lovecraft's stories would have been bet-ter left dead, and all those involved in the reanimations suffer from the effects of their experiences, whether they are the innocent or the guilty. What is learned cannot be unlearned, and what is seen cannot be unseen.

9

GENTEEL DECAY

I n many respects, Lovecraft was his own worst enemy when it came to his career as a professional freelance writer. He fought against success tenaciously, and in the end he won the battle. His biographer L. Sprague de Camp called this pigheadedness "Lovecraft's invincible will-to-failure."[1] In spite of his moderate popularity and name recognition, his extensive network of professional and amateur friends and colleagues, his considerable talent as both a writer and an editor, and his knowledge of the publishing industry, Lovecraft contrived to eke out his last years in abject poverty, and lived to see his name on the spine of only one book.

The sole book of Lovecraft's fiction issued from a printing press during his lifetime was an edition of *The Shadow Over Innsmouth*, published by William L. Crawford (1911–84) of the Visionary Publishing Company of Everett, Pennsylvania, in 1936. Four hundred copies were printed, but only two hundred copies were actually bound, and the unbound copies were later destroyed. As may be imagined, Lovecraft did not grow rich on the proceeds. The edition was riddled with errors, and many surviving copies bear Lovecraft's corrections in pencil in the margins.[2]

He had come close to seeing his name on a hardcover book when his story "The Shunned House" was printed up for publication in 1928 by fellow amateur journalist and onetime president of the NAPA, William Paul Cook (1881–1948). Due to the poverty and nervous breakdown of the publisher, it was never bound between covers or sold, although some years later Robert H. Barlow did discuss with Lovecraft the possibility of binding the printed sheets. As was so often the case with young Barlow's enthusiastic but impractical schemes, little came of the matter. Only a few sets of sheets were bound by Barlow. The majority remained loose for three decades, until finally bound by Arkham House between 1959 and 1961.

Barlow did manage to publish Lovecraft's story "The Cats of Ulthar" as a separate booklet in 1935, under the imprint of his Dragon-Fly Press of Cassia, Florida. The edition had a print run of only forty-two copies. It was a kind of Christmas gift to Lovecraft, and of course it earned Lovecraft not a single dime.

Several of Lovecraft's stories found their way into hardcover anthologies during his lifetime. In 1929 the anthology *Beware After Dark!*, which was published by Macaulay of New York, included "The Call of Cthulhu." Three stories were selected for anthologies put out by the London publisher Selwyn & Blount—"The Horror at Red Hook" appeared in *You'll Need a Nightlight* (1927), "Pickman's Model" was included in *By Daylight Only* (1929), and "The Rats in the Walls" was one of the stories in *Switch on the Light!* (1931). In this same anthology appeared Lovecraft's ghostwritten story "The Curse of Yig," but under the author's name Zealia B. Reed. The Selwyn & Blount anthology *Terror by Night* (1934) contained Lovecraft's ghostwritten story "The Horror in the Museum," but under the author's name Hazel Heald. Their large anthology *Not At Night Omnibus* (1937) reprinted from the previous anthologies "Pickman's Model," "The Curse of Yig," and "The Horror in the Museum."

Farnsworth Wright talked about bringing out a book of Lovecraft's stories—but that is all it was: talk.[3] In 1930 Simon and Schuster inquired about publishing Lovecraft, but what they really wanted was a novel. The following year G. P. Putnam's Sons looked at a collection of his stories for a possible book. In the end they decided against it. William Morrow and Company also turned down a selection of short stories, but indicated to Lovecraft's agent in 1936 that they would be more receptive to a novel.[4] Lovecraft was steadfast in his determination not to write to order. He felt that he could only do his best work when the impulse to write arose spontaneously, and that this impulse must not be forced. He wrote, "All good work must come from the subconscious, without regard for markets."[5]

Arguing against this belief is the excellent work he did as a ghost-writer for others, notably the stories he wrote for Zealia Bishop and Hazel Heald, and the one he penned for the escape artist Harry Houdini. The quality of the ghosted tales is uneven, and they are generally ranked lower in worth than the stories that bear his own name, but two of them, "The Mound" and "The Curse of Yig," are among his very best. They prove that Lovecraft could write to order, when he was in the frame of mind to do so and his subconscious cooperated with him.

His later works such as "The Shadow Out of Time" tend to be longer stories and suggest that Lovecraft was moving toward the novel format. Had he lived another few decades, it seems almost certain that he would have written novels, probably in the science-horror genre he pioneered, and that they would have found publishers beyond the pulp magazines. But during his life, he fled from success as though it were a pursuing demon. He wrote defiantly, "If I can't get cash without twisting my writing, I'm willing to starve."[6]

In 1924 J. C. Henneberger, the owner and publisher of *Weird Tales*, asked Lovecraft to replace Edwin Baird as editor. As an incentive, he dangled the prospect that under Lovecraft's leadership the magazine would be devoted to weird fiction on a higher level of literary quality than the potboilers that had been its usual staple. Lovecraft turned him down. Lovecraft's reasons were sound enough at the time—he assumed that the struggling magazine would fail, and he did not wish to move to Chicago only to be stranded there when it went belly-up. However, his refusal to consider the proposition illustrates his self-defeating attitude. Even at the beginning of his marriage when his optimism about life reached its high-water mark, he was unwilling to take a chance on success, and this reluctance to attempt achievement only became more pronounced after his return to Providence.

It was this unwillingness to speculate that kept him at his desk at 10 Barnes Street, grinding out ghosted stories and nonfiction for other writers. True, this work paid less than sales of his own stories to the magazines, but when he did ghost work he had the confident expectation of getting paid, because the fee had been agreed to in advance. For example, when he extensively revised the story "A Sacrifice to Science" for Adolphe de Castro, he was paid sixteen dollars for his work. The story was published in the November 1928 issue of *Weird Tales* under the title "The Last Test," and de Castro was paid one hundred and seventy-five dollars for it.[7] Lovecraft generally asked for half of his modest fee up front, and the other half upon delivery of the finished manuscript.

The assurance of payment was the thing that mattered to Lovecraft. He wrote to one of his clients, "My only object in accepting revision is to eliminate the element of chance—to accept lesser returns *because they are certain* instead of contingent upon acceptance."[8] When he wrote for *Weird Tales* and other pulp magazines, he never knew if his stories would be accepted or rejected. Many of his best stories were rejected by Farnsworth Wright, and Lovecraft hated rejection. He could not deal with it. Rejection of his work broke his spirit and destroyed any shred of self-confidence in his abilities as a writer. When his stories were declined, he would make no effort to place them elsewhere or to revise them. He just gave up and set them aside. They were only eventually published when his friends sent them to the pulps on his behalf.

Rejections during the last few years of his life discouraged him so greatly that he toyed with the idea of giving up fiction-writing completely, on the grounds that his creative talent was used up. In a 1935 letter to August Derleth, he wrote, "It is possible that I have wholly lost the knack of fiction formulation, and ought to cease altogether from attempting stories."[9] Derleth was not the most supportive of friends. Three years earlier he had criticized the literary worth of Lovecraft's story "The Dreams in the Witch-House" so harshly that it led Lovecraft to protest in a mild way that he had not felt that his story was all that bad, but Lovecraft then added with his characteristic insecurity: "the whole incident shows that my fictional days are probably over."[10]

What must be understood is that while Lovecraft was moaning that his fiction-writing days were probably behind him, he was doing the best fiction work of his entire life. He was only in his mid-forties, the very prime of life for a writer. Yet so fragile was his ego that he was ready to stop writing stories entirely. Paradoxically, for this man who refused to call himself a professional, but continued to refer to himself as an amateur throughout his entire life, it was the lure of payment from professional outlets such as *Weird Tales*, either directly or indirectly through his ghosted work, that kept him writing.

In July of 1931 the rejection by Farnsworth Wright of his short novel *At the Mountains of Madness* had been a terrible blow. Lovecraft wrote that the rejection "did more than anything else to end my effective literary career."[11] However, in 1935 an agent was able to place it with *Astounding Stories* for $350, and at nearly the same time a friend, Donald Wandrei, sold Lovecraft's latest story, "The Shadow Out of

Time," to *Astounding Stories* for $280—in spite of Lovecraft's neurotic misgivings that it was not good enough to type, and that he might be better off to just "tear it up and start all over again."[12] The total, after the agent deducted his 10 percent from the first story sale, was $595. This sudden influx of money boosted Lovecraft's spirits somewhat and helped convince him that there might be some purpose in continuing with his fiction writing after all. In December of 1935 he wrote in a letter, "This dual stroke gave me such a psychological boost that I've just written a new tale—a short specimen called 'The Haunter of the Dark.'"[13]

Lovecraft needed the money. During the Hungry Thirties he was extremely poor, as was a good portion of the population of the United States. Good jobs were almost impossible to find. Virtually his only sources of income were his ghostwriting and his occasional fiction sales, and these were not enough to sustain even a modest lifestyle. What little money Lovecraft made from his own stories he regarded as a windfall, and usually spent on travel. He tried to live on his revision income and on a miniscule fixed income that he received in the form of interest payments on promissory notes secured by the mortgage on a stone quarry.[14] This interest income gradually dwindled away over the years, so that at the time of his death it amounted to only thirty dollars a year, on three notes worth five hundred dollars.

Even though he was ascetic by nature, and cared little or nothing for the minor sensual luxuries of life such as restaurant dining, alcohol, and tobacco, he had so little money that he half-starved himself. His time on Clinton Street had taught him how to eat on less than fifty cents a day, and he continued this practice after his return to Providence. He had written to August Derleth in 1931 that "$3.00 per week sees me fully fed."[15] His diet during the last years of his life consisted mainly of starches and sugars in such simple fare as bread, beans, doughnuts, chili, cake—Lovecraft always had a sweet tooth, perhaps in part because he was calorie-deprived most of the time. His meager daily diet provided enough energy to run his body, and that was all Lovecraft cared about. Toward the end he became so thin, he was almost skeletal.

Neither did he waste money on clothes. His hats, suits, and coats were secondhand or years out of date. In 1931 he was still using a topcoat that he had purchased in 1909, although his good topcoat was more up-to-date, having been bought in 1917.

Expensive suits were one thing Lovecraft might have indulged in had he possessed the money to afford them. Even back in his Red Hook period he was more than a bit of a clothes snob, and had very decided ideas about what a gentleman should wear, and what cuts of suits marked what he characterized in a 1925 letter to his Aunt Lillian as "flashy young 'boobs' and foreigners."[16] He deplored the lack of refined taste he observed on the streets of New York, and thought that the modern tendency to adopt pastel colors in fabrics was a sign of effeminacy and moral decadence, whereas his favored style of "subdued and loosely but finely hung garments" was characteristic of a "genuinely refined and wholesomely masculine ruling or conquering class or race-stock."[17] He must have approved of his dead father's fashion sense, because he continued to wear various articles of his father's clothing well into his adulthood, long after they had passed out of style in the opinion of even the most conservative fashion critic.

What vexed him the most about being poor was his inability to travel as much as he would have wished. During the decade of the Thirties, travel became his escape from depression and the frustrations of daily life. Poverty prevented him from touring Europe and viewing the ancient walled towns that he would have loved so much. He never voyaged to his beloved and revered England, even though some of his stories, such as "The Rats in the Walls" and "The Horror in the Museum," were set in that country.

In 1932 he found the money to visit Edgar Hoffmann Price (1898–1988) in New Orleans. Price was a fellow pulp writer whose stories were published in *Weird Tales*. Lovecraft had a high regard for his best work, which he considered uncommonly original, although Price, who was out of a job, was forced by his need to earn a living to write in haste many stories that were far from his best. Robert E. Howard learned that Lovecraft was vacationing in New Orleans, and telegraphed his friend Price with Lovecraft's hotel phone number so that Price could introduce himself. Lovecraft ended up paying Price a call on June 12 at his room in the Vieux Carré that lasted twenty-five-and-a-half hours! The men talked about writing and life in general from Sunday evening until around midnight on Monday without a break. Lovecraft wrote, "Nobody seemed to get sleepy, and the hours slipped away imperceptibly amidst discussions and fictional criticisms."[18] This was typical of Lovecraft. He did his visiting in the middle of the night, and had no regard for the passage of time. Several subsequent visits with Price lasted ten hours each.

Price talked about collaborating with Lovecraft on a sequel to his story "The Silver Key," and Lovecraft, who was not averse to the idea of explaining to readers what had happened to his favorite character and alter ego, Randolph Carter, gave his approval for Price to write an initial draft of the sequel.

On the return leg of his epic southern vacation, which included at least in passing Richmond, Fredericksburg, Washington, Annapolis, and Philadelphia, Lovecraft stopped in Brooklyn to see Samuel Loveman, and while he was there he received a telegram informing him that his Aunt Lillian was dying. He returned to Providence on the first of July to find his aunt in the hospital in a coma. Lillian died on July 3, and was buried in the Phillips family plot in Swan Point Cemetery. Her death was an emotional shock, but also a domestic inconvenience for

Lovecraft. She had been acting as his unpaid housekeeper at 10 Barnes Street.

Price completed his version of the sequel to "The Silver Key," which Price titled "The Lord of Illusion," in late August and mailed it to Lovecraft. Lovecraft wrote back to Price on October 3 telling him that the story would require extensive revision to make it a natural continuance of the first story. The upheavals in his personal life caused Lovecraft to set the story aside for several months.

In late May of 1933, Lovecraft moved out of his rooms at 10 Barnes Street and into the upper flat of the historic Samuel B. Mumford House, a two-story yellow clapboard colonial house located at 66 College Street, right behind the John Hay Library on the campus of Brown University. The schoolteacher living in the lower level of the house was a close friend of Aunt Annie, and when the tenants of the upper level announced their intention of moving out, she told Annie of the opportunity. It was too good a chance to pass up.

This was to be Lovecraft's final home in life. His Aunt Annie moved into the flat with him to replace the deceased Aunt Lillian and take care of his domestic needs, as she had done off and on for various periods of time in earlier years. Both aunts had looked after him after his mother's death. Even at the age of forty-two, Lovecraft was still being mothered. Indeed, the mothering never really ceased throughout his life, save only for the brief period he roomed on Clinton Street near Red Hook, and even then he had Sonia to turn to in emergencies.

Lovecraft was delighted with both the Mumford House and its location. He found the experience of actually living in a historic Providence colonial house "magical and dreamlike."[19] To Lovecraft, it was like living in a museum, and he could not have been happier. He had two rooms for his own use, and shared the kitchenette and bathroom with his aunt. He could not easily have afforded to pay the rent for the entire flat on his own with his dwindling income. It was forty dollars a month, the same as the rent on his Barnes Street rooms, and that was becoming an increasingly heavy burden. "I wish I knew how people manage to acquire cash!"[20] he wrote to a friend. However, by splitting the rent with his aunt it became bearable.

In the spring of 1933, Lovecraft revised Price's manuscript, which became "Through the Gates of the Silver Key." After an initial rejection by Farnsworth Wright, it was published in *Weird Tales* in July of 1934, bearing the names of both Price and Lovecraft. During this period, Lovecraft continued to travel extensively, did considerable revision work, and wrote several of his best stories, including "The Thing on the Doorstep," which was written in August of 1933, and the story that many critics consider his very best, "The Shadow Out of Time," begun in November of 1934 and finished in March of the following year. Both stories are concerned with the displacement of the mind from the body—as indeed is "Through the Gates of the Silver Key."

In "The Thing on the Doorstep," an evil wizard forcibly transposes his mind with that of his daughter in an act of incestuous psychic violation, and while inhabiting the body of his daughter, marries an impressionable young poet with the intention of stealing the young man's body for his own. In "The Shadow Out of Time," it is an alien intelligence that forcibly transposes its mind with that of a professor at Miskatonic University in Arkham. In "Through the Gates of the Silver Key," the mind of Randolph Carter ends up forcibly displacing the mind of an alien wizard on a distant star system and inhabiting the alien's body. The forcible transposition of minds between a human and an alien also occurs the 1935 four-way collaborative story "The Challenge from Beyond," and is a theme introduced into the story by Lovecraft, who seems to have been a bit obsessed with this concept during the mid-1930s.

This obsession is understandable. Even though Lovecraft did not believe in possession or the transmigration of souls, over the course of his life he had many experiences that most other people would have called past-life experiences. He suffered powerful sensations of déjà vu when visiting places such as Marblehead and Salem, the absolute inner certainty that he had been there before centuries previously, and in his dreams he was often someone living in the past. He never dreamed that he was a famous historic figure, which is almost a certain indication that past-life experiences are mere fantasies of wish fulfillment, but his dream identities were remarkable for their clarity and detail.

Lovecraft was painfully aware of his steadily worsening financial circumstances. In 1935 he wrote, "Within a decade, unless I can find some job paying at least $10.00 per week, I shall have to take the cyanide route through inability to keep around me the books, pictures, furniture, and other familiar objects which constitute my only remaining reason for keeping alive."[21] He feared that poverty would force him to sell or pawn his beloved possessions, relics of his childhood days in the Phillips mansion that he had dragged from Providence to Flatbush, from Flatbush to Clinton Street, and back to Providence again, the way a turtle drags it heavy shell wherever it goes.

He found himself growing more distant from his friends, even those who had corresponded with him for years. The young did not share enough of his views for him to converse with them on a meaningful level, and the old were too set in their thinking to provide him with much in the way of stimulating discussion. As for his acquaintances in Providence, such as Muriel and Clifford Eddy, Lovecraft had no real use for them at all on the intellectual level. He wrote, "In Providence I have never seen a congenial mind with which I could exchange ideas . . ."[22]

His depression deepened. It seems likely he would have become a heavy drinker were it not for his utter detestation of alcohol and his unwavering support for the ideals of the temperance movement. He would certainly have been placed on anti-depression medications today, but such medications were not available to him. He had always, since the passing of his childhood, found life more of a burden than a blessing, but during the Thirties the regular rejection of his stories caused him increasingly to doubt not only his talent as a writer and the worth of his fiction, but his very reasons for continuing to exist at all.

When the first signs of lower intestinal problems began to show themselves in 1935, he dismissed them as the grippe—what we might refer to as stomach flu. He did what many willful people do under similar circumstances—he ignored the discomfort with the hope that it would go away on its own. Had he consulted a doctor, there is a good chance than an operation might have preserved his life.

The growing cancer obstructed his bowels and gave him ever longer and more trying bouts of constipation. Whether it was the burden that the cancer put on his vitality, or some other cause, he accomplished very little in the final year of his life. Lovecraft put it down to vision problems. His eyes would suddenly and with no warning give out on him, producing a vortex effect in his field of view that made writing impossible for him. The last story published exclusively under his own name was "The Haunter of the Dark," which was written early in November 1935 and published in *Weird Tales* in December 1936. He did some revision work in 1936, making relatively minor edits and additions to Barlow's story "The Night Ocean" and Kenneth Sterling's science fiction tale "Within the Walls of Eryx," but produced no fiction of his own.

Poverty pressed upon him. He was forced to put off a trip to Florida to visit with Barlow in the spring of 1936 due to a lack of funds, pleading "the lamentable state of the treasury."[23] Instead, Barlow made an extended visit to Providence, arriving on July 28 and staying until September 1. After his houseguest departed, an exhausted Lovecraft wasted the last energies for writing he possessed in the autumn of 1936 on the revision of a textbook titled *Well Bred Speech* by the amateur journalist Anne Tillery Renshaw, for which he was paid a meager one hundred dollars. De Camp called it "disorganized, superficial, amateurish, and worthless."[24] Lovecraft did it purely for the money, and had hoped to get at least twice what he was paid, but with his typical pose of the English gentleman, he had told the author that any amount she felt was merited would be satisfactory—naturally Renshaw paid him less than his labor was worth.

Frank Belknap Long, Jr. and his parents invited Lovecraft to vacation in New York over the Christmas season, as had been their custom for the previous four years, but Lovecraft declined. The effects of his bowel cancer were becoming impossible to ignore. As 1937 began, he found himself losing weight and had increasing difficulty writing with a pen—in early February he was still able to peck out his correspondence on his Remington typewriter, an activity that he hated with a passion. "I detest the typewriter, and could not possibly compose a story on one," he had written in 1935. "The mechanical limitations of the machine are death to good style . . ."[25] Necessity compels compromise. Toward the end of the month of February he could no longer even sit up to type, but took to lying in his bed, propped up on pillows, while dictating to his Aunt Annie postcard replies to his never-ending river of correspondence.

Lovecraft found some relief from his lower abdominal pain by sitting in a bathtub filled with hot water. He could no longer eat solid food. His aunt became alarmed, and at last induced him to allow her to summon a doctor, who took no immediate action but put Lovecraft on medications. A specialist examined him on March 2 and told him what he must already have guessed: that he had cancer, and that it had progressed so far that it was inoperable. Lovecraft entered the Jane Brown Memorial Hospital in Providence on March 10. For the next five days he was kept sedated to control his pain. He died on the morning of March 15, at the age of forty-six.

A noon funeral service was held three days later in the chapel of a local funeral parlor, and Lovecraft was buried in the Phillips family plot at Swan Point Cemetery, where he had so often walked with enjoyment during life. Only four mourners were in attendance at the service—Aunt Annie and one of her friends, and Lovecraft's second cousin and his friend. The Eddys came late and missed the service, but were just in time to see the hearse carry Lovecraft's corpse from the chapel to the grave.[26] Lovecraft received no separate stone, but his name was carved on the stone pillar that carried the names of his parents.

Lovecraft had shown his high opinion and trust of young Robert Barlow by making him literary executor of his estate. It fell to Barlow to dispose of Lovecraft's papers, and to finalize any pending story sales. De Camp pointed out in his biography that literary executor was an honorary post having no legal standing.[27] By the terms of a will Lovecraft had signed in 1912, all of his estate went to his surviving aunt. Before his death, Lovecraft had granted August Derleth the rights to a collection of his stories that Derleth had proposed publishing as a book. This gave Derleth, who never met Lovecraft in the flesh, a legal interest in some of Lovecraft's works.

Lovecraft had a middling opinion of both Derleth's intellect and his attempts at weird fiction, although in his correspondence with Derleth he graciously encouraged the younger man. In a letter to Frank Belknap Long, Jr. in 1931, in which Lovecraft expounded on his philosophical beliefs, he referred to Derleth as "little Augie Derleth" and characterized him as a self-blinded earth-gazer.[28] In a letter that Lovecraft wrote shortly after the death of Robert E. Howard, he compared unfavorably the writings of both Robert Bloch and August Derleth with those of Howard, damning Bloch and Derleth with faint praise by referring to them as "clever enough technically" but nowhere in

Howard's league when it came to "real emotions of fear and of dread suspense."[29]

The carelessness with which young Barlow carried out his duties as literary executor soon aroused the ire of Derleth and other correspondents of Lovecraft, such as Donald Wandrei and Clark Ashton Smith. Some of Lovecraft's papers Barlow gathered up and took away with him to Kansas, where he was now attending the Kansas City Art Institute. Others he left scattered around Lovecraft's rooms, but this was not known until years later. He kept the papers he had taken with him for months, doing nothing with them and disregarding Derleth's pleas for access. Clark Ashton Smith wrote to sever all connection with Barlow on the grounds that Barlow's conduct toward Lovecraft's aunt had been unethical. Smith was acting in defense of his dead friend's memory, prompted by rumors spread by Derleth and Wandrei, but it is impossible to know whether his opinion of Barlow was justified.

Barlow stopped responding to letters. He was caught up in his art studies and in his awakening homosexuality, and found little time or interest for Lovecraft's literary remains. At last, in 1938, Barlow decided to rid himself of the burden he had so rashly taken on. He divided the papers between Derleth and the Brown University Library, where they formed the nucleus of the university's Lovecraft collection. He also edited *The Notes and Commonplace Book of H. P. Lovecraft*, a notebook filled with story ideas. This was published by Futile Press of California in June 1938.

When Derleth tried and failed with both Charles Scribner's Sons and Simon and Schuster to get his planned collection of Lovecraft's stories published, he decided that the only recourse was to publish it himself. For this purpose he formed Arkham House, along with Donald Wandrei. Both men put their savings into the fledgling publishing house, although Derleth took the larger financial risk. In 1939 *The Outsider and Others* issued from the press in 1,268 copies. This was the very title Lovecraft himself had once suggested for a proposed collection of his tales. It is a large hardcover containing thirty-six of Lovecraft's stories and his essay "Supernatural Horror in Literature," as well as an introduction by Derleth and Wandrei. The dust jacket is illustrated by Virgil Finley, a popular *Weird Tales* illustrator who had corresponded with Lovecraft.

After the death of Annie Gamwell, Lovecraft's aunt, on January 29, 1941, Lovecraft's library was appraised for sale by a local bookseller. He discovered a heap of papers and dozens of manuscripts left behind by Barlow in 1937, and unnoticed by the elderly aunt. They were piled in front of the furnace, about to be burned as trash. He bought them and offered them for sale to Brown University, which purchased them and added them to its Lovecraft collection.

In her will, Gamwell gave back her royalty rights to *The Outsider and Others* to Derleth and Wandrei, to be divided between the two men "in equal shares." This was largely a symbolic gesture. It took four years for the first printing of the book to sell out, so not a lot of money was involved. However, it gave Derleth a tighter hold over Lovecraft's literary works, and in future years he used it as the base from which to gradually gain near total control over Lovecraft's writings. The bequest may not even have been legal—there is a contention that Lovecraft's divorce was never formally fulfilled, and if this is true, Sonia would have had claim to the royalties from the book, as Lovecraft's wife.

While *The Outsider and Others* was slowly selling to Lovecraft's friends and fans, in 1941 Derleth published under the Arkham House imprint a book of his own horror stories titled *Someone in the Dark*, and the following year a book of stories by Clark Ashton Smith titled *Out of Space and Time*. Wandrei began to work on a collection of Lovecraft's letters. The two men got as many of Lovecraft's correspondents as they could locate to send them whatever batches of Lovecraft's letters they might have saved, hired a professional typist to transcribe the letters, and then returned the originals.

He and Derleth soon realized that a single volume of letters would never be enough. Lovecraft's letters have been called one of "the pinnacles of his literary achievement."[30] Maurice W. Moe, a member of Lovecraft's early circle of correspondents who referred to themselves as the Kleicomolo Club and exchanged letters with each other from 1916 to 1918, suggested that Lovecraft was "the greatest letter-writer in history."[31] There were thousands of letters, some as long as thirty to fifty pages, and this was only the tip of the iceberg. L. Sprague de Camp wrote that "it had been guessed" that Lovecraft wrote 100,000 letters in the course of his life.[32]

Donald Wandrei joined the navy in 1942, as did so many young American men. His influence at Arkham House was greatly diminished, and Derleth took full control of the business, but Wandrei continued to edit Lovecraft's letters. Eventually, they would run to five large volumes, and even at that, only the cream had been skimmed from Lovecraft's correspondence. It is unfortunate that Sonia burned in an open field hundreds of Lovecraft's letters to her two years after her last meeting with Lovecraft in March 1933, in a bid to irrevocably rid herself of the shadow of her past, but many others to whom Lovecraft had written valued his letters enough to squirrel them away, and the prodding of Derleth and Wandrei brought many of these precious packets back into the light.

Derleth, who did not go to war, published in 1943 a second large hardcover collection of Lovecraft's stories, *Beyond the Wall of Sleep*. The print run was slightly smaller than that of the first book—only 1,217 copies. It contains the two full novels Lovecraft wrote, *The Case of Charles Dexter Ward* and *The Dream-Quest of Unknown Kardath*, as well as some of his revision work, his early dream-cycle stories, and a selection of Lovecraft's poetry. This book in its original printing, along with the earlier Arkham House edition of stories, is a rare collector's item today, and commands steep prices at book auctions. At the time of its publication, *The Outsider and Others* sold for five dollars, or for only three dollars and fifty cents to those 150 optimistic souls who paid for it prior to its actual printing.

After the war, Derleth began to write stories set in what he referred to as the Cthulhu mythos, based on brief fragments or ideas by Lovecraft. This was a continuation of a practice he had adopted during the final years of Lovecraft's life, when he was encouraged by Lovecraft to use Lovecraft's Yog-Sothothery in his fiction. Derleth wrote "The Return of Hastur" in 1931, and revised it in 1937. Derleth has received criticism for placing Lovecraft's name on his Cthulhu mythos stories, implying a collaboration where none existed. His motives are difficult to know. It could not have been done for the money, since Arkham House never had a profitable year during Derleth's lifetime. Perhaps it was an attempt to expand and improve the mythos, or it may have been Derleth's way of honoring Lovecraft's memory and keeping it alive in the public eye. Derleth sold several of these mythos pastiches to *Weird Tales* under the editorship of Dorothy McIlwraith shortly before the magazine went bankrupt in 1954.

In a sense, by writing his Cthulhu mythos pastiches, Derleth was doing the same thing Lovecraft himself had done for most of his career in his "revision" works—composing what were essentially original stories based on a few sentences or an idea by another person, and placing that person's name on the result. His novel *The Lurker at the Threshold*, published in 1945 by Arkham House, does have a very small amount of Lovecraft in it, but Lovecraft's name was featured prominently on the dust jacket. Lovecraft ghostwrote for money, Derleth for some other motive—perhaps a desire to elevate the stature or fame of his writings by associating them with Lovecraft's name, perhaps as a homage to a man he considered both mentor and friend, perhaps as a way of controlling the Cthulhu mythos by reshaping it in his own image.

Whatever his motives, Derleth is said to have gained an almost absolute control over the use of Lovecraft's work from 1937 until his own death in 1971.[33] He was fiercely protective of the copyrights he claimed to hold for Lovecraft's fiction, and of the Cthulhu mythos in general. He let some writers produce mythos tales while arbitrarily denying other writers the same privilege. During his life, Lovecraft had always encouraged other writers, including the younger Derleth, to make as extensive a use of his mythological background as they wished, but Derleth was not nearly as generous. In justification for his prohibitions and refusals of use, he asserted that mythos stories from second-rate writers would only cheapen Lovecraft's memory. He obviously did not consider himself a second-rate writer.

Derleth purchased some rights to Lovecraft's stories from *Weird Tales*, but there is doubt as to whether *Weird Tales* had any rights to sell. It seems that at least some of the stories, probably most of them, that Derleth claimed for many years to own were actually in the public domain. The whole question of Lovecraft's copyrights is one of the most murky and convoluted chapters in American copyright law, and I will not even attempt to enter into it, but will only observe that through his draconian control over Lovecraft's works, Derleth inhibited and delayed the expansion of the mythos that took place following Derleth's death and that continues to this day. Whether this is a good or bad thing perhaps depends on one's point of view.

In 1977 a group of Lovecraft's fans raised enough money to erect a marble stone in the Phillips family plot in Swan Point Cemetery. The marker bears the name *Howard Phillips Lovecraft* and the dates of his birth and death. Below is carved the motto "I Am Providence." The quotation comes from a letter Lovecraft wrote while in emotional turmoil over his possible liberation from New York and his return to

Providence. It is a fitting epitaph for this man who called himself an impersonal dreamer. Just as Randolph Carter saved himself from the ultimate abyss of chaos by holding in his imagination the architecture and streets of his beloved Boston, so had Lovecraft saved himself from the hell that was Red Hook by clinging to his childhood memories of Providence.

It was for Lovecraft more than a place—it was a way of life, an island of sanity and order, a refuge from the madness of the twentieth century. Throughout his life Lovecraft had always been largely indifferent to direct individual human relationships. He preferred to carry on relationships by letter. Toward the mass of humanity as a whole he had a positive dislike. But for the architecture and environment of old New England he felt a deep love, and toward the city of Providence that love rose to the level of a passion rivaled only by his infatuation with Marblehead. Place was everything for Lovecraft. He identified with the place of his birth and childhood happiness. It is fitting that he be remembered in death for the place he loved in life.

n 1944 Lovecraft was such a nonentity on the American literary scene that when the prominent critic Edmund Wilson (1895–1972) wrote a spring article for the *New Yorker* magazine about American writers of horror stories, he did not even think it necessary to mention Lovecraft's name. Readers of the magazine suggested to Wilson that he really should pay attention to Lovecraft, who was just beginning to gain some minor recognition thanks to the promotional efforts of August Derleth and Arkham House. In response to this admonishment, Wilson wrote a short article in November of the following year that was devoted to the Lovecraft phenomenon. It is titled "Tales of the Marvellous and the Ridiculous." His central conclusion was anything but flattering.

He reported to his readers, "I regret that, after examining these books, I am no more enthusiastic than before."[1] The books he referred to were Derleth's biography of Lovecraft, *H. P. L.: A Memoir*; Lovecraft's essay "Supernatural Horror in Literature;" *The Lurker at the Threshold*, which he described as an unfinished novel that had been completed by Derleth; a collection of miscellaneous writings by Lovecraft and brief biographical notes by other writers on Lovecraft's life,

titled *Marginalia*; and a collection published in 1945 containing four-
teen of Lovecraft's stories that is titled *Best Supernatural Stories of H. P.
Lovecraft*.

The collection was published by World Publishing Company of
Cleveland, Ohio, and offers a fairly good sampling of Lovecraft's fiction. It contains such excellent stories as the "Colour Out of Space,"
"The Call of Cthulhu," "The Dunwich Horror," "The Whisperer in
Darkness," and "The Music of Erich Zann." August Derleth wrote the
introduction to the book. As Joshi and Schultz have pointed out, it was
pretty much impossible to escape Derleth when reading anything by
Lovecraft that was published after his death.[2] Over a short period of
time, Derleth simply took control of all of Lovecraft's writings.

Apart from *The Lurker at the Threshold*, which is really a Derleth
novel, not a Lovecraft novel, Wilson had a fair if somewhat narrow
basis upon which to judge Lovecraft's literary merits, both as a writer
of fiction and nonfiction. His judgement of the fiction was predominantly one of amused contempt, and was summed up in a single sentence that has been widely quoted: "The only real horror in most of
these fictions is the horror of bad taste and bad art."[3] Wilson was an
advocate of the sparse American prose style exemplified in the writings of Faulkner and Hemingway. He was simply incapable of appreciating on any level Lovecraft's florid, antique, verbose prose style.

His criticism of Lovecraft's style is still used today by Lovecraft's
detractors, and for very good reason—there is some basis for criticism
of Lovecraft's writing style. Wilson mocked Lovecraft for his excessive
use of adjectives such as *hellish*, *unhallowed*, and *blasphemous*. He concluded, "Surely one of the primary rules for writing an effective tale
of horror is never to use any of these words . . ."[4] Lovecraft himself,
toward the end of his life, had reached a similar if less absolute conclusion about his style, and was making the effort to prune his adjectives,[5]

but he died before his more streamlined style could make a substantial impact on his fiction as a whole.

Wilson took time to mock Professor T. O. Mabbott of Hunter College, an expert on Edgar Allan Poe, for daring to write in an essay in *Marginalia* that he had "enjoyed every word" of Lovecraft's stories, and for making comparisons between Poe and Lovecraft. As far as Wilson was concerned, the linking of Lovecraft with Poe was merely an indication of how degenerate literary criticism had become. "I have never yet found in Lovecraft a single sentence Poe could have written,"[6] Wilson wrote in arch dismissal of the comparison, perhaps failing to consider that this bespoke originality on Lovecraft's part. Elsewhere he concluded, "The truth is these stories were hackwork contributed to such publications as *Weird Tales* and *Amazing Stories*, where, in my opinion, they ought to have been left."[7]

When it came time to eviscerate Lovecraft's nonfiction, Wilson was a little more kind. He called "Supernatural Horror in Literature" "a really able piece of work,"[8] but could not resist criticizing Lovecraft for his enthusiastic approval of the fiction of Machen and Dunsany. It is somewhat amusing that Wilson reported Lovecraft "strong in the Gothic novelists" when, in one of his letters, Lovecraft himself admitted to merely skimming through some the Gothic novels to get an idea of their contents for his essay.[9] As to Lovecraft's poetry, Wilson wasted no time on it, but dismissed it as "quite second-rate."

Wilson's little essay is significant because it set the general tone for Lovecraft criticism for several decades, at least in intellectual circles. As it happens, the essay is riddled with factual errors. Wilson had only the most superficial acquaintance with Lovecraft, both the man and his works. This is to be expected of someone who dismissed Lovecraft's fiction as "hackwork" and "second-rate"—for why would Wilson study in depth the works of a man he held in contempt? Thanks to the able criticism of such scholars as S. T. Joshi, Wilson's errors of fact and judgement are glaringly obvious to the modern reader of his essay. He was wrong about Lovecraft and, incidentally, also wrong about Machen, and perhaps Dunsany as well.

Where is it incised into stone that a writing style must eschew the use of adjectives? True, this is the common statement of modern critics of literary style, but what edict of God makes it so? When I read Hemingway's story "The Killers," I find his chopped, short little sentences, stripped of all color, to be at least as unnatural as Lovecraft's ramblings through the flowery purple fields of verbiage. Indeed, the piling on of adjective after adjective has its own distinct stylistic effect, and it is quite a powerful effect. That it was out of fashion among the literati in Lovecraft's time does not negate it.

Wilson saved his parting shot for those who dared to suggest that Lovecraft's work had merit and should be remembered. "Lovecraft, since his death in 1937, has rapidly become a cult,"[10] he asserted, adding at the end of his essay, "But the Lovecraft cult, I fear, is on an even more infantile level than the Baker Street Irregulars and the cult of Sherlock Holmes."[11] By *cult*, Wilson meant both the tendency of other writers to reproduce in their fiction artifacts of Lovecraft's mythos, such as references to the Old Ones and the *Necronomicon*, and also the enthusiasm of readers for this interconnected world of the mythos.

This essay marks one of the earliest appearances in print of the term *Cthulhu mythos*,[12] which was coined by August Derleth in the slightly variant form "Cthulhu mythology." Wilson's references to a cult of Lovecraft are fascinating because they reveal how soon after Lovecraft's death the mythos took hold on the imagination of readers. Derleth's efforts to make Lovecraft's stories known to a wider audience, and to extend the mythos by writing his own original stories set in Lovecraft's mythological world, were evidently producing results. It is true that the quality of Derleth's mythos stories is inferior to the quality of Lovecraft's stories, but readers were sufficiently enthralled by the wonder of the mythos itself that they were willing to overlook this unevenness. The power of the *Necronomicon* mythos transcended Derleth's weaknesses as a writer of weird tales.

Lovecraft's posthumous progress along the road from obscurity to notable figure in modern American literature has not been without its bumps. The English writer Colin Wilson (1931–), who gained recognition for himself in 1956 with his book of literary criticism *The Outsider*, a title derived from Lovecraft's short story of the same name, wrote of Lovecraft in 1962, "It must be admitted that Lovecraft is a very bad writer."[13] He not only criticized Lovecraft's writings, but Lovecraft himself, calling him "a horrifying figure" and declaring "he is sick." Wilson's main problem with Lovecraft the man seems to have been his perception that Lovecraft had turned his back on life. He projected his disapproval of Lovecraft's attitudes and lifestyle onto his fiction, and characterized it as similarly diseased and unhealthy. But the power of the mythos was not to be denied. Five short years later, Wilson changed his mind. After corresponding with August Derleth, he wrote in 1967, "I am now willing to admit that my assessment of Lovecraft . . . was unduly harsh."[14]

In the 1921 story "The Nameless City," Lovecraft quoted a couplet supposedly penned by the mad Arab, Abdul Alhazred, in his *Necronomicon*:

That is not dead which can eternal lie
And with strange aeons, death may die.

The exact meaning of this mysterious couplet has remained obscure. Lovecraft deliberately left it that way. It has been applied to the things under his Nameless City in the desert of Arabia, and also to dreaming Cthulhu who lies beneath the waves of the Pacific Ocean in his stone house in R'lyeh. It seems that the couplet may also be applied to the

Necronomicon mythos as a whole, which has not faded as Edmund Wilson and other literary authorities expected, but has survived and flourished. With every passing year, Lovecraft's memory is more revered, his fiction more widely read and appreciated, and his mythos expanded by the writings of appreciative fans and professionals alike.

The popularity of Lovecraft's mythos cannot be attributed to the quality of his writing, much less to the quality of the writings of those others who enlarged its boundaries both during his life and after his death. No, the mythos has continued to haunt the consciousness of humanity because its essential components were drawn from the deepest recesses of Lovecraft's dreaming mind, which lay in contact with the racial consciousness of our species. His Old Ones are archetypical in their potency. The mythos offers a replacement for both religion and magic, while exalting as it renders mysterious and strange the future potential of science.

Science cannot replace either religion or magic, but it can encompass and transform them, making them an organic part of its totality. In this way, they are not abandoned but are renewed and reborn. Lovecraft firmly believed in the oneness of both spirit and matter—that what was called spirit was actually a form of matter, or else it did not exist at all. He drew upon Einstein's theory of relativity in support of this view, maintaining that Einstein's demonstration of the oneness of time and space, matter and energy, did not indicate that at its root reality was nonphysical, as the Theosophists and Spiritualists asserted, but rather proved that the spiritual was a subtle form of the material.

Lovecraft's world view, uncommon in his own day, is increasingly becoming the popular world view of our age, at least in the West. In the underdeveloped world, religion and magic still reign supreme, but in the West science has toppled them from their thrones, at least in the common consciousness of the population. Yet the needs and perceptions that religion and magic address in the depths of the human mind have not vanished, and can never vanish. They are real needs, real perceptions, and unless they are addressed the mind becomes unbalanced.

The *Necronomicon* mythos offers a solution to this problem. Religion and magic are embraced by a science that has been expanded and metamorphosed by beings from beyond human consciousness. The mythic agents of this transformation of science are Lovecraft's Old Ones. Infinitely wise and strange, the Old Ones offer the possibility via their alien sciences for us to once again consider questions of religion and magic without outraging reason. The terms of religion and magic are redefined and accommodated by a science released from the constraints of mechanical three-dimensional thinking. The universe of the Old Ones is multidimensional and extends far beyond the boundaries of normal space-time, yet for all its strangeness it is still a part of the material oneness of the universe in which we live.

The *Necronomicon* is central to Lovecraft's mythology, and central to the book is the promise of answers to the most obscure occult mysteries. What else has made the book so fascinating to modern readers, but the lure of forbidden knowledge from unimagined realms beyond our conventional reality? This knowledge is transformative—merely to become aware of it causes irrevocable changes in the life of the person who possesses the book, or who comes into contact with it. To hold the book is to be close to those creatures of the other worlds who are attracted by its power, and such proximity is in itself dangerous.

We cannot know exactly what is in the *Necronomicon* because Lovecraft never wrote the book. It exists, if it exists at all, only on the astral plane, and is accessible solely by dreams or visions. Others suggested that he should write it, and he considered doing so from time to time, but the task daunted him, in part because the book is supposed to be very large—the John Dee translation was said in "The Dunwich Horror" to have more than 751 pages. Ultimately, he decided that the book was more potent if left unwritten, confiding to science fiction writer

James Blish that "one can never *produce* anything even a tenth as terrible and impressive as one can awesomely *hint* about."[15] Its power comes not from what has been quoted from its pages by Lovecraft, but from what is left unrevealed. Its power is the promise of a revelation so terrifying, a truth so shocking and so impossible to accept, that it unhinges the reason.

To a lesser degree, this was the promise of all the forbidden grimoires—the grammars of magic—that circulated under the rose in medieval and Renaissance times in Europe. Unpublished texts such as the *Goetia*, the *Key of Solomon*, and the *Picatrix* gained their reputations from vague rumors about their contents and the dreadful consequences of reading them, or worse still, of practicing the methods they described. The grimoires were forbidden by the Catholic Church. This only made them more desired by those with a yearning to acquire occult knowledge and the power its acquisition promised. Curiously, the eventual publication of these texts and others like them did not increase their reputation, but diminished it.

The reality of the grimoires is somewhat different from the rumor. Those who have made an extensive study of their contents have noticed that they are rather tedious to read. E. M. Butler observed, "That so-called black magic is rarely as black as it has been painted is one of the conclusions to which I have been irresistibly drawn by a close scrutiny of the texts available."[16] They are like magical cookbooks, and list various ingredients and tools and practices that must be carried out to attain the conversation or service of various spiritual beings. The wonders that they possess lie not in the words on the page, which are prosaic, but in the promise of those words. Since that promise is not to be attained without long and difficult training of the mind and body, and since its attainment does not take the form that is commonly conceived by the general population, reading the grimoires proves disappointing to the average person, who is looking for some magic button he can press that will transform his life.

The *Necronomicon* promises that magic button. Merely to hold the book is to be transformed by it, and to read it is to have thrust upon you the two-edged sword of forbidden knowledge and madness. The *Necronomicon* is like an untameable stallion that can be ridden by a few brave and resourceful adventurers, but never without grave danger. The rider cannot be sure where the horse will carry him, or when it will choose to throw him into a pit, but in the meanwhile it is an exhilarating ride.

A few serious modern magicians—those who actually work the techniques of magic described in the grimoires—have decided to treat both the *Necronomicon* and the Great Old Ones of Lovecraft's dreams as real, if not on the physical plane of common waking consciousness, then on the astral level of dreams and visions. The underlying premise they rely on is quite simple—they believe that Lovecraft could never have conceived the *Necronomicon* or the Old Ones unless they had some existence in a different dimension or in an alternative reality. Accepting Lovecraft's underlying assumption that all the universe with its myriad levels is a unity, then the Old Ones do exist and can be reached. Mythos magicians can be confident of this because Lovecraft reached the Old Ones in dreams.

During his life, Lovecraft always laughed at the notion that his Old Ones might be real. He denied them existence with unwavering determination. But then, he denied his own duality of nature, embracing his rational scientific side and relegating his mystical side, which he could not suppress, to the status of entertainment. Perhaps the only reason he was able to retain his sanity throughout his life was his success in diminishing the terrors of his night visions to the level of mere fantasies to be shuddered over for a short time, and then dismissed. Had he not been able to dismiss these persistent, uncannily tangible visions, he might have shared the fate of many of his characters, and ended up locked in an insane asylum, or dead.

The fear of madness was Lovecraft's overriding terror, both by day and by night. The examples of his father and mother were forever before him. While awake he was able to hold with rigid determination to the rational methods of science. They became the firm foundation of his waking life. But while asleep, he slipped into a dreamworld in which reason was snatched from under his feet, precipitating him into a pit of shadows where he confronted the very madness that he feared always stalked his footsteps, waiting for any sign of mental weakness to assert its natural sovereignty over him forever. Each night for Lovecraft was a battle for sanity itself, and he was never completely sure he would prevail.

Serious modern magicians have taken the step that Lovecraft could never have taken—they have chosen to treat the mythos as magical reality. The cults of Cthulhu, Dagon, Nyarlathotep, and Shub-Niggurath, which Lovecraft only dreamed about, have in a sense been manifested upon the material level. Kenneth Grant (1924–), leader of the Typhonian branch of the occult society known as the Ordo Templi Orientis, referred to this system of magic as the *"Necronomicon* cycle" in his 1981 book *Outer Gateways*. He pointed out that Cthulhu in the depths of the Pacific Ocean, awaiting the stars to come right before it can emerge into our world, is analogous on the microcosmic level to Cthulhu in the depths of the subconscious, "awaiting certain astrological configurations that will both announce and facilitate its manifestation on earth, projected via the minds of its chosen votaries."[17]

Grant believes the name *Cthulhu* that was transcribed by H. P. Lovecraft is a variant form or corruption of *Tutulu*, a word heard by Aleister Crowley while sitting in a trance in North Africa on November 24, 1909, as Crowley was scrying the 27th Enochian Aethyr of Zaa.[18] It is significant Grant wrote that Lovecraft "transcribed" the name, rather than invented it or imagined it, as it indicates his belief in the pre-existence of the name. Grant equated the word *Tutulu* with the number 66, a number of Aleister's Crowley's Great Work—communication by the magician with his or her Holy Guardian Angel, and the subsequent fulfillment of the magician's True Will. Through Kabbalistic numerology he found an "essential identity of the *Necronomicon* (555) and Therionic (666) Currents."[19] (Therion was one of Crowley's magical titles.)

The Enochian Aethyrs, the scrying of which preoccupied Aleister Crowley, are invocations that form a part of the system of Enochian angel magic received from 1583 to 1587 by the Elizabethan sage John Dee through the agency of his crystal gazer, the alchemist Edward Kelley. Dee has a prominent place in Lovecraft's "History of the *Necronomicon*" as one of the translators of the book. Lovecraft wrote in his brief essay, "An English translation made by Dr. Dee was never printed, and exists only in fragments recovered from the original manuscript." This perhaps refers to the copy of Dee's translation that was for a time in the possession of Wilbur Whateley, as described in "The Dunwich Horror."

In a note accompanying his vision of the 27th Aethyr, Crowley wrote concerning the word *Tutulu* "this word cannot be translated."[20] In this sense it is equivalent to the Tetragrammaton, the Hebrew name of God with four letters that has no explicit translation. It is a mystery, just as the knowledge of the grimoires is veiled in mystery, and is made all the more potent due to its concealment in the depths of the subconscious. In his best-known book, *Magick in Theory and Practice*, Crowley wrote that "formidable words that roar and moan . . . have a real effect in exalting the consciousness."[21] It is the very mystery of these barbaric words of evocation, these obscure and untranslatable names, that empowers them when they are incanted.

The purpose of practical magic dealing with the Great Old Ones is communication. Most modern magicians working in Lovecraft's mythos—the *Necronomicon* cycle, as Grant calls it—would probably not consider themselves worshippers of the Old Ones. In general, Western magicians have never worshipped the things they invoke, but rather have sought to command them in the name and authority of higher powers with which the magicians are in rapport. Worship is a religious impulse, and the impulse of magic is control.[22] Even so, the invocation of higher beings such as the Pagan gods in magic approaches a kind of worship, in which offerings or sacrifices are made to the invoked deity and praises are given in acknowledgement of its greatness and power. This is true of the invocation of archangels in the Judeo-Christian tradition of magic, and it is true of the invocation of the Old Ones of the *Necronomicon* cycle.

The compact paperback version of the *Necronomicon* published by Avon Books in March of 1980 caused a minor sensation, at least among the general public. For the first time, the *Necronomicon*—or what claimed to be the *Necronomicon*—was made widely available at a low price. The book was initially published in 1977 by Schlangekraft Inc., a small publishing house owned by L. K. Barnes, who ran a graphics business, in a limited leather-bound first edition of 666 copies at the high price of seventy-five dollars. Kenneth Grant made reference to this first edition in his *Outer Gateways*.[23] So quickly did it sell out, it was soon followed by a hardcover edition of 3,333 copies, also by Schlangekraft, before the rights were sold to Avon Books.

The book is often asserted to have been the brainchild of Herman Slater (1935–92), proprietor of the Magickal Childe bookstore of New York, who is said to have hired a writer and an illustrator to create it. Whatever its genesis, its author chose to pass as its editor, and remains anonymous under the pseudonym Simon, but copyright records indicate that he is Peter Levenda. The illustrator who designed the various seals in the book is Khem Caigan. The Avon paperback edition, first published in 1980, has never been out of print. It immediately proved itself enormously successful for a book of its subject matter—so much so that Levenda, under his pseudonym of Simon, wrote a kind of sequel that was published in 1981, also by Avon Books: a much more slender companion volume called the *Necronomicon Spellbook*.

The Simon *Necronomicon*, as it is known, is a grimoire that offers the reader actual techniques of ritual magic that are supposedly part of Lovecraft's *Necronomicon*, which is presented by Levenda as a genuine, existing ancient text from Sumeria. In his lengthy prefatory material, the author claimed to have received a copy of the manuscript in the Greek language from a wandering priest of dubious provenance.[24]

The text of the grimoire is in the first person and purports to be the very words of the Mad Arab, who is not named in the body of the text itself. The Arab introduces himself and declares, "I have found the Gate that leads to the Outside, by which the Ancient Ones, who ever seek entrance to our world, keep eternal watch."[25] He goes on to teach a variety of barbarous names, demonic seals, incantations, and rituals that are a mixture of Sumerian mythological fragments and medieval European spirit evocation. Names of Lovecraft's Old Ones are given variant forms—Cthulhu becomes *Kutulu*, for example.

As a literary pastiche of Lovecraft's apocryphal *Necronomicon*, Levenda's book is not without merit. He had the inspiration to use as his background the mythology of Sumer, which is virtually unknown to modern magicians. This gave the work an air of freshness and novelty, while insuring that few would be able to easily identify his factual errors. The more ancient, the more mysterious, and Sumer is the most ancient of all the lands recorded in histories, with the exception of fanciful realms such as Atlantis or Hyperborea. As a practical grimoire, the book is somewhat less impressive. It relies heavily on incantations, exorcisms, seals, and barbarous names of power, but lacks coherent structure and offers few practical ritual techniques of use to the modern practitioner.

Other versions of the *Necronomicon* have been written by fans of Lovecraft and his mythos, who refuse to allow that which is eternal to die. Just a year after the limited first edition of the Simon *Necronomicon* was published by Schlangekraft, the so-called Hay *Necronomicon* was published by Neville Spearman Ltd. It boasted an introduction by none other than Colin Wilson, who had by this time repented of his 1961 acid criticism of Lovecraft and his writing style, and had become an instrument of the Old Ones, albeit tongue-in-cheek. George Hay is listed as the book's editor, hence its common designation.

The Hay *Necronomicon* is an awkward grouping of parts—the introduction by Wilson, a treatise on ciphers, the text supposedly decoded from John Dee's enigmatic letter tables, and a collection of literary essays on Lovecraft. The letter tables, which are not reproduced in the book, make up only a part of the complex system of Enochian magic. No scholar has ever been able to understand the construction of these Enochian tables or to decipher their meaning, but this is the claim made in the Hay *Necronomicon*. The result is disappointing—a simplistic grimoire written in pseudo-antique English of the sort that Lovecraft would have enjoyed, although Lovecraft would have done a better job mocking it up. The text is, however, much more closely based on Lovecraft's fictional mythology than the text of the Simon *Necronomicon*, which barely refers to it.

There is no indication that the modern cultural phenomenon commonly called the Cthulhu mythos shows any signs of weakening. Like a plant nourished by the color out of space, it continues to flourish and sprout in unexpected directions, taking on strange shapes and uncouth associations. Cthulhu has been offered as candidate for the office of president of the United States of America in several past elections under the slogan "Why choose the lesser evil?" Novels and stories based in the mythos continue to be written by amateur and professional writers. The Old Ones and the *Necronomicon* form the subject of Tarot decks, video games, comic books, and films for both the cinema and television. Those seeking to dip their toes into the shallow end of the mythos pool can buy plush toys in the shape of Cthulhu, T-shirts emblazoned with the logo of Miskatonic University, and jewelry bearing Derleth's version of the Elder Seal.

Lovecraft was convinced that he would find only oblivion after death, and he welcomed the prospect. But if by strange design his consciousness could look down upon what his mythos has brought forth upon the world, he would react with bemusement and perhaps a secret satisfaction. The creation of the mythos was for him a wonderful game, and it could only give him pleasure to see so many others deriving enjoyment by playing it. He never expected anyone to take it seriously, yet perhaps he would be gratified that the work to which he devoted the creative energies of a lifetime has not been forgotten but has continued to offer meaning to an ever-increasing number of admirers.

It remains to be seen whether the *Necronomicon* mythos will collapse and rot under its own dead weight, or will spring up from a hidden root and put forth a new flower beneath the moon. The area of the mythos that has barely been tapped is its potential use as the basis for serious esoteric work. The teenagers who recite the incantations of the Simon *Necronomicon* are not to be taken seriously, but Kenneth Grant and the Typhonian Order are an entirely different matter. What Lovecraft created, without ever really intending to do so, is an entirely new mythology for our technological, space-faring Western culture. It may become the root of a new system of magic, or even of a new religion. Only the passing of years will show whether these hidden shoots have the hardiness to rise up and bear fruit.

RELATIONS
AND FRIENDS

RELATIONS

Winfield Scott Lovecraft (1853–98)—Lovecraft's father. Born October 26, died July 19. He worked as a blacksmith from 1871–73, but in 1889 he was a traveling salesman for Gorham & Co., Silversmiths, of Providence, Rhode Island, selling jewelry and precious metals to jewellers and retail outlets. By religion, Anglican. He was regarded as pompous by some of those who knew him due to his affectation of an English accent. He married Lovecraft's mother, Sarah Phillips, at St. Paul's Episcopal Church in Boston on June 12, 1889. Became insane while on a business trip to Chicago in the spring of 1893, probably due to syphilis contracted in the 1870s. Institutionalized April 25, 1893, at Butler Hospital in Providence. Died in that institution, 1898. He left an estate worth approximately ten thousand dollars.

Sarah Susan (Phillips) Lovecraft (1857–1921)—Lovecraft's mother. Born October 17, died May 24. Commonly called "Susie." She was descended from old Rhode Island stock, and could trace her ancestors back to the Massachusetts Bay Colony of 1630. Attended the Wheaton Seminary in Norton, Massachusetts. Died in Butler Hospital, Providence, from complications of a gall-bladder operation. She had been committed to Butler Hospital for mental problems March 13, 1919, after suffering from hallucinations and disorientation culminating in a nervous breakdown, and never left the grounds of the institution until the time of her death. The examining doctor observed that some mental disorder had been in evidence since 1904 (the year her father, Whipple Phillips, died).

Lillian Delora (Phillips) Clark (1856–1932)—Lovecraft's elder maternal aunt. Born April 20, died July 3. She helped Lovecraft's mother raise and care for him in childhood, then continued to look after him when he became an adult. She was the eldest child in the Phillips family. Studied at the Wheaton Seminary in Norton, Massachusetts, and at the Rhode Island Normal School before becoming a schoolteacher. A talented painter, she had paintings exhibited at the Providence Art Club. Married Dr. Franklin Chase Clark, who became the Phillips' family physician. The marriage was childless. Widowed in 1915. After Susie Lovecraft was institutionalized, she took care of the Lovecraft flat at 598 Angell Street from 1919 to 1924. She rented a room above Lovecraft's room when he moved to 10 Barnes Street in 1926 in order to be close enough to care for his needs. Lovecraft described the cause of her death as "collapse of the general organic system."

Annie Emeline (Phillips) Gamwell (1866–1941)—Lovecraft's younger maternal aunt. Born July 10, died January 29. Youngest child of the Phillips family. On June 3, 1897, she married the newspaper editor Edward Francis Gamwell, and moved with him to Cambridge, Massachusetts. She had two children: Marion Roby Gamwell, who died at the age of five days in 1900, and Phillips Gamwell, who died of tuberculosis on December 31, 1916. The marriage was not happy. In October 1916, Annie left her husband to take their son to Roswell, Colorado, in the hope that the dry climate would arrest his disease. It is possible that she and her husband were separated even before this date. After Phillips died, Annie returned, not to Edward in Cambridge, but to Providence. Edward and Annie were never legally divorced. She moved with Lovecraft into a flat at 66 College Street, Providence, on May 15, 1933, and kept house for him until his death. The cause of her own death was cancer.

Whipple Van Buren Phillips (1833–1904)—Lovecraft's maternal grandfather. Born November 22, died March 28. He was a prominent Rhode Island industrialist. Whipple attended school in Foster, Rhode Island, and later at the East Greenwich Academy (then called the Providence Conference Seminary), and went on to teach in country schools. He left teaching to build a mill in the western Rhode Island village of Coffin's Corner, which he eventually renamed Greene. On January 27, 1856, he married his first cousin, Robie Alzada Place—a closeness of blood that was always a source of worry to Lovecraft—and sired with her a son and four daughters, one of whom died in early childhood. When Lovecraft was a young boy, his grandfather told him ghost stories and encouraged Lovecraft to read his library of classics. He was a Freemason, and founded Ionic Lodge No. 28 in Greene in 1870. The Lodge Hall still stands and contains his portrait. At the height of his prosperity in 1881, he had the Phillips' family mansion built at 194 Angell Street in Providence. In 1889 he formed the Owyhee Land and Irrigation Company for the purpose of constructing a dam across the Bruneau River in Idaho, but the project was fraught with problems and lost money. A few weeks before his death, spring floods washed away the irrigation canal of the company, driving it into bankruptcy and ruining Whipple. This may have brought on the cerebral hemorrhage that killed him.

Robie (or Rhoby) Alzada (Place) Phillips (1827–96)—Lovecraft's maternal grandmother. Born April 18, died January 26. She was devoted to astronomy, which she studied at the Smithville Seminary, a Baptist teachers' college founded in 1839 at North Scituate, Providence, which was renamed the Lapham Institute in 1863. Lovecraft inherited her astronomical library. She was the only member of the Phillips household who kept an emotional distance from young Lovecraft and did not demonstrate physical affection toward him, yet he was devastated by her death and began to have horrific nightmares that kept him awake. Lovecraft spelled her name "Rhoby" in his letters, but it is spelled "Robie" on her grave marker.

Edwin Everett Phillips (1864–1918)—Lovecraft's maternal uncle. Born February 14, died November 14. The only son of Whipple Phillips. He married Martha Helen Mathews on July 30, 1894. They were divorced, but remarried on March 23, 1903. Edwin was involved in the businesses of his father, Whipple Van Buren Phillips, until Whipple's death in 1904. After that, he worked in real estate and for a time as a salesman, and served as a notary public. Lovecraft claimed that he mismanaged his mother's investments in 1911 and caused them to lose considerable money.

Franklin Chase Clark (1847–1915)—Lovecraft's maternal uncle by marriage. Born April 10, died April 26. He went to high school in Warren, Rhode Island, and in 1869 he received his Bachelor of Arts from Brown University. In 1872 he was awarded a medical degree from the College of Physicians and Surgeons in New York City. He did his internship at Rhode Island Hospital in Providence and set up his own medical practice. On April 10, 1902, he married Lovecraft's Aunt Lillian. The marriage was happy but there were no children. For a hobby he wrote classical poetry and articles on genealogy and natural history.

His papers were placed in the University Archives at Brown following his death from cerebral hemorrhage.

Edward Francis Gamwell (1869–1936)—Lovecraft's maternal uncle by marriage. Born May 22, died May 10. Received his Bachelor of Arts degree from Brown University in 1894, and became city editor of the *Cambridge Chronicle* in 1896, a position he held until 1901. He married Lovecraft's Aunt Annie on June 3, 1897, and the couple set up house in Cambridge, Massachusetts. From 1901 until 1912 he was the owner and editor of the *Cambridge Tribune*. He spent 1913–15 as the editor of the *Budget* and the *American Cultivator*, then went into freelance commercial writing. Around 1916 Edward and Annie separated, but were never divorced. He went to live in Boston in 1931.

Phillips Gamwell (1898–1916)—Lovecraft's cousin, son of his younger aunt. Died December 31, of tuberculosis, in Roswell, Colorado, where he was undergoing a rest cure with his mother. He began to correspond by letter with Lovecraft around 1910 and continued to do so until his death. Lovecraft was quite fond of his cousin, and gave the boy his stamp collection.

Sonia Haft (Greene) Lovecraft (1883–1972)—Lovecraft's wife. Born March 16, died December 26. Sonia Haft Shafirkin was born of Jewish parents in Ichnya, near Kiev, in the Ukraine. She emigrated with her mother from the Ukraine to England in 1890, and from there traveled to New York City in 1892. On December 24, 1899, Sonia married Samuel Seckendorff, who changed his name during the marriage to Samuel Greene. He died in 1916, probably by suicide. During this marriage Sonia gave birth to two children, a son who died before he reached four months of age and a daughter, Florence Carol, born March 19, 1902. Sonia was working as an executive at the clothing store Ferle

Heller's in Manhattan when Lovecraft met her in July 1921. Sonia married Lovecraft on March 3, 1924, at St. Paul's Chapel in Manhattan, and the couple set up house at her fashionable flat at 259 Parkside Avenue, Brooklyn. Sonia's daughter moved out of the flat shortly after Lovecraft moved in—the two never got along due to the intense enmity of Florence for Lovecraft. The marriage ended on March 25, 1929, although the final divorce papers were never signed. After divorcing Lovecraft, Sonia eventually burned all of Lovecraft's letters and moved to California, where she married a Jewish doctor, Nathaniel A. Davis, becoming Sonia H. Davis.

George Lovecraft (c. 1818–95)—Lovecraft's paternal grandfather. A harness-maker by trade, he married Helen Allgood in Rochester, New York, and sometime in the 1860s moved to Mount Vernon, New York. The marriage produced two girls and a boy, Lovecraft's father. Lovecraft appears to have had little or no contact with his paternal aunts. George sent Lovecraft the family library after the institutionalization of Lovecraft's father at Butler Hospital.

FRIENDS

Miss Louise Imogen Guiney (1861–1920)—New England poet. Born January 7, died November 2. An acquaintance of Lovecraft's mother, who came to know her while Guiney was attending the Academy of the Sacred Heart in Providence from 1872 to 1879. Lovecraft's parents boarded with her at her home in Auburndale, Massachusetts, over the winter of 1892–93—Guiney occasionally rented out rooms in her large house as a way of earning additional income. Among her literary friends was Oliver Wendell Holmes. She kept mastiffs as pets, one of which became attached to the infant Lovecraft and would follow him about. She trained Lovecraft to recite bits of poetry for her guests. In 1901 she moved to England, where she lived until her death.

Winslow Upton (1853–1914)—Director of Ladd Observatory at Brown University, and a friend of the Phillips family. Born October 12, died January 8. He was born in Salem, Massachusetts, where he attended Salem High School, and graduated from Brown University in 1871. He received his MA at the University of Cincinnati in 1877. After various appointments in different institutions, he returned to Brown in 1884 as Professor of Astronomy, a chair that he held until his death in Providence. He taught classes in mathematics, meteorology, and logic. When the ground was broken for Ladd Observatory, a gift of the late Governor H. W. Ladd to the university, a mile from Brown University on Tin-top Hill in May 1890, he took upon himself the supervision of its construction and equipping, then became its director upon its opening on October 21, 1891. For one year he served as Dean of Brown University, but did not enjoy the administrative work and gave up the position. He often permitted young Lovecraft to use the 12-inch refractor telescope at the observatory.

John Edwards—Assistant at Ladd Observatory, a Cockney from England who helped Lovecraft in the use of the observatory telescope, and made for him a set of photographic lantern slides from pictures in books, which Lovecraft employed while giving lectures on astronomy at local clubs.

Chester Pierce Munroe (1889–1943)—School friend with Lovecraft at Slater Avenue School in Providence. Born September 1. Along with Lovecraft, he was one of the Slater Avenue Army, a group of boys from the neighborhood. They were also members of a Sherlock Holmes fan club calling itself the Providence Detective Agency and of the Blackstone Military Band. His house at 66 Paterson Street was only four blocks away from the Phillips mansion at 454 Angell Street. Later in life he joined the United Amateur Press Association at Lovecraft's urging. Moved to Asheville, North Carolina, around 1915, where he is presumed to have entered the hotel business.

Harold Bateman Munroe (1891–1966)—School friend with Lovecraft at Slater Avenue School. Born September 11, died February 18. One of the "Slater Avenue Army." Harold and his brother Chester were almost inseparable when Lovecraft knew them. Their father was Addison Munroe, member of the Rhode Island Senate from 1911–14.

Edward F. Daas (1879–1962)—Amateur journalist of Milwaukee, he was president of the United Amateur Press Association from 1907–16, and editor of *The United Amateur* when he invited Lovecraft to join the UAPA in 1914, after reading Lovecraft's letters in *The Argosy*. This invitation marked the turning point in Lovecraft's life. Daas visited Lovecraft's home in Providence on June 21, 1920.

Samuel Loveman (1887–1976)—Poet and bookseller in Cleveland, fellow member of the UAPA, and Lovecraft's close friend in spite of Lovecraft's prejudices—Loveman was Jewish and a homosexual. Lovecraft first wrote to him in 1917. He was in the 1919 dream that formed the basis for Lovecraft's story "The Statement of Randolph Carter" and also in the 1920 dream that was the basis for the story "Nyarlathotep." The two men met in New York in April 1922. In August Lovecraft visited him in Cleveland. His 1922 story "Hypnos" is dedicated to Loveman. In September of 1924 Loveman came to live in New York, and the following year was working in the Dauber and Pine book store, at the corner of Fifth Avenue and 12th Street. He later worked at the Rowfant Book Shop at 103 East 59th Street, and the Bodley Book Shop at 104 Fifth Avenue. After Lovecraft's death, Loveman's feelings turned against him due to Lovecraft's prejudices.

Rheinhart Kleiner (1892–1949)—A member of the UAPA and a correspondent with Lovecraft. Together with Maurice Moe and Ira A. Cole, they formed the Kleicomolo Club, a group of correspondents who circulated letters amongst themselves. Kleiner published an amateur magazine, *The Piper*, predominantly devoted to poetry. He visited Lovecraft in Providence on July 1, 1916, and several times in the following few years. They met frequently while Lovecraft was living in New York from 1924–26, where Kleiner was a member of the Kalem Club, a group of writer friends centered around Lovecraft.

Alfred Galpin (1901–83)—A fellow member of the UAPA and a correspondent of Lovecraft's. He had been one of Maurice W. Moe's students at Appleton High School, in Wisconsin. In 1919 Galpin and Moe were members of the Gallomo circle of correspondents, who circulated letters with Lovecraft. Lovecraft met Galpin when he came to Cleveland on July 30, 1922. He stayed with Galpin at his residence at 2931 Birchdale Avenue until August 15. Galpin later moved to Italy and became a professional musician.

Maurice Winter Moe (1882–1940)—He taught high-school English at Appleton High School in Appleton, Wisconsin, and at West Division High School in Milwaukee, Wisconsin, and was a member of the UAPA. He began his correspondence with Lovecraft in 1914 and continued it until Lovecraft's death. It was Moe who came up with the idea in 1916 for the Kleicomolo Club, and he was later part of the Gallomo. In a letter written to Moe in 1918, Lovecraft related the dream that became the story "Polaris." Moe met Lovecraft August 10, 1923, on a visit to Providence. They then went together to Boston, and the following day took a walking tour through Marblehead. Moe visited Providence a second time on July 18, 1936.

Jacob Clark Henneberger (1890–1969)—He founded Rural Publications Inc. in 1922 for the purpose of publishing a line of magazines. The first issue of *Weird Tales* was published in March 1923, with Edwin Baird as editor. Baird had trouble getting submissions from well-known writers, which opened the magazine to the speculative submissions of unknowns. In the spring of 1924, Henneberger commissioned Lovecraft to ghostwrite a story for Harry Houdini, which was published as "Imprisoned with the Pharaohs." In the same year, Henneberger offered Lovecraft the job as editor of a renewed *Weird Tales* that was to focus more on classic horror stories. Lovecraft refused the offer because it would have meant moving to Chicago, and the job went to Farnsworth Wright. In the fall of 1924 he talked with Lovecraft about editing a proposed new humor magazine, but the magazine never materialized.

Edwin Baird (1886–1957)—The editor of *Weird Tales* from its inception in March 1923 until April 1924, Baird reacted very favorably to Lovecraft's submissions to the magazine despite Lovecraft's self-defeating cover letters. When the magazine began to founder, the publisher J. C. Henneberger replaced Baird with Farnsworth Wright. Baird became the editor of Henneberger's magazine *Detective Tales*.

Farnsworth Wright (1888–1940)—A music critic in Chicago, he was editor of *Weird Tales* from 1924 until 1940. For the final two decades of his life he suffered from Parkinson's disease. It was Wright who gave Lovecraft his first rejection at the magazine, when he turned down "The Shunned House" in 1925. Wright was not nearly as receptive to Lovecraft's work as Edwin Baird had been. He considered many of Lovecraft's stories too cerebral and lacking in action for the magazine's readership. He rejected "In the Vault" and "Cool Air" out of fear that they were too shocking, and might provoke demands that the magazine be censored. When Wright rejected *At the Mountains of Madness* in 1931, Lovecraft was so disheartened he stopped sending in stories to *Weird Tales* for five years.

Clark Ashton Smith (1893–1961)—Contributor to *Weird Tales*. Born January 13, died August 14. Poet, painter, sculptor, and writer of fantasy fiction. Smith was born in Long Valley, California, and spent much of his life living in a small cabin in the town of Auburn in the Sierra hills, caring for his elderly parents. Although he had little formal education, at the age of nineteen he achieved critical acclaim as a poet, but was still forced to chop wood and pick fruit to earn a basic living. Lovecraft wrote to Smith on August 12, 1922, and the two continued to correspond for the rest of Lovecraft's life. They never met face to face. It was Lovecraft's example that caused Smith to begin selling fantasy fiction to *Weird Tales*. He wrote over a hundred stories in only a six-year period, but his work was too esoteric to be widely acclaimed by the *Weird Tales* readership, and rejections caused him to turn his interests away from story writing to sculpture.

Robert Ervin Howard (1906–36)—Contributor to *Weird Tales*. Born January 22, died June 11. Writer of weird and heroic fiction for the pulps. A native of Cross Plains, Texas, he is best known as the creator of Conan the Barbarian, but also coined other notable characters such as King Kull and Solomon Kane. It is sometimes said that he invented sword and sorcery—if he did not invent it, he certainly perfected it. He committed suicide by shooting himself with a semi-automatic handgun in a bout of depression over his mother's failing health. His mother died the following day, and both mother and son were buried on June 14 in a double funeral at Greenleaf Cemetery in Brownwood, Texas.

Frank Belknap Long, Jr. (1901–94)—Contributor to *Weird Tales*. Born April 27, died January 3. A native of Manhattan, Long began to correspond with Lovecraft in 1920, when he was only eighteen years old. Around this same time he joined the UAPA. He decided to give up a university degree to become a freelance writer of pulp fiction. The first meeting between Lovecraft and Long took place in April 1922, when Lovecraft visited New York. They were often together during 1924–26, while Lovecraft lived in the city. Both Lovecraft and Long were members of the Kalem Club. It was Long who suggested to Lovecraft's aunts that it would be better for his mental health if they invited him to return home to Providence. Lovecraft thought of himself as Long's mentor. From 1932 to 1935 Lovecraft spent his Christmases and New Years as a guest at the Manhattan apartment of Long's parents. Long's 1929 novel, *The Horror From the Hills*, is based on one of Lovecraft's dreams.

Robert Bloch (1917–94)—Contributor to *Weird Tales*. Born April 5, died September 23. Writer of stories and novels, he corresponded with Lovecraft at the end of the older man's life, from 1933 to 1937. His story "The Shambler from the Stars," published in *Weird Tales* in September 1935, prompted Lovecraft to compose the sequel, "The Haunter in the Dark," published in *Weird Tales* in December 1936. Many years after Lovecraft's death, Bloch turned the two stories into part of a trilogy with "The Shadow from the Steeple," in *Weird Tales*, September 1950.

Fritz Leiber (1910–92)—Contributor to *Weird Tales*. Born December 24, died September 5. Writer of horror, fantasy, and science fiction stories, and editor of story anthologies, who corresponded with Lovecraft in the final year of Lovecraft's life.

August William Derleth (1909–71)—Contributor to *Weird Tales*. Born February 24, died July 4. Writer of mystery and horror novels and stories. A native of Wisconsin, he was the co-founder and prime mover of Arkham House, a small publishing house created specifically to publish the works of Lovecraft in hardcover editions. He never met Lovecraft face to face. Although he was sometimes critical of Lovecraft's work, he tried to get Lovecraft to be more aggressive about marketing his stories, and when this attempt failed, he began to market the stories himself on Lovecraft's behalf but without Lovecraft's knowledge. Following Lovecraft's death, Derleth gradually gained total control over the publication and use of Lovecraft writings, a control that was only ended by Derleth's own death.

Donald Albert Wandrei (1908–87)—Contributor to *Weird Tales*. Born April 20, died October 15. A native of Saint Paul, Minnesota. Wandrei's friend and correspondent Clark Ashton Smith first put Wandrei in touch with Lovecraft in 1926. He exchanged fiction manuscripts with Lovecraft and was helped by Lovecraft's comments, although the two never collaborated. In the summer of 1927, he visited Providence to meet Lovecraft, who later suggested that Wandrei should correspond with August Derleth. Wandrei became co-founder with Derleth of Arkham House, but when the Second World War began, he went to fight and the running of Arkham House fell wholly into Derleth's hands. Wandrei is, however, responsible for most of the editing of Lovecraft's collection of letters, published by Arkham House.

Winifred Virginia Jackson (1876–1959)—Collaborator with Lovecraft. A Boston poet, she was a member of the UAPA and a correspondent and friend of Lovecraft between the years 1918–21. Under the pseudonym Elizabeth Berkeley, she collaborated with Lovecraft on two stories, both based on dreams—"The Green Meadow" and "The Crawling Chaos." Lovecraft used the pseudonym Lewis Theobald, Jun. Their names appeared together when the stories were published. In amateur writing circles, they were rumored to be romantically involved, although it was purely a romance of the heart, and ended abruptly when Lovecraft met Sonia Greene.

Zealia Brown Reed Bishop (1897–1968)—Collaborator with Lovecraft. Zealia B. Reed wrote to Lovecraft first in 1927, seeking advice. At the time she was a widow and inclined to try her hand at romantic fiction. Lovecraft encouraged her to try weird fiction, and he ghostwrote three stories for her: "The Curse of Yig," "The Mound," and "Medusa's Coil," for which he was not fully paid. They are Lovecraft's best work as a ghostwriter and are almost entirely his own work—Reed contributed next to nothing. She later married D. W. Bishop.

Edgar Hoffmann Price (1898–1988)—Collaborator with Lovecraft. He was a prolific writer for the pulps, including *Weird Tales*, and a correspondent with Lovecraft. Price first met Lovecraft on June 12, 1932, when Lovecraft came to visit him at his home in New Orleans. The two men kept in touch by letters. Price wrote a sequel to Lovecraft's story "The Silver Key" in the summer of 1932, and Lovecraft revised it in the spring of 1933, retitling it "Through the Gates of the Silver Key."

Henry St. Clair Whitehead (1882–1932)—Collaborator with Lovecraft. A native of New Jersey and writer of supernatural stories, he was an Anglican priest who served as Acting Archdeacon in the Virgin Islands from 1921–29. Lovecraft knew him during the years 1931–32. From May 21 to June 10, 1931, he visited with Whitehead at his home in

Dunedin, Florida. It may have been during this visit that Lovecraft revised Whitehead's story "The Trap."

Clifford Martin Eddy, Jr. (1896–1971)—Collaborator with Lovecraft. A resident of Providence and a writer of mystery and horror stories, he sold his first story to *Mystery Magazine* in 1919. Eddy met Lovecraft in August of 1923. Lovecraft revised Eddy's story about necrophilia, "The Loved Dead," which appeared in the *Weird Tales* May-June-July 1924 issue, and is reputed to have rescued *Weird Tales* from oblivion with its notoriety (it almost caused the magazine to be banned in Indiana). He also revised Eddy's stories "Ashes," "The Ghost-Eater," and "Deaf, Dumb, and Blind." Lovecraft often paid evening visits to Eddy and his wife, Muriel, at their home prior to Lovecraft's departure to live in New York. Upon Lovecraft's return to Providence, the friendship was resumed. Lovecraft went for long walks at night through the town with Eddy, and explored the countryside around Providence with him. Eddy wrote a brief memoir of his friend, "Walks with H. P. Lovecraft."

Robert Hayward Barlow (1918–51)—Collaborator with Lovecraft. Writer, poet, and artist, a native of DeLand, Florida. He was only thirteen years old when he began to write to Lovecraft in 1931, but the maturity of his letters disguised his age from Lovecraft. Barlow became Lovecraft's protégé. When Barlow invited Lovecraft to visit him in Florida in the summer of 1934, Lovecraft was amazed and somewhat shocked to find out his age. However, Barlow's parents were completely in favor of Lovecraft's visit, and Lovecraft was loath to leave because he loved the heat. Lovecraft made another extended visit in the summer of 1935, but in the summer of 1936 it was Barlow who traveled to visit with Lovecraft in Providence. The two collaborated on Barlow's short story "The Night Ocean," but Lovecraft made only minor changes to Barlow's text. Lovecraft named Barlow his literary executor, a task he executed poorly under Derleth's glaring eye.

Anne Vyne Tillery Renshaw—Collaborator with Lovecraft. A poet and amateur journalist from Mississippi who was a frequent contributor to UAPA's official periodical, *The United Amateur*, she also ran a school for proper speaking—presumably, elocution and grammar. She prevailed upon her amateur-journalist association with Lovecraft to have him ghostwrite in 1936 her rough draft of a nonfiction book titled *Well Bred Speech*. Work on it was a great drain on both the time and energies of Lovecraft, who was dying of cancer. He rewrote the book completely, but she paid him only one hundred dollars.

TIMELINE

1818—Born George Lovecraft, Lovecraft's paternal grandfather.

1827—Born April 18, Robie Alzada Place, Lovecraft's maternal grandmother.

1833—Born November 22, Whipple Van Buren Phillips, Lovecraft's maternal grandfather.

1853—Born October 26, Winfield Scott Lovecraft, Lovecraft's father.

1856—Whipple Phillips marries Robie Place, January 27. They are first cousins. Robie is pregnant at the time of the marriage.

   —Lillian Delora Phillips, Lovecraft's elder maternal aunt, born April 20.

1857—Born October 17, Lovecraft's mother, Sarah Susan Phillips. She is called Susie by her family and friends.

1864—Born February 14, Edwin Everett Phillips, Lovecraft's maternal uncle.

1866—Born July 10, Annie Emeline Phillips, Lovecraft's younger maternal aunt.

1889—On June 12, Winfield Lovecraft and Sarah S. Phillips are married in Boston, at St. Paul's Episcopal Church. He is Anglican, she is Baptist. They move to Dorchester, Massachusetts.

1890—Howard Phillips Lovecraft born, August 20 at 9 a.m., at the Phillips' family home at 194 Angell Street, on the East Side of Providence. He is an only child. The house address is renumbered 454 Angell Street in 1895 or 1896. The house is torn down in 1961.

1892—(age 1–2) Lovecraft's parents rent quarters at Dudley, Massachusetts, for a vacation during the summer.

  —The Lovecraft family boards during June and July at Auburndale, Massachusetts, in the home of Susie Lovecraft's school friend, the poet Miss Louise Imogen Guiney, with the intention of eventually having a new house of their own built on a lot they have purchased. This intention is never realized.

  —Lovecraft learns the alphabet.

  —He is taught by Guiney to memorize and recite bits of poetry, and to perform them for visitors to her house.

1893—(age 2–3) Winfield becomes psychotic in a Chicago hotel room in April while on a business trip. He begins to cry out that his wife is being assaulted in a room above. He is institutionalized on April 25 at Butler Hospital, Providence, where he remains until his death. Probable cause is syphilis (general paresis of the insane, also known as paralytic dementia). Lovecraft and mother move back to 194 Angell Street, Providence, to live with his grandparents.

  —Lovecraft is reading at age 3.

1894—(age 3–4) He reads such works as *Grimm's Fairy Tales* and the novels of Jules Verne. Lovecraft would later assert that at age 4 he could "read with ease."

  —His maternal uncle, Edwin Everett Phillips (1864–1918), marries Martha Helen Mathews on July 30.

1895—(age 4–5) The *Arabian Nights* is his favorite book. He adopts the pseudonym of "Abdul Alhazred." Later in life he is uncertain whether he dreamed the name or it was suggested to him.

1896—(age 5–6) Begins to compose original poetry.

—Begins to write in script, rather than in block letters.

—The death of his grandmother, Robie Alzada (Place) Phillips, on January 26, shocks his family circle.

—Nightmares of the night-gaunts begin shortly after his grandmother's death.

—He discovers Greek mythology through Hawthorne's *Wonder Book* and *Tanglewood Tales*, then later through Bulfinch's *Age of Fable*.

—Begins to write literary works. First short story of two hundred words, "The Noble Eavesdropper" (not extant).

—In the winter he attends his first stage play, *The Sunshine of Paradise Alley* by Denman Thompson, at the Providence Opera House, which is run by Mr. Manow, a neighbor from across the street, who gives one of Lovecraft's aunts free tickets.

1897—(age 6–7) His earliest surviving composition is written, "The Poem of Ulysses" (published 1959), a paraphrase of Homer's *Odyssey* in eighty-eight lines of rhyming verse.

—His Aunt Annie marries Edward F. Gamwell on June 3. The newlyweds move to Cambridge, Massachusetts, where Edward takes a job as a newspaper editor.

—First extant story, "The Little Glass Bottle," written at age 6 (published 1959).

—Begins taking violin lessons from the music teacher Mrs. Wilhelm Nauck. Takes them for two years, from age 7 to age 9.

—In December he sees Shakespeare's *Cymbeline* at the Providence Opera House.

1898—(age 7–8) He attends his first full year of school (Slater Avenue School), but withdraws after only a year.

> —His father dies at Butler Hospital on July 19. Buried in Swan Point Cemetery.

> —Suffers a "near-breakdown" that may have been connected with the death of his father.

> —He discovers the works of Edgar Allan Poe.

> —Becomes interested in chemistry, encouraged by his Aunt Lillian, and then in astronomy. Professor John Howard Appleton, a professor of chemistry at Brown University, presents Lovecraft with his own book for beginners—*The Young Chemist* (published 1876).

> —Writes the stories the "Secret Cave, or John Lees Adventure" and "The Mystery of the Graveyard" (both published 1959).

1899—(age 8–9) Begins publishing a small periodical titled *The Scientific Gazette* for family and friends, first using carbon copies, then using the hectograph (also known as the jellygraph) process. Continues this for seven years as a weekly periodical.

> —Gives public recital on the violin before a considerable audience, playing a solo piece from Mozart. Loses interest in the violin and never plays again.

1900—(age 9–10) He translates fragments of the Latin poetry of Ovid.

> —Another "near-breakdown" occurs, cause unknown.

1901—(age 10–11) Writes a two-volume book of original poetry, *Poemata Minora*, dedicated "To the Gods, Heroes, and Ideals of the Ancients." Only the second volume is extant.

> —At age 11 he is the drummer in the Blackstone Military Band, a band of children who play an instrument called the zobo.

1902—(age 11–12) Writes the short story "The Mysterious Ship" (published 1959).

—Aunt Lillian is married to Dr. Franklin Chase Clark on April 10. He becomes the Phillips' family physician.

—Returns to the Slater Avenue School (1902–03 school year). Not generally liked, and makes only a few friends, among them the three Banigan brothers and the Munroe brothers, Chester Pierce Munroe and Harold Bateman Munroe. He rebels against the strict school discipline.

—Becomes fascinated by astronomy.

1903—(age 12–13) February 12, he buys his first new book on astronomy, *Lessons in Astronomy* by Young.

—Begins in August of this year to publish an amateur periodical, the *Rhode Island Journal of Astronomy*. (Lovecraft peddled this publication and the *Scientific Gazette* door to door on his bicycle.)

—In a letter to Rheinhart Kleiner, November 16, 1916, he writes that in the summer of this year (other sources say February), his mother gives him an astronomical refractor telescope with a 2.5-inch objective lens. In a letter to Alfred Galpin, August 21, 1918, Lovecraft states that he purchased the telescope, and that it was equipped with a 2.25-inch objective lens. He uses it mainly to view the moon and Venus.

—Inspired by the Sherlock Holmes stories, at age thirteen he organizes the Providence Detective Agency, a group of boys who reenact crime-solving in a deserted house on the outskirts of town.

—Of the years 1903–04, Lovecraft later wrote, "I had private tutors."

1904—(age 13–14) Grandfather dies of apoplectic stroke (cerebral hemorrhage) on March 28. Lovecraft will later refer to this as the worst event of his life.

—In the spring, he writes the first draft of "The Beast in the Cave."

—Estate mismanaged. Lovecraft and his mother forced to move two blocks east into a smaller house at 598 Angell Street (later transformed into a duplex, numbered 598–600 Angell Street). Lovecraft and his mother occupy the ground floor, and have the use of part of the attic and of the basement—Lovecraft later referred to it as a "five-room-and-attic flat." This move provokes thoughts of suicide in young Lovecraft (he will have similar thoughts many times in the course of his life).

—With the help of his friends Chester and Harold Munroe, he attempts to recreate the imaginary play-village of New Anvik in a vacant lot near his new house.

—Lovecraft's beloved black cat, Nigger-Man, disappears.

—He begins to attend Hope Street High School in the fall.

—Writes the nine-volume *Science Library*, of which only three volumes have survived.

1905—(age 14–15) On April 21, he does a finished draft of his short story "The Beast in the Cave," a tale of around two thousand words. It is his first real attempt at serious fiction. Later, he would describe this April draft of the story as "ineffably pompous and Johnsonese."

—Convinces his mother to buy him a small hand press to print greeting cards.

—Does not return to Hope Street High School in the fall due to his "nervous condition." Nervous breakdown occupies winter 1905–06. Nickname at school—"Lovey."

1906—(age 15–16) June 3, a letter (written May 27) is published in the *Providence Sunday Journal*—his first writing to be published professionally. It is an attack against the superstition of astrology.

—July 6, Lovecraft receives a used Remington typewriter. He will use it for the rest of his life to type out finished drafts of his stories, which he composes in longhand by pen or pencil. He never learns to touch-type, and hates typing with a passion.

—July 16, a letter is published in *Scientific American* urging astronomical observatories to make a cooperative effort to find a planet beyond Neptune.

—In July he begins writing a weekly astronomy column for the professional newspaper the *Pawtuxet Valley Gleaner*, and in August begins monthly astronomy columns for the *Providence Tribune*—columns in the *Tribune* run from 1906–08.

—Puts his small hand press up for sale.

—He views his first moving picture show.

—Re-enters Hope Street High School in September. Nickname changes to "the Professor."

—Suffers another "near-breakdown."

—In December the *Pawtuxet Valley Gleaner* fails, ending his weekly astronomy column.

1907—(age 16–17) January 25, Lovecraft is invited to lecture on astronomy at the Boys' Club of the First Baptist Church.

—He ceases to publish the *Scientific Gazette* and the *Rhode Island Journal of Astronomy.*

—During his basement chemical experiments, he sustains a "mighty phosphorous burn" on the inner surface of the third finger of his right hand. The burn scars him for life, but his uncle Dr. Clark saves his finger. Later in life the finger is always stiff and aches in cold weather.

—Lovecraft is introduced to the astronomer Percival Lowell by Professor Upton, head of Ladd Observatory at Brown University, when Lowell comes to Providence to give a lecture at the University in Sayles Hall. At this time, Lovecraft is writing an astronomy column for the *Providence Tribune.*

—He purchases a two-dollar Number 2 Brownie camera, but uses it infrequently.

—Writes a short horror story, "The Picture," which is not extant. In the story, an artist in a Paris garret paints a picture embodying the essence of all evil, only to be found clawed to death before the destroyed painting. In one remaining corner of the work is a painted claw the size of which matches the scratch marks on his corpse. An entry in Lovecraft's Commonplace Book (notebook of story ideas and fragments) reads: "19 Revise 1907 tale—painting of ultimate horror." The story is never revised.

1908—(age 17–18) In the spring, Lovecraft drops out of high school. He still has a year and a half remaining before he can gain his high school diploma. He suffers a nervous breakdown. Later in life, Lovecraft will claim that he did graduate from high school, and that his nervous collapse prevented him from entering university. His desire to attend Brown University and study astronomy is frustrated by this lack of a diploma (he had great difficulty with algebra).

—He lives the life of a hermit from 1908–14, seeing few people other than his immediate family, and composing a great deal of poetry.

—Writes the short story "The Alchemist."

1909—(age 18–19) In the fall of the year, an attack of measles almost kills him. His constitution is weakened by poor diet, coupled with lack of sun and exercise.

1910—(age 19–20) Writes a bulky manuscript titled *A Brief Course in Inorganic Chemistry* while studying chemistry in his mother's basement.

—Visits Cambridge, Massachusetts.

1911—(age 20–21) On August 20, Lovecraft's 21st birthday, he spends the entire day riding aimlessly around Providence on trolley cars.

1912—(age 21–22) His poem, "Providence in 2000 AD," a sixty-two line satire, appears in the *Evening Bulletin* of March 4. It is his first published poem. In it, he ridicules the attempts of Italians living in the Federal Hill slums of Providence to change the name of one of their streets from Atwells Avenue to Columbus Avenue.

—Writes the racist poem "New England Fallen" in April.

—Suffers one of his periodic "near-breakdowns."

1913—(age 22–23) Writes the satirical poem "The Creation of Niggers." Lovecraft's bigotry and racist feelings are intense during this period, and he never entirely loses them throughout his life.

> —His letter attacking the love stories of writer Fred Jackson is published in the September issue of the magazine *The Argosy*. It provokes heated responses, and proves to be a key turning point in Lovecraft's life.

1914—(age 23–24) A second satirical letter in verse is written, and is published in the January 14 issue of *The Argosy*, and a third in the spring of this year. They attract the notice of Edward F. Daas, president of the United Amateur Press Association, who invites Lovecraft to join the UAPA in March. He does so on April 6.

> —Begins writing an astronomy column in the *Providence Evening News* (column runs from 1914 until 1918).

> —Conducts a letter-writing campaign against the astrologer Joachim Friedrich Hartmann (1848–1930) in the *Providence Evening News*, using the pseudonym "Isaac Bickerstaffe, Jr."

> —Ends the poetic feud in *The Argosy* in its October issue.

1915—(age 24–25) His first article for *The United Amateur*, official literary organ of the UAPA, is published in January.

> —Death of his uncle Franklin Chase Clark on April 26 greatly saddens him. Clark's unpublished papers are placed in the archives of the Rhode Island Historical Society.

> —Begins in April to publish his own amateur journal, *The Conservative* (thirteen issues, published between 1915–23).

> —Replaces Ada P. Campbell as Chairman of the Department of Public Criticism at the UAPA.

—Writes astronomical articles for the *Gazette-News* of Asheville, North Carolina, at the suggestion of his old friend Chester Munroe, who had moved there to work in the hotel business.

—He holds the office of First Vice-President of the UAPA (1915–16).

—He contracts chicken pox.

—Gives his stamp collection to his young cousin Phillips Gamwell, who has at this time only a year to live.

—This year, or the following, Lovecraft's mother begins to suffer from hallucinations during which she sees weird creatures at twilight that rush out at her from around corners and from behind buildings.

1916—(age 25–26) Visits Boston in January.

—Suffers a relatively minor "nervous collapse."

—Steady output of articles on social issues and poetry written in the archaic style of the eighteenth century.

—Rheinhart Kleiner visits Lovecraft in Providence, while on his way to an amateur journalist convention in Boston. He is struck by Lovecraft's formal manner and youthful appearance (Lovecraft suffered from an age mania, and began referring to himself in his correspondence as an old man while still a teenager).

—In late October, Lovecraft attends a performance of the modern classic opera *Katinka*.

—Lovecraft's aunt Annie and her husband Edward F. Gamwell separate in October when she takes her sick son to Roswell, Colorado, for treatment. Phillips Gamwell, Lovecraft's cousin, dies of tuberculosis on December 31 in Roswell. After the death, Annie returns not to her husband in Cambridge, Massachusetts, but to Providence, where she stays at the flat of Lovecraft's mother.

—His short story "The Alchemist," written in 1908, is published in *The United Amateur* in its November issue.

—During this year he attends meetings of a Providence literary group called the Providence Amateurs. He is regarded as a bit of a joke by other members, because he sits stiffly, looking forward and never turning his head unless spoken to.

1917—(age 26–27) Attempts to enlist in the army in May, and is accepted in the Coast Artillery—but when his mother is informed of his action, she prevails upon their family physician to have his medical examination voided and Lovecraft rejected on grounds of poor health, although the army physician states, in Lovecraft's words, that "such an annulment was highly unusual and almost against the regulations of the service."

—Writes the short story "The Tomb" in June, after walking with his Aunt Lillian through Swan Point Cemetery.

—Writes the story "Dagon" in August.

—Begins the story "Psychopompos" in August, lays it aside, and finishes it in the summer of 1918.

—Serves as president of the UAPA (1917–18).

—Joins the National Amateur Press Association (NAPA), which was founded in 1876, and was thus older than the UAPA, founded in 1895. The two amateur writing organizations were rivals, and Lovecraft joined both in an attempt to reconcile them.

1918—(age 27–28) Writes the story "Polaris," which is based on a dream he had around May 12 of floating as a disembodied observer over a strange city.

—"The Beast in the Cave" is published in *The Vagrant* in its June issue.

—Writes the serial story "The Mystery of Murdon Grange" (not extant).

—Collaborates on "The Green Meadow" with Winifred Jackson.

—Becomes a ghostwriter, by revising for money the works of other writers.

—November 14, Lovecraft's maternal uncle Edwin dies.

—Mother suffers nervous breakdown in the winter of 1918–19.

1919—(age 28–29) In January, his mother leaves her home at 598 Angell Street to stay with her elder sister, Lillian, due to nervous problems. Separated from Susie for the first time, Lovecraft, who is left in the care of his Aunt Annie, becomes distraught.

—Mother is committed to Butler Hospital on March 13 after suffering a nervous breakdown. Lovecraft contemplates suicide. He experiences yet another of his "near-breakdowns."

—In spring, he writes the story "Beyond the Wall of Sleep." It is published in the October issue of the amateur magazine *Pine Cones*.

—Also in the spring, he writes the story "Memory." It is published in the June issue of the *United Co-operative*.

—In September he reads the book *A Dreamer's Tales,* a collection of short stories by Lord Dunsany (Edward John Moreton Drax Plunkett, 18th Baron of Dunsany), which has a profound effect on his writing.

—September 16, writes the story "The Transition of Juan Romero." It is never published in Lovecraft's lifetime, but appears in the Arkham House collection *Marginalia* in 1944.

—October 20, he attends a lecture delivered by Dunsany in Boston, traveling from Providence to Boston and back again in the same day just to hear the lecture. On the way home, he reads Dunsany's book of stories *The Gods of Pegana*.

—Late October, writes the story "The White Ship" in imitation of Dunsany's style. It is published in the November issue of *The United Amateur*.

—Reads Dunsany's collection of stories *Time and the Gods*.

—His story "Dagon" is published in the November issue of the professional periodical *The Vagrant*.

—December 3, he obtains Dunsany's newly published book *Unhappy Far-Off Things*.

—Also December 3, writes the story "The Doom that Came to Sarnath."

—Writes story "The Statement of Randolph Carter" in December. It is based entirely on a dream.

1920—(age 29–30) January 28, writes the story "The Terrible Old Man."

—Writes the story "The Tree" sometime in the spring.

—"The Statement of Randolph Carter" is published in the May issue of *The Vagrant*.

—"The Cats of Ulthar" written on June 15. The story is published in the November issue of *Tryout*.

—"The Doom that Came to Sarnath" is published in the June issue of the amateur magazine *The Scot*.

—Sometime in the summer or early fall, writes the story "The Temple."

—In the fall of this year, writes the story "Facts Concerning the Late Arthur Jermyn and His Family."

—November, he writes the story "Celephaïs," which is heavily influenced by Dunsany's style.

—November 16, writes the story "From Beyond."

—December, writes the story "Nyarlathotep" based on a vivid dream.

—Collaborates with Winifred Virginia Jackson on the story "The Crawling Chaos" in December.

—Late in the year he writes the story "Ex Oblivione."

—December 12, writes the story "The Picture in the House."

—"Polaris" is published in December in *The Philosopher*, an amateur newspaper put out by Lovecraft's friend Alfred Galpin.

1921—(age 30–31) In January he writes the story "The Nameless City." It is published in the November issue of *The Wolverine*.

—February 22, attends the Boston Conference of Amateur Journalists held at Quincy House, Boston.

—February 28, writes the short story "The Quest of Iranon."

—"Nyarlathotep" is published in *The United Amateur* in an issue marked November 1920, but this issue of the magazine was actually printed in the spring of 1921.

—Early in March, writes the story "The Moon-Bog."

—On March 17, attends St. Patrick's Day gathering of amateur writers in Boston held at 20 Webster Street. He reads "The Moon-Bog" aloud at the gathering.

—"Ex Oblivione" is published in *The United Amateur* in March.

—"Facts Concerning the Late Arthur Jermyn and His Family" is published in *The Wolverine* (March and June).

—April, "The Crawling Chaos" is published in *The United Co-operative* under the dual pseudonymous byline Elizabeth Berkeley (Jackson) and Lewis Theobald, Jun. (Lovecraft).

—May 24, mother dies from complications during gall-bladder surgery. Lovecraft again expresses suicidal longings.

—Sometime in the spring or early summer he writes the story "The Outsider."

—"The Picture in the House" is published in the summer in *The National Amateur*, in an issue falsely dated July 1919.

—Aunt Lillian moves in to live with him at 598 Angell Street.

—"The Terrible Old Man" is published in the July issue of *The Tryout*.

—On July 4, Lovecraft meets Sonia Haft Greene at the NAPA amateur journalist convention in Boston.

—August 14, he writes the story "The Other Gods."

—September 4, Sonia Greene arrives in Providence for a two-day visit with Lovecraft. She stays at the Crown Hotel.

—In September, he begins the six-part series "Herbert West—Reanimator" for the professional magazine *Home Brew*, which publishes it the following year.

—"The Tree" is published in the October issue of *The Tryout*.

—In December, he writes the story "The Music of Erich Zann."

1922—(age 31–32) Writes his autobiographical essay "A Confession of Unfaith" in February. It is published that same month in the amateur journal *The Liberal*.

—March, writes the story "Hypnos."

—"The Tomb" is published in the March issue of *The Vagrant*.

—"The Music of Erich Zann" is published in the March issue of *The National Amateur*.

—Visits Sonia Greene in her Brooklyn apartment at 259 Parkside Avenue, April 6–12. Meets for the first time Samuel Loveman, who is in New York looking for work, and Frank Belknap Long Jr. They remain lifelong friends.

—Finishes the last parts of "Herbert West—Reanimator" in April or May. The six parts are published in *Home Brew* successively in its February, March, April, May, June, and July issues.

—"Celephaïs" is published in the May issue of Sonia Greene's amateur periodical *The Rainbow*.

—June 5, writes the story "What the Moon Brings."

—Writes the five-hundred-word fragment "Azathoth" in June. It is part of a projected novel that is never written.

—Sonia Greene visits Providence in June.

—Visits Sonia at the seaside resort town of Magnolia, Massachusetts, from June 26 to July 5. The story "The Horror At Martin's Beach" is co-written with her. They kiss for the first time.

—Visits Cleveland, Ohio, from July 30 to August 15, where he first meets his letter correspondent Alfred Galpin. Stays at Galpin's family house, at 9231 Birchdale—Samuel Loveman's flat is "just around the corner" at the Lenore Apartments.

—Returning home from Cleveland, he stops at New York for a second visit with Sonia, August–October.

—He is chosen president of the National Amateur Press Association.

—Writes his first letter to Clark Ashton Smith.

—October, writes the story "The Hound."

—Writes the story "The Lurking Fear" in November.

—In December he travels to Salem and Marblehead, the latter of which he first views on December 17.

1923—(age 32–33) "The Lurking Fear" is published in four successive parts in the January, February, March, and April issues of *Home Brew*.

—In May, Lovecraft submits five of his stories to the new magazine *Weird Tales* (the first issue is published in March). He is told to retype them double-spaced and submit them again. He retypes only "Dagon." *Weird Tales* publishes "Dagon" in its October issue.

—"Hypnos" and "What the Moon Brings" are published in the May issue of *The National Amateur*.

—He refers to Einstein's theory of relativity in a letter to James F. Morton dated May 26.

—Reads stories of Arthur Machen for the first time.

—Antiquarian tours of New England.

—Visits to Providence by Sonia Greene.

—Lovecraft suffers a temporary bout of deafness.

—Late summer, writes the story "The Rats in the Walls."

—September, writes the story "The Unnamable."

—Writes the story "The Festival" in the autumn of this year.

—October, collaborates with Clifford Martin Eddy on the story "The Ghost Eater." Much of this story is Eddy's.

—Also in October, he collaborates with C. M. Eddy on the story "The Loved Dead." Much of the story appears to have been written by Lovecraft.

—Collaborates with C. M. Eddy on the story "Ashes." Lovecraft makes only minor changes to the story.

—"The Horror at Martin's Beach" is published in the November issue of *Weird Tales* (under the title "The Invisible Monster").

1924—(age 33–34) In February, he writes the story "Under the Pyramids" (retitled by *Weird Tales* editor Edwin Baird as "Imprisoned with the Pharaohs") for escape artist Harry Houdini, and it is published under Houdini's name in the oversized May-June-July issue— Lovecraft is paid one hundred dollars.

—Collaborates in February with Clifford M. Eddy on the story "Dead, Dumb and Blind." Most of the story is Eddy's.

—"The Hound" is published in the February issue of *Weird Tales*.

—"The Rats in the Walls" is published in the March issue of *Weird Tales*.

—On March 3, Lovecraft and Sonia Greene marry in New York City at Saint Paul's Chapel, an Episcopal church located at the corner of Broadway and Vesey Street.

—The couple honeymoons in Philadelphia.

—April, "The Ghost Eater" is published in *Weird Tales*.

—Lovecraft stays with his new wife to live in her apartment at 259 Parkside Avenue, Brooklyn, but cannot find work.

—"The Loved Dead" is published in the May-June-July issue of *Weird Tales*. So explicit in the necrophilia in the story, the authorities in Indiana try but fail to have this issue of the magazine banned.

—Attends gatherings of the Kalem Club (the last names of all its original members began with the letters K, L, or M). Members are George Kirk, Rheinhart Kleiner, Lovecraft, Frank B. Long, Samuel Loveman, James Morton, and Everett McNeil.

—He turns down an offer from J. C. Henneberger, the owner of *Weird Tales*, to edit a revised version of *Weird Tales*, which is to be a magazine of classic horror in the style of Poe and Machen, on the grounds that it will necessitate a move to Chicago and because he fears the venture will fail.

—In July, Sonia's attempt to start her own hat shop fails. Sonia loses a job with another millinery firm, suffers a nervous breakdown, and is hospitalized. She goes to live by herself for a time at a New Jersey farm to recover.

—In October, Lovecraft writes the short story "The Shunned House."

—He visits Sonia at the New Jersey farm in November.

—"Ashes" is published in the March issue of *Weird Tales*.

—Toward the end of the year, Sonia leaves New York to seek work in Cincinnati, Ohio. Lovecraft remains behind with his Kalem Club friends.

1925—(age 34–35) On January 1, Lovecraft moves alone into an apartment consisting of a bedroom and an entrance alcove, located in the northwest corner of a rooming house at 169 Clinton Street, on the fringe of the depressed Brooklyn district of Red Hook, while his wife travels from Cincinnati to Cleveland to seek a job for herself. During this year, he contemplates suicide and carries a bottle of poison around with him at all times.

—In January, he takes a freezing train and walks with friends into northern Yonkers to see a total solar eclipse, his first (he views a second one in 1932 at Newburyport).

—"The Festival" is published in the January issue of *Weird Tales*.

—April, visits Washington, D.C.

—"Deaf, Dumb and Blind" is published in the April issue of *Weird Tales*.

—In late May, the outer alcove of his apartment is robbed while he sleeps in the inner room, by a thief with a key to his door. The thief takes all his suits except an old one, and his overcoat, as well as a wicker suitcase belonging to Sonia and radio parts belonging to Loveman.

—July, he buys a new suit for twenty-five dollars.

—"The Unnamable" is published in the July issue of *Weird Tales*.

—On the first two days in August, he writes the short story "The Horror at Red Hook," based on his impressions of the area. (It is his first story to receive book publication, in the British anthology of Selwyn & Blount, Ltd., which is titled *You'll Need A Nightlight* and is published in 1927.)

—August 11, writes the short story "He."

—"The Temple" is published in the September issue of *Weird Tales*.

—September 18, writes the story "In the Vault." It is published in the November issue of *Tryout*.

—Begins the literary essay "Supernatural Horror in Literature" in November.

—October, he buys a Perfection oil stove to heat his room, since his landlady, Mrs. Burns, won't turn up the heat.

1926—(age 35–36) The story "Cool Air" is written in February or March.

—In early March, Lovecraft gets temporary work addressing envelopes for catalogs at the New York bookstore where his friend Samuel Loveman works. The job lasts several weeks.

—In April, his aunts send Lovecraft a train ticket to come home to Providence, since he is flat broke at the time. Lovecraft returns to Providence on April 17, and moves into a ground-floor room in a house at 10 Barnes Street, west of his former family home and north of Brown University, with his elder aunt, Lillian Clark, who takes a room on the second floor.

—"The Outsider" is published in the April issue of *Weird Tales*.

—UAPA collapses, temporarily halting Lovecraft's contributions to amateur journals.

—He finishes "Supernatural Horror in Literature."

—"The Moon-Bog" is published in the June issue of *Weird Tales*.

—Reads up on astrology in order to ghostwrite an exposé on the subject for Houdini.

—Receives his first letter from August W. Derleth, whom Lovecraft will never actually meet in person.

—The story "Two Black Bottles" is revised for Wilfred Blanch Talman over the summer and fall.

—Writes the story "The Call of Cthulhu" in August or September.

—Writes the story "Pickman's Model" in early September.

—"He" is published in the September issue of *Weird Tales*.

—Begins *The Dream-Quest of Unknown Kadath* in October.

—October 31, Harry Houdini dies, ending Lovecraft's plans for a collaboration on a book exposing fraudulent spiritualism.

—November 9, writes the story "The Strange, High House in the Mist."

—Writes the story "The Silver Key" early in November.

1927—(age 36–37) Finishes *The Dream-Quest of Unknown Kadath* on January 22. This novel is not published until 1943, in the Arkham collection *Beyond the Wall of Sleep*.

—"The Horror at Red Hook" is published in the January issue of *Weird Tales*.

—Writes *The Case of Charles Dexter Ward* from late January to March 1.

—Writes the story fragment "The Descendant" early this year.

—Also in March, writes "The Colour Out of Space." The story is published in the September issue of *Amazing Stories*.

—"The Green Meadow" is published in the spring issue of *The Vagrant*. The pseudonymous byline is Elizabeth Neville Berkeley (Winifred Jackson) and Lewis Theobald, Jun. (Lovecraft).

—"Supernatural Horror in Literature" is published in *The Recluse*. (Lovecraft revises it in 1933.)

—Meets Donald Wandrei in Providence.

—"Two Black Bottles" is published in the August issue of *Weird Tales*.

—Writes "The Thing in the Moonlight" based on a dream. Later on, J. Chapman Miske adds a small amount of text at the beginning and end to turn this dream vision into a short story.

—Receives his first letter of correspondence from Zealia Reed (later Zealia Bishop).

—In the autumn, he travels to Deerfield, Massachusetts, and to Vermont.

—Brief essay "History of the *Necronomicon*" written in the autumn (first published in 1938).

—"Pickman's Model" is published in the October issue of *Weird Tales*.

—November 2, he records the dream "The Very Old Folk" in a letter to Donald Wandrei.

—In the autumn, he ghostwrites the novelette "The Last Test" for Adolphe de Castro. It is a radical rewriting and expansion of de Castro's non-supernatural story "A Sacrifice to Science."

1928—(age 37–38) The sheets for W. Paul Cook's edition of "The Shunned House" are printed up, but they are not bound, and this booklet is never released in Lovecraft's lifetime.

—Early in this year he ghostwrites the story "The Curse of Yig" for Zealia Bishop, based on her vague synopsis. Lovecraft later wrote, "this story is about 75% mine."

—"The Call of Cthulhu" is published in the February issue of *Weird Tales*.

—"Cool Air" is published in the March issue of *Tales of Magic and Mystery*.

—April-May, he stays with his wife Sonia in Flatbush at her insistence, when she returns to New York in an attempt to start a new hat shop. The effort puts him on the verge of a nervous breakdown.

—Visits the region near Brattleboro, Vermont, in mid-June, where he meets the artist Bert G. Akley, the model for his character Henry Wentworth Akeley in "The Whisperer in Darkness."

—In late June, he visits a ravine known as the Bear's Den in Massachusetts, and enters a cave that is incorporated into his story "The Dunwich Horror."

—Spends eight days in July visiting Wilbraham, Massachusetts.

—Travels through Virginia in July, and visits the Endless Caverns, which he describes as the first "real cave" he has been in.

—August, writes "The Dunwich Horror."

—Writes satirical essay "Ibid."

—Sonia Greene Lovecraft visits with her husband in Providence in the latter part of this year.

—"The Last Test" is published in the November issue of *Weird Tales*.

1929—(age 38–39) "The Silver Key" is published in the January issue of *Weird Tales*.

—Lovecraft and Greene divorce, but the paperwork is never finalized. Lovecraft writes that the marriage ended March 25.

—In April he visits Virginia, and sees Jamestown and Williamsburg.

—"The Dunwich Horror" is published in the April issue of *Weird Tales*.

—July, he revises an existing published story by Adolphe de Castro and retitles it "The Electric Executioner."

—"The Curse of Yig" is published in the November issue of *Weird Tales*.

—Begins composing "The Mound" in December. This story is ghostwritten for Zealia Bishop, but it is entirely Lovecraft's work.

—December 27, he starts the sonnet cycle "Fungi from Yuggoth."

1930—(age 39–40) January 4, finishes the initial thirty-five-sonnet set of "Fungi from Yuggoth." A thirty-sixth sonnet is added in 1936. The complete sonnet cycle is first published 1943 in the Arkham collection *Beyond the Wall of Sleep*.

—Finishes writing "The Mound" in January.

—Writes the story "The Whisperer in Darkness" from February to September.

—The dwarf planet Pluto is discovered on February 18. Lovecraft later incorporates the discovery into his fiction, calling it Yuggoth.

—In late April he visits Charleston, South Carolina.

—Late in May he visits Loveman in New York, and meets Hart Crane once again. Lovecraft had first met him in Cleveland in 1922. Crane is now a famous poet, but an alcoholic.

—In July, attends the National Amateur Press Association convention at Boston.

—Over the summer he ghostwrites the novelette "Medusa's Coil" for Zealia Bishop. Much of the story is Lovecraft's

—"The Electric Executioner" is published in the August issue of *Weird Tales*.

—Sees the movie *All Quiet on the Western Front*.

—In early September he makes his first trip out of the United States, to visit Quebec City, Canada.

—October, begins an essay on Quebec City that becomes the 75,000-word travelogue *A Description of the Town of Quebeck*, written in his early archaic eighteenth-century style.

—Simon and Schuster ask Lovecraft for a novel, but he only offers them a collection of stories, which they are not interested in publishing, even though he has the manuscript of the novel *The Case of Charles Dexter Ward* sitting in his files.

1931—(age 40–41) In January he finishes his essay on Quebec City.

—He writes the novella *At the Mountains of Madness* from February 24 to March 22.

—Robert Barlow first writes to Lovecraft, who has no way of telling from his letter that Barlow has barely reached his teens.

—In May and June he visits with the writer Henry S. Whitehead in Dunedin, Florida, and also spends time in Key West. Lovecraft does not have the money to take a boat ride to Cuba.

—Collaborates with Henry S. Whitehead on the story "The Trap" during his spring visit. Lovecraft writes to August Derleth that he "revised and totally recast" this story, and elsewhere states that the "central part" is his.

—The publisher G. P. Putnam's Sons asks to look at several of Lovecraft's stories for a possible hardcover collection, but decides against the project.

—"The Whisperer in Darkness" is published in the August issue of *Weird Tales*.

—In the summer, Farnsworth Wright, editor at *Weird Tales*, rejects *At the Mountains of Madness*. Lovecraft's confidence as a writer is greatly shaken.

—He becomes a member of the Bureau of Critics in the NAPA.

—July, visits New York City.

—The stable at Lovecraft's birthplace, the Phillips' mansion at 454 Angell Street, is pulled down.

—In a letter, Lovecraft remarks that his groceries cost him only three dollars per week.

—"The Strange, High House in the Mist" is published in the October issue of *Weird Tales*.

—August Derleth convinces *Weird Tales* to buy the story "In the Vault," which Farnsworth Wright had rejected in November 1925 as too gruesome. The magazine pays Lovecraft fifty-five dollars.

—He writes the novelette *The Shadow Over Innsmouth* in November, finishing it December 3.

1932—(age 41–42) The story "The Dreams in the Witch-House" is written in pencil during January-February.

—"The Trap" is published in the March issue of *Strange Tales*.

—Visits Edgar Hoffmann Price at his home in New Orleans. Price tries to talk him into collaborating on a sequel to Lovecraft's story "The Silver Key."

—On his way back from New Orleans, he visits New York City. Receives word that his aunt is dying on the sixth day of the visit, and returns to Providence on July 1.

—His elder aunt, Lillian Clark, dies on July 3. Buried July 6 in the Clark lot of Swan Point Cemetery (Anglican burial service). At this time his younger aunt, Annie Gamwell, is living a mile from Lovecraft's rooming house.

—On August 31 he travels to Newburyport in order to view the totality of the solar eclipse on that date. It is his second viewing of the solar corona.

—Late summer, he spends some time in Montreal, and makes his second visit to Quebec City, where he stays four days. Stops at Salem and Marblehead on his way home.

—Ghostwrites "The Man of Stone" in the summer for Hazel Heald. Most of the story is Lovecraft's work. It is published in the October issue of *Wonder Stories*.

—Ghostwrites the novelette "Winged Death" in the summer for Hazel Heald. Lovecraft later writes that "90 to 95%" of the story is his work.

—Ghostwrites "The Horror in the Museum" in October for Hazel Heald. Lovecraft later admits that this story is "virtually my own work."

—E. Hoffmann Price sends Lovecraft his proposed six-thousand-word sequel to "The Silver Key."

1933—(age 42–43) March, Lovecraft extensively revises E. Hoffmann Price's sequel to "The Silver Key," producing the story he calls "Through the Gates of the Silver Key."

—In May, he moves out of his room at 10 Barnes Street, Providence, and into the five-room upper-level flat of a yellow, historic colonial two-story house at 66 College Street. The house, built around 1825, was located right behind the John Hay Library. His remaining aunt, Annie Gamwell, moves in to the upper flat with him. Lovecraft has two rooms to himself, and shares the kitchenette and bathroom with his aunt. He also has the use of two storerooms in the attic. The house has since been moved to 65 Prospect Street.

—Annie Gamwell breaks her leg, and Lovecraft takes care of her, grumbling in his letters about his loss of freedom to travel.

—"The Dreams in the Witch-House" is published in July by *Weird Tales*, which pays $140 thanks to the marketing efforts of August Derleth, who nonetheless is critical of the story.

—"The Horror in the Museum" is published in the July issue of *Weird Tales*.

—In August, he ghostwrites the story "Out of the Aeons" for Hazel Heald. The story is almost all Lovecraft's work. He writes about the story that it "may be regarded as a story of my own."

—Writes the story "The Thing On the Doorstep" in late August. It is written in pencil because Lovecraft does not have the confidence to use a pen.

—Writes an autobiographical essay, "Some Notes on a Non-Entity."

—Trip to Quebec, Lovecraft's third trip there.

—Robert Bloch, seventeen years old, writes to Lovecraft for the first time.

—Excursions around New England in the fall.

—October, a letter to Bernard Austin Dwyer contains the dream that becomes the story "The Evil Clergyman."

—"The Other Gods" is published in the November issue of *The Fantasy Fan*.

—Story fragment "The Book" is written late in the year.

—Lovecraft visits New York City at New Year's.

1934—(age 43–44) "Winged Death" is published in the March issue of *Weird Tales*.

—In May he writes the story "The Tree on the Hill" with Duane Rimel, who later declares that Lovecraft wrote the entire final chapter.

—In the spring he visits sixteen-year-old Robert Barlow for the first time in DeLand, Florida, and stays from May 2 to June 21.

—"From Beyond" is published in June in *The Fantasy Fan*.

—"Through the Gates of the Silver Key" is published in the July issue of *Weird Tales*.

—Spends a week in Nantucket.

—November 10, he begins the novelette "The Shadow Out of Time."

1935—(age 44–45) The "Shadow Out of Time" is finished on February 22.

—"Out of the Aeons" is published in the April issue of *Weird Tales*.

—In June Lovecraft begins his second extended visit with Robert Barlow in DeLand, Florida. Lovecraft stays two months, and returns to Providence in mid-August.

—The first symptoms of intestinal cancer begin to show themselves in the form of cramps and constipation.

—"The Quest of Iranon" is published in the July-August issue of *The Galleon*.

—On August 14 at 8 p.m., Lovecraft sees with a group of friends a rare astronomical phenomenon, a lunar rainbow in the northwestern night sky.

—Writes "The Horror in the Burying Ground" with Hazel Heald (this story may have been written 1933).

—Contributes the central part of the composite story commissioned by *Fantasy Magazine*, "The Challenge from Beyond." It is Lovecraft's portion, written by him late in August, that sets the direction for the plot. The story is published in the September issue of *Fantasy Magazine*.

—September, collaborates on the story "The Disinterment" with Duane Rimel. Most of the story is Rimel's work.

—October, he ghostwrites the story "The Diary of Alonzo Typer" with William Lumley. Lovecraft worked from a rough draft by Lumley, but much of the story, including the ending, is his own creation.

—From November 5–9, he writes the story "The Haunter of the Dark."

—Toward the end of the year, *Astounding Stories* buys both *At the Mountains of Madness* and "The Shadow Out of Time" for a total of $630, of which Lovecraft gets to keep $595. In one of his letters Lovecraft calls the check a "lifesaver."

1936—(age 45–46) January, he collaborates with another resident of Providence, Kenneth Sterling, on the science fiction story "In the Walls of Eryx."

—Lovecraft's health is poor during January and February.

—*At the Mountains of Madness* is published in sections in the February, March, and April issues of *Astounding Stories*.

—"The Shadow Out of Time" is published in the June issue of *Astounding Stories*.

—Annie Gamwell hospitalized to have a cancerous breast removed.

—On the morning of June 11, writer Robert E. Howard commits suicide by shooting himself in the head.

—July 22, Lovecraft views Peltier's Comet through the 12-inch refractor at the Ladd Observatory of Brown University. The observatory is located a mile north of 66 College Street.

—Lovecraft remarks in a letter that he is surviving on two dollars per week of groceries.

—Robert Barlow visits Providence for two months.

—Over the summer, Lovecraft collaborates on the story "The Night Ocean" with Robert Barlow, but it is mostly Barlow's work. It is published in the Winter issue of *Californian*.

—Adolphe de Castro visits.

—Maurice Moe visits.

—October 9, he attends a meeting of the amateur astronomical association known as the Skyscrapers, who are associated informally with Brown University.

—*The Shadow Over Innsmouth* is published as a book by William Crawford, publisher of a small magazine called *Marvel Tales*. Lovecraft is unhappy with the number of printing mistakes. Of the 400 copies, only 150 are sold.

—Sonia Greene Lovecraft marries Dr. Nathaniel Abraham Davis in California.

—"The Haunter of the Dark" is published in the December issue of *Weird Tales*.

—Late in this year Lovecraft is diagnosed with cancer of the intestine.

1937—(age 46) "The Thing on the Doorstep" is published in the January issue of *Weird Tales*.

—"The Disinterment" is also published in the January issue of *Weird Tales*.

—Writes his last letter in March, to James Morton, in which he talks about Roosevelt winning his second term as president in 1936.

—He enters Jane Brown Memorial Hospital in Providence on March 10, and dies March 15 from cancer, at age 46. An unfinished letter is found on the desk in his hospital room. Buried March 18 in the Phillips family plot in Swan Point Cemetery. C. M. Eddy tries to attend the funeral ceremony at the funeral home with his wife, but they are late and just miss it.

1938—February, "The Diary of Alonzo Typer" is published in *Weird Tales*.

—In June, Robert Barlow publishes *The Notes and Commonplace Book of H. P. Lovecraft* through Futile Press of California.

—"Azathoth" is published in the magazine *Leaves*.

—"The Book" is published in *Leaves*.

—"The Descendant" is published in *Leaves*.

—"History of the *Necronomicon*" is published as a pamphlet by Wilson Shepherd of Rebel Press, Oakman, Alabama.

1939—First collection of Lovecraft's stories, *The Outsider and Others*, published by Arkham House.

—"Medusa's Coil" is published in the January issue of *Weird Tales*.

—"The Evil Clergyman" is published in the April issue of *Weird Tales*.

—"In the Walls of Eryx" is published in the October issue of *Weird Tales*.

1940—"The Very Old Folk" is published in the Summer issue of *Scienti-Snaps*.

—"The Tree on the Hill" is published in the September issue of *Polaris*.

—"The Mound" is published in an abridged form in the November issue of *Weird Tales*.

1941—Lovecraft's remaining aunt, Annie Emeline (Phillips) Gamwell, dies on January 29.

—"The Thing in the Moonlight" is published in *Bizarre* in January.

—*The Case of Charles Dexter Ward* is published in an abridged form in the May and July issues of *Weird Tales*.

1943—Second collection of Lovecraft's stories, *Beyond the Wall of Sleep*, published by Arkham House.

1944—Arkham House collection *Marginalia*.

1972—Sonia H. Davis, Lovecraft's ex-wife, dies on December 26.

1977—A group of fans raises money to erect a separate headstone for Lovecraft inscribed with the motto "I Am Providence."

CHAPTER 1

1. I am not the first to harbor this suspicion. Kenneth W. Faig wrote in his essay "Parents of Howard Phillips Lovecraft" that the location of the marriage at Boston, rather than at Providence as would be expected, raises the speculation that it "took place against the wishes of Susie's parents." See Schultz & Joshi, *An Epicure in the Terrible*, pp. 46–47.

2. De Camp, p. 14.

3. Letter to J. Vernon Shea dated February 4, 1934. Referred to by de Camp, p. 15. A similar reference occurs in a letter to Rheinhart Kleiner dated November 16, 1916—see Schultz & Joshi, *Lord of a Visible World*, p. 9.

4. De Camp, photograph facing p. 246. De Camp is wrong in asserting that the photo was taken in 1891—see Joshi, *A Dreamer and a Visionary*, p. 34.

5. De Camp, p. 15, citing Koki, p. 9.

6. Joshi, *A Dreamer and a Visionary*, p. 33.

7. Ibid., p. 2.

8. Joshi & Schultz, *An H. P. Lovecraft Encyclopedia*, p. 203.

9. De Camp, photograph facing p. 246.

10. Letter to Rheinhart Kleiner dated November 16, 1916. Lovecraft, *Letters to Rheinhart Kleiner*, p. 64.

11. See references to this superstition of dressing boys as girls in Clodd, p. 131.

12. Joshi, *A Dreamer and a Visionary*, p. 33.

13. Ibid., p. 44.

14. *Selected Letters*, Vol. I, p. 104. Quoted in Schultz & Joshi, *An Epicure of the Terrible*, p. 64.

15. Letter to Edwin Baird dated February 3, 1924. Lovecraft, *Selected Letters*, Vol. I, pp. 299–305.

16. Letter to Robert E. Howard dated January 16, 1932. Quoted by Joshi, *Call of Cthulhu and Other Weird Stories*, pp. 380–81.

17. "A Confession of Unfaith" was first published in *The Liberal* in February 1922.

18. Lovecraft, *Supernatural Horror in Literature*, p. 53.

19. Ibid.

20. Joshi, *H. P. Lovecraft: A Life*, p. 153.

21. Letter to J. Vernon Shea dated February 4, 1934. *Selected Letters*, Vol. IV.

22. "A Confession of Unfaith." *The Liberal*, February 1922.

23. Letter to Maurice W. Moe dated January 1, 1915. *Selected Letters*, Vol. I.

24. Letter to Rheinhart Kleiner dated November 16, 1916. *Letters to Rheinhart Kleiner*, p. 73.

25. Letter to Maurice W. Moe dated January 1, 1915. *Selected Letters*, Vol. I.

26. Joshi, *A Dreamer and a Visionary*, p. 40.

27. Letter to Alfred Galpin dated August 21, 1918. Lovecraft, *Letters to Alfred Galpin*, p. 27.

CHAPTER 2

1. Letter to Rheinhart Kleiner, November 16, 1916. *Letters to Rheinhart Kleiner*, p. 68.

2. Ibid.

3. Jung, *Alchemical Studies*, pp. 265–66.

4. De Camp, p. 29.

5. Joshi, *A Dreamer and a Visionary*, p. 32.

6. Letter to Rheinhart Kleiner, November 16, 1916. *Letters to Rheinhart Kleiner*, p. 70.

7. Letter to Alfred Galpin dated August 29, 1918. *Letters to Alfred Galpin*, p. 38.

8. Letter to J. Vernon Shea dated November 8, 1933. Schultz & Joshi, *Lord of a Visible World*, p. 22.

9. De Camp, p. 31.

10. De Camp, pp. 18–19. De Camp has quoted from Lovecraft's short biographical essay "A Confession of Unfaith."

11. Letter to Rheinhart Kleiner dated November 16, 1916. *Letters to Rheinhart Kleiner*, p. 70.

12. Letter to Rheinhart Kleiner dated November 16, 1916. *Letters to Rheinhart Kleiner*, p. 68.

13. Joshi, *A Dreamer and a Visionary*, p. 43.

14. Ibid., 32.

15. Eddy & Eddy, p. 8. Susie Lovecraft confided to Muriel Eddy over the telephone that Lovecraft was "tormented with facial ingrown hairs" that caused him discomfort, and said that it was an inherited condition. This can only refer to Lovecraft's facial twitches and grimaces.

16. Joshi, *A Dreamer and a Visionary*, p. 33.

17. Fodor, p. 19.

18. Letter to J. Vernon Shea dated February 4, 1934. De Camp, p. 32.

19. Joshi. *H. P. Lovecraft: A Life*, p. 60.

20. De Camp, p. 34.

21. Letter to Robert E. Howard dated March 25, 1933. *Selected Letters*, Vol. IV.

22. De Camp, p. 60.

23. Letter to E. Baird dated February 3, 1924. *Selected Letters*, Vol. I.

24. De Camp, p. 29.

25. De Camp, p. 73.

26. De Camp, p. 61.

27. Letter to Rheinhart Kleiner dated December 4, 1918. *Letters to Rheinhart Kleiner*, p. 152.

28. De Camp, p. 60.

29. For the full text of this Thanksgiving Day note, see de Camp, p. 72.

30. De Camp, p. 16.

31. De Camp, p. 4.

CHAPTER 3

1. Those interested will find Lovecraft's poem "On the Creation of Niggers" reproduced by de Camp, p. 95.

2. In America, Christie's novel was published in January 1940, under the title *And Then There Were None*.

3. Letter to Lillian D. Clark dated September 29, 1922. *Lord of a Visible World*, p. 111.

4. De Camp, p. 61.

5. De Camp, p. 63.

6. Letter to Rheinhart Kleiner dated November 16, 1916. *Letters to Rheinhart Kleiner*, p. 77.

7. This poem was titled *"Ad Criticos,"* and according to de Camp it has 46 lines, not 44. See de Camp, p. 77.

8. The final pair of poems is given in full by de Camp, pp. 78–79.

9. In Lovecraft's biographical essay "What Amateurdom and I Have Done for Each Other," written in 1921, and published in *Boys' Herald*

46, no. 1, in August of 1937. Schultz & Joshi, *An Epicure of the Terrible*, p. 18; Lovecraft, *Lord of a Visible World*, p. 43.

10. Joshi & Schultz. *An H. P. Lovecraft Encyclopedia*, p. 4.

11. Letter to Rheinhart Kleiner dated May 23, 1917. *Letters to Rheinhart Kleiner*, p. 109.

12. Ibid.

13. Letter to Rheinhart Kleiner dated November 8, 1917. *Letters to Rheinhart Kleiner*, p. 119; de Camp, p. 110.

14. The racist comment appears in Lovecraft's essay "Something About Cats."

15. De Camp, p. 74.

16. Letter to Lillian D. Clark dated March 29, 1926. *Lord of a Visible World*, p. 187.

17. Letter to Rheinhart Kleiner dated January 20, 1916. *Letters to Rheinhart Kleiner*, p. 29.

18. De Camp, p. 127.

19. Letter from Clara L. Hess to August Derleth dated October 9, 1948. De Camp, p. 66.

20. Letter to Rheinhart Kleiner dated January 18, 1919. *Letters to Rheinhart Kleiner*, p. 154.

21. Ibid.

22. Eddy & Eddy, p. 5.

23. Letter to Rheinhart Kleiner dated March 30, 1919. *Letters to Rheinhart Kleiner*, p. 158.

24. Ibid.

25. Letter to Anne Tillery Renshaw dated June 4, 1921. *Lord of a Visible World*, p. 85.

26. Letter to Clark Ashton Smith dated April 14, 1929. *Lord of a Visible World*, p. 69. See de Camp, p. 139, where the Dunsany book is incorrectly identified as *Time and the Gods*.

27. Joshi, *H. P. Lovecraft: A Life*, p. 218.

28. De Camp, p. 141.

29. De Camp, p. 178.

30. Letter to Edward Baird, published in *Weird Tales 2*, no. 2, September 1923, pp. 81–82. *Lord of a Visible World*, p. 120.

31. De Camp, p. 179.

32. Letter to August Derleth dated March 4, 1932. *Lord of a Visible World*, p. 271.

33. Houellebecq, p. 57.

34. Joshi, *A Subtler Magick*, p. 13; Lovecraft, *Selected Letters*, Vol. I, p. 110.

35. De Camp, p. 196.

CHAPTER 4

1. Letter to Rheinhart Kleiner dated May 21, 1920. *Letters to Rheinhart Kleiner*, p. 189.

2. Letter to Rheinhart Kleiner dated December 14, 1920. *Letters to Rheinhart Kleiner*, p. 201.

3. Automatic writing may be preceded by involuntary movements of the hand which can at times become violent; automatic speaking is similarly often preceded by involuntary movements of the jaw and lips. See Fodor, Nandor. *Encyclopaedia of Psychic Science*, pp. 23 and 25.

4. The dream is related at length in a letter to a group of correspondents known collectively as the Gallomo, and is dated December 11, 1919. *Lord of a Visible World*, p. 76.

5. Letter to Maurice Moe, dated May 15, 1918. *Lord of a Visible World*, pp. 57–58.

6. Schweitzer, Darrell. "Lovecraft and Lord Dunsany" (essay). *Discovering H. P. Lovecraft*, p. 75.

7. Fox, Oliver. *Astral Projection*, pp. 32–37.

8. Ibid., p. 36.

9. For references to headaches following dreams, see *Lord of a Visible World*, pp. 76, 79, 82.

10. De Camp, p. 149.

11. Letter to Rheinhart Kleiner dated May 21, 1920. *Letters to Rheinhart Kleiner*, p. 189.

12. Letter to J. Vernon Shea dated November 8, 1933. *Lord of a Visible World*, p. 23.

13. Letter to Maurice W. Moe, May 15, 1918. *Lord of a Visible World*, p. 58.

14. Letter to Maurice W. Moe dated December 8, 1914. *Lord of a Visible World*, p. 64.

15. Letter to Lillian D. Clark dated March 29, 1926. *Lord of a Visible World*, p. 188.

16. Letter to August Derleth, 1926. *Lord of a Visible World*, p. 232.

17. Letter to Rheinhart Kleiner dated November 16, 1916. *Letters to Rheinhart Kleiner*, p. 69.

18. First published in January 1929, in *Weird Tales*, Vol. 13, No. 1, pp. 41–49 and 144.

19. Letter to the Gallomo dated September 3, 1920. *Lord of a Visible World*, p. 26.

20. Letter to Maurice W. Moe, May 15, 1918. *Lord of a Visible World*, p. 58.

21. Burleson's essay "On Lovecraft's Themes: Touching the Glass" appears in Schultz & Joshi, *An Epicure in the Terrible*, 1991.

22. Letter to the Gallomo [January 1920]. *Lord of a Visible World*, p. 69.

CHAPTER 5

1. Letter to Anne Tillery Renshaw dated June 4, 1921. *Lord of a Visible World*, p. 85.

2. Ibid.

3. Letter to Rheinhart Kleiner dated June 12, 1921. *Letters to Rheinhart Kleiner*, p. 207.

4. Ibid.

5. In a letter to Rheinhart Kleiner dated September 21, 1921, Lovecraft mentions that he has as yet traveled no farther afield than Hampstead, New Hampshire, referring to his meeting with Miss M. A. Little. See *Letters to Rheinhart Kleiner*, p. 218.

6. Joshi & Schultz, *An H. P. Lovecraft Encyclopedia*, p. 59.

7. Lovecraft's need to find a replacement for his mother was noted by L. Sprague de Camp, who wrote, "Evidently the 'wife' whom Lovecraft wanted was not a mate in the sexual sense but a surrogate mother, who would flutter around him, coddle him, and relieve him of all chores, errands, and responsibilities." De Camp, p. 307.

8. Harms & Gonce, *Necronomicon Files*, p. 197.

9. Crowley, *Confessions*, p. 714.

10. Ibid., p. 782.

11. Letter to Rheinhart Kleiner dated August 30, 1921. *Letters to Rheinhart Kleiner*, p. 213.

12. Letter to Rheinhart Kleiner dated September 21, 1921. *Letters to Rheinhart Kleiner*, p. 216.

13. Letter to Maurice W. Moe dated May 18, 1922. *Lord of a Visible World*, p. 99.

14. Letter to Maurice W. Moe dated June 21, 1922. *Lord of a Visible World*, p. 91.

15. De Camp, p. 153.

16. De Camp, p. 27.

17. Letter to Lillian D. Clark dated August 4, 1922. *Lord of a Visible World*, p. 108.

18. Letter to Lillian D. Clark dated March 9, 1924. *Lord of a Visible World*, pp. 127–28.

19. Letter to James F. Morton dated March 10, 1930. *Lord of a Visible World*, p. 115.

20. Letter to Lillian D. Clark dated March 9, 1924. *Lord of a Visible World*, p. 129.

21. Letter to Bernard Austin Dwyer dated March 26, 1927. *Lord of a Visible World*, p. 165.

22. Ibid., p. 166.

23. De Camp, p. 201.

24. Letter to Lillian D. Clark dated January 11, 1926. *Lord of a Visible World*, p. 181.

25. Letter to Bernard Austin Dwyer dated March 26, 1927. *Lord of a Visible World*, p. 167.

26. De Camp, p. 156.

27. Letter to Lillian D. Clark dated December 22–23, 1925. *Lord of a Visible World*, p. 184.

28. Letter to Frank Belknap Long dated May 1, 1926. *Lord of a Visible World*, p. 189.

29. De Camp wrote that Sonia had intended to travel to Providence with Lovecraft but was delayed by a job offer and followed him later—see de Camp, p. 259. Joshi and Schultz disagree—see *An H. P. Lovecraft Encyclopedia*, p. 60.

30. Letter to Frank Belknap Long dated May 1, 1926. *Lord of a Visible World*, p. 192.

31. Joshi & Schultz, *An H. P. Lovecraft Encyclopedia*, p. 60.

32. Letter to Maurice W. Moe dated July 2, 1929. *Lord of a Visible World*, p. 196.

33. De Camp, p. 194.

34. Letter to Maurice W. Moe dated July 2, 1929. *Lord of a Visible World*, p. 196.

35. A few of Lovecraft's postcards to Sonia have survived—see Joshi & Schultz, *An H. P. Lovecraft Encyclopedia*, p. 61. De Camp (p. 308) wrote that Sonia had burned "a trunkful of Lovecraft's letters."

CHAPTER 6

1. Joshi & Schultz, *An H. P. Lovecraft Encyclopedia*, p. 64.

2. Ibid., pp. 53–54.

3. Letter to Farnsworth Wright dated July 5, 1927. *Lord of a Visible World*, p. 209.

4. This is the third of three laws proposed by Clarke. It appeared in the 1973 revised edition of his collection of essays, *Profiles of the Future*, in the essay "Hazards of Prophecy: The Failure of Imagination."

5. Letter to Lillian D. Clark dated March 29, 1926. *Lord of a Visible World*, p. 187.

6. Letter to Farnsworth Wright dated July 5, 1927. *Lord of a Visible World*, p. 210.

7. From Gray's 1742 poem "Ode on a Distant Prospect of Eton College."

8. Joshi & Schultz, *An H. P. Lovecraft Encyclopedia*, p. 53.

9. Letter to Frank Belknap Long, February 1931. *Lord of a Visible World*, p. 257.

10. Ibid., p. 258.

11. Letter to Frank Belknap Long dated November 22, 1930. *Lord of a Visible World*, p. 222.

12. Ibid, pp. 221–22.

13. Ibid., p. 222.

CHAPTER 7

1. Letter to Donald Wandrei dated February 10, 1927. *Lord of a Visible World*, p. 198.

2. *The Tryout* was a small amateur magazine published out of a dilapidated cottage on 408 Groveland Street, Haverhill, Massachusetts. Lovecraft visited Smith there in June 1921, in the company of Miss. M. A. Little. The visit is described in a letter to Kleiner dated June 12, 1921. *Letters to Rheinhart Kleiner*, pp. 207–08.

3. Eddy & Eddy, pp. 7–8. Muriel Eddy speculated that Lovecraft's curious sensitivity to the cold and immunity to the heat might have inspired the story "Cool Air."

4. Letter to Frank Belknap Long dated May 1, 1926. *Lord of a Visible World*, p. 190.

5. Letter to Lillian D. Clark dated March 29, 1926. *Lord of a Visible Word*, p. 187.

6. Ibid.

7. Letter to Maurice W. Moe dated May 18, 1922. *Lord of a Visible World*, p. 93.

8. Letter to Lillian D. Clark dated March 9, 1924. *Lord of a Visible World*, p. 130.

9. Joshi & Schultz, *An H. P. Lovecraft Encyclopedia*, p. 286.

10. Ibid., p. 151.

11. Eddy & Eddy, p. 23.

12. Ibid., p. 24.

13. Joshi & Schultz. *An H. P. Lovecraft Encyclopedia*, p. 302.

14. Ibid., p. 116.

15. Eddy & Eddy, p. 20.

16. Letter to Lillian D. Clark dated August 4, 1922. *Lord of a Visible World*, p. 108.

17. Joshi & Schultz, *An H. P. Lovecraft Encyclopedia*, p. 247.

18. Letter to E. Hoffmann Price dated June 20, 1936. *Lord of a Visible World*, p. 338.

19. Ibid.

20. Quoted from C. A. Smith's 1935 short story "The Treader of the Dust."

21. Joshi & Schultz, *An H. P. Lovecraft Encyclopedia*, p. 22.

22. Price, p. 11, footnote 11.

23. Letter to J. Vernon Shea dated September 25, 1933. *Lord of a Visible World*, p. 294.

24. Letter to Elizabeth Tolridge [September 1930]. *Lord of a Visible World*, p. 251.

25. Letter to J. Vernon Shea dated September 25, 1933. *Lord of a Visible World*, p. 293.

CHAPTER 8

1. Letter to Rheinhart Kleiner dated March 7, 1920. *Letters to Rheinhart Kleiner*, p. 184.

2. Letter to Rheinhart Kleiner dated November 16, 1916. *Letters to Rheinhart Kleiner*, p. 69. See de Camp, p. 19.

3. Letter to Robert E. Howard dated August 16, 1932. *Selected Letters* Vol. IV, p. 57.

4. Letter to Anne Tillery Renshaw dated June 4, 1921. *Lord of a Visible World*, p. 85.

5. Letter to Woodburn Harris dated February 25, 1929. *Lord of a Visible World*, p. 226.

6. Letter to Frank Belknap Long dated February 20, 1929. *Lord of a Visible World*, p. 215.

7. Letter to Edwin Baird dated February 3, 1924. *Lord of a Visible World*, p. 27.

8. Letter to Frank Belknap Long [February 1931]. *Lord of a Visible World*, p. 259.

9. Letter to Rheinhart Kleiner dated October 1916. *Letters to Rheinhart Kleiner*, p. 56.

10. Genesis 3:24.

11. Matthew 19:14. King James Version.

12. Burleson, p. 136.

13. Letter to the Gallomo [January 1920]. *Lord of a Visible World*, p. 67.

14. Eddy & Eddy, p. 54.

15. Letter to Maurice W. Moe dated April 5, 1931. *Lord of a Visible World*, pp. 3–7.

16. Eddy & Eddy, p. 9.

17. Letter to August Derleth dated March 4, 1932. *Lord of a Visible World*, p. 271.

CHAPTER 9

1. De Camp, p. 421.

2. Joshi & Schultz, *An H. P. Lovecraft Encyclopedia*, p. 239.

3. De Camp, p. 303.

4. De Camp, pp. 423–24.

5. De Camp, p. 412.

6. Ibid.

7. Joshi & Schultz, *An H. P. Lovecraft Encyclopedia*, p. 142.

8. Letter to Richard F. Searight dated August 23, 1933. *Lord of a Visible World*, p. 300.

9. Letter to August Derleth dated February 25, 1935. De Camp, p. 401.

10. Letter to August Derleth dated June 6, 1932. Joshi & Schultz, *An H. P. Lovecraft Encyclopedia*, p. 76.

11. Letter to E. H. Price dated February 2, 1936. De Camp, p. 414.

12. Letter to E. Hoffmann Price dated March 14, 1935. *Lord of a Visible World*, p. 330.

13. Letter to Lee White dated December 20, 1935. *Lord of a Visible World*, p. 331.

14. De Camp, p. 157.

15. Letter to August Derleth dated January 16, 1931. *Lord of a Visible World*, p. 278.

16. Letter to Lillian D. Clarke dated October 24–27, 1925. *Lord of a Visible World*, p. 159.

17. Ibid.

18. Letter to J. Vernon Shea dated October 13, 1932. *Lord of a Visible World*, p. 290.

19. Letter to E. Tolridge dated June 8, 1933. De Camp, p. 371.

20. De Camp, p. 370.

21. Letter to Helen Sully dated August 15, 1935. *Lord of a Visible World*, p. 305.

22. Ibid.

23. Letter to Robert H. Barlow dated April 29, 1936. De Camp, p. 416.

24. De Camp, p. 417.

25. Letter to Alvin Earl Perry dated October 4, 1935. *Lord of a Visible World*, p. 264.

26. Eddy & Eddy, p. 26.

27. De Camp, p. 430.

28. Letter to Frank Belknap Long [February 1931]. *Lord of a Visible World*, p. 259.

29. Letter to E. Hoffmann Price dated June 20, 1936. *Lord of a Visible World*, p. 338.

30. Joshi & Schultz, *An H. P. Lovecraft Encyclopedia*, p. 144.

31. Maurice W. Moe in the 1937 essay "Howard Phillips Lovecraft, the Sage of Providence." Quoted by Joshi & Schultz, *An H. P. Lovecraft Encyclopedia*, p. 144. The essay is published in full in Joshi's *Caverns Measureless to Man*, p. 16.

32. De Camp, p. 112. Joshi and Schultz dispute the number of 100,000 letters. "The actual number of Lovecraft's letters has probably been somewhat exaggerated, and the figure of a hundred thousand casually bandied about since the 1970s is probably much too high." (Joshi & Schultz, *Lord of a Visible World*, p. vii.) They speculate that the number may have been nearer to 75,000. It is to be noted that de Camp himself did not assert that the number of letters was 100,000.

33. Joshi & Schultz, *An H. P. Lovecraft Encyclopedia*, p. 65.

CHAPTER 10

1. Edmund Wilson, p. 287.

2. Joshi & Schultz, *An H. P. Lovecraft Encyclopedia*, p. 65.

3. Edmund Wilson, p. 288.

4. Ibid.

5. De Camp, p. 399.

6. Edmund Wilson, p. 288.

7. Ibid.

8. Ibid., p. 289.

9. Letter to James F. Morton dated January 5, 1926. *Lord of a Visible World*, p. 178.

10. Edmund Wilson, p. 286.

11. Ibid., p. 290.

12. Ibid., p. 289.

13. De Camp, p. 438. De Camp has quoted from Colin Wilson's book *The Strength to Dream*, pp. 1–10.

14. Ibid. De Camp has quoted *The Arkham Collector* I, 1 (Summer 1967), p. 17.

15. Joshi & Schultz, *An H. P. Lovecraft Encyclopedia*, p. 187.

16. Butler, p. ix.

17. Grant, p. 6.

18. Crowley, *Vision and the Voice*, p. 43.

19. Grant, p. 14.

20. Crowley, *Vision and the Voice*, note 34.

21. Crowley, *Magick in Theory and Practice*, p. 69.

22. Butler, p. 3: "The fundamental aim of all magic is to impose the human will on nature . . ."

23. Grant, p. 13.

24. Simon, p. xxxi.

25. Ibid., p. 7.

Burleson, Donald R. "On Lovecraft's Themes: Touching the Glass." Essay in *An Epicure in the Terrible: A Centennial Anthology of Essays in Honor of H. P. Lovecraft*. Edited by David E. Schultz and S. T. Joshi. Cranbury, NJ: Associated University Presses, 1991.

Burritt, Elijah Hinsdale. *Geography of the Heavens, and Class Book of Astronomy*. New York: Huntington and Savage, 1833.

Butler, E. M. *Ritual Magic* [1949]. Hollywood, CA: Newcastle Publishing Company, 1971.

Clarke, Arthur C. *Profiles of the Future*. New York: Harper and Row, 1963.

Clodd, Edward. *Tom Tit Tot: An Essay on Savage Philosophy in Folk-tale*. London: Duckworth and Co., 1898.

Crowley, Aleister. *The Confessions of Aleister Crowley* (corrected edition). London: Arkana Books, 1989.

———. *The Vision and the Voice*. First published in the periodical *The Equinox*, Vol. 1, No. 5 (March 1911). Dallas, TX: Sangreal Foundation Inc., 1972.

De Camp, L. Sprague. *H. P. Lovecraft, A Biography* [1975]. New York: Barnes and Noble Books, 1996.

Eddy, Muriel E., and C. M. Eddy, Jr. *The Gentleman From Angell Street: Memories of H. P. Lovecraft*. Narragansett, RI: Fenham Publishing, 2001.

Fodor, Nandor. *Encyclopaedia of Psychic Science* [1934]. New York: University Books, 1966.

Fox, Oliver (Hugh Callaway). *Astral Projection: A Record of Out-of-the-Body Experiences* [1938]. Secaucus, NJ: The Citadel Press, 1962.

Grant, Kenneth. *Outer Gateways*. London: Skoob Books Publishing, 1994.

Harms, Daniel, and John Wisdom Gonce III. *The Necronomicon Files: The Truth Behind Lovecraft's Legend*. Boston: Weiser Books, 2003.

Hay, George. *The Necronomicon: The Book of Dead Names* [1978]. London: Corgi Books, 1980.

Houellebecq, Michel. *Atomised*. Translated from the French by Frank Wynne. London: Vintage Books, 2001.

———. *H. P. Lovecraft: Against the World, Against Life*. Translated from the French by Dorna Khazeni. San Francisco: Believer Books, 2005. Published in French as *H. P. Lovecraft: contre le monde, contre la vie* [2001].

Joshi, S. T. *A Dreamer and a Visionary: H. P. Lovecraft in His Time*. Liverpool, UK: Liverpool University Press, 2001.

———. *A Subtler Magick*. Third Edition. Gillette, NJ: Wildside Press, 1982, 1996.

———. *Caverns Measureless to Man: 18 Memoirs of H. P. Lovecraft*. West Warwick, RI: Necronomicon Press, 1996.

———. *H. P. Lovecraft: A Life*. West Warwick, RI: Necronomicon Press, 2004.

———. *H. P. Lovecraft: The Decline of the West*. Berkeley Heights, NJ: Wildside Press, 1990.

Joshi, S. T. (editor). *The Call of Cthulhu and Other Weird Stories by Howard Phillips Lovecraft*. New York: Penguin, 1999.

Joshi, S. T., and David E. Schultz. *An H. P. Lovecraft Encyclopedia*. Westport, CT: Greenwood Publishing Group, 2001.

Jung, C. G. *Alchemical Studies*. Translated from the German by R. F. C. Hull. Princeton, NJ: Princeton University Press, 1967.

Koki, Arthur. S. *H. P. Lovecraft: An Introduction to His Life and Writings*. Master's thesis, Columbia University, 1962.

Lovecraft, H. P. *Letters to Alfred Galpin*. New York: Hippocampus Press, 2003.

———. *Letters to Rheinhart Kleiner*. New York: Hippocampus Press, 2005.

———. *Lord of a Visible World: An Autobiography in Letters*. Edited by S. T. Joshi and David E. Schultz. Athens, OH: Ohio University Press, 2000.

———. *Selected Letters of H. P. Lovecraft, Vol. I (1911–1924)*. Sauk City, WI: Arkham House, 1964.

———. *Selected Letters of H. P. Lovecraft, Vol. II (1925–1929)*. Sauk City, WI: Arkham House, 1968.

———. *Selected Letters of H. P. Lovecraft, Vol. III (1929–1931)*. Sauk City, WI: Arkham House, 1976.

———. *Selected Letters of H. P. Lovecraft, Vol. IV (1932–1934)*. Sauk City, WI: Arkham House, 1976.

———. *Supernatural Horror in Literature*. New York: Dover Punblications Inc., 1973.

Park, T. Peter. "H. P. Lovecraft: An Abductee?" Essay in *The Anomalist*, No. 9, Winter 2000/1, pp. 82–91.

Price, Robert M. "H. P. Lovecraft and the Cthulhu Mythos." Essay in *Crypt of Cthulhu*, issue no. 35. Mount Olive, NC: Cryptic Publications, 1985.

Schultz, David E., and S. T. Joshi (editors). *An Epicure in the Terrible: A Centennial Anthology of Essays in Honor of H. P. Lovecraft*. Cranbury, NJ: Associated University Presses, 1991.

Schweitzer, Darrell. *Discovering H. P. Lovecraft, Revised & Expanded.* Holicong, PA: Wildside Press, 2001.

Simon (Peter Levenda). *Necronomicon Spellbook.* New York: Avon Books, 1981.

———. *The Necronomicon.* New York: Avon Books, 1980.

Szumskyj, Ben J. S., and S. T. Joshi (editors). *Fritz Leiber and H. P. Lovecraft: Writers of the Dark.* Holicong, PA: Wildside Press, 2003.

Van Eeden, Frederik. "A Study of Dreams." Essay in the *Proceedings of the Society for Psychical Research*, vol. 26, 1913.

Waugh, Robert H. *The Monster in the Mirror: Looking for H. P. Lovecraft.* New York: Hippocampus Press, 2005.

Wilson, Colin. *The Outsider.* Boston: Houghton Mifflin, 1956.

———. *The Strength to Dream: Literature and the Imagination.* Boston: Houghton Mifflin, 1962.

Wilson, Edmund. "Tales of the Marvelous and Ridiculous." Essay first published November 24, 1945, in the *New Yorker* magazine. Republished in *Classics and Commercials: A Literary Chronicle of the Forties*, pp. 286–90. New York: Farrar, Straus & Giroux, 1950.

Young, Charles Augustus. *Lessons in Astronomy Including Uranography: A Brief Introductory Course Without Mathematics.* Boston: Ginn and Company, 1891.

Necronomicon
The Wanderings of Alhazred
Donald Tyson

The first *Necronomicon* created in the true spirit of H. P. Lovecraft! Anyone familiar with H. P. Lovecraft's work knows of the *Necronomicon*, the black-magic grimoire he invented as a literary prop in his classic horror stories. There have been several attempts at creating this text, yet none stand up to Lovecraft's own descriptions of the *Necronomicon* . . . until now.

Fans of Lovecraftian magic and occult fiction will delight in Donald Tyson's *Necronomicon*, based purely within Lovecraft's own fictional universe. This grimoire traces the wanderings of Abdul Alhazred, a necromancer of Yemen, on his search for arcane wisdom and magic. Alhazred's magical adventures lead him to the Arabian desert, the lost city of Irem, the ruins of Babylon, the lands of the Old Ones, and Damascus, where he encounters a variety of strange creatures and accrues necromantic secrets.

978-0-7387-0627-6, 288 pp., 7 x 10 $17.95

To order, call 1-877-NEW-WRLD
Prices subject to change without notice
Order at Llewellyn.com 24 hours a day, 7 days a week!

Grimoire of the Necronomicon

Donald Tyson

On the heels of his widely successful series of works honoring H. P. Lovecraft, Donald Tyson now unveils a true grimoire of ritual magic inspired by Lovecraft's *Necronomicon* mythos. *The Grimoire of the Necronomicon* is a practical system of ritual magic based on Lovecraft's mythology of the alien gods known as the Old Ones.

Fans of Lovecraft now have the opportunity to safely get in touch with the Old Ones and draw upon their power for spiritual and material advancement. Tyson expands upon their mythology and reintroduces these "monsters" in a new, magical context—explaining their true purpose for our planet. As a disciple, you choose one of the seven lords as a spiritual mentor, who will guide you toward personal transformation. Daily rituals provide an excellent system of esoteric training for individual practitioners. This grimoire also provides structure for an esoteric society—the Order of the Old Ones—devoted to the group practice of this unique system of magic.

978-0-7387-1338-0, 216 pp., 7 x 10   **$18.95**

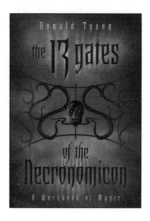

The 13 Gates of the Necronomicon

A Workbook of Magic

DONALD TYSON

On the heels of his successful and critically acclaimed *Necronomicon* books, Donald Tyson now unveils an authentic sourcebook for magicians inspired by H. P. Lovecraft's *Necronomicon* mythos. Tyson uses Lovecraft's story elements and characters—alien races, ancient sorceries, the Dreamlands, deities, witches, and ghouls—as the foundation for a workable and coherent system of modern ritual magic. This authoritative guide, based on actual zodiacal constellations, presents essential elements of the *Necronomicon* mythos for use in esoteric practices such as dream scrying, astral projection, and spirit communication.

978-0-7387-2121-7, 432 pp., 7 x 10   **$21.95**

To order, call 1-877-NEW-WRLD
Prices subject to change without notice
Order at Llewellyn.com 24 hours a day, 7 days a week!

Necronomicon Tarot

DONALD TYSON; ARTWORK BY ANNE STOKES

Gruesome gods, sinister monsters, and other strange creatures lurk throughout this fully functional tarot deck. All seven rulers of the Old Ones from Tyson's *Necronomicon* star among the deck's trumps, including the great amphibian deity Dagon as the Hierophant and the ancient witch I'thakuah as the Hermit. The symbolism of these vividly illustrated cards corresponds with astrology, the elements, and the Golden Dawn, while the deck's structure honors the boundaries of traditional tarot.

The enclosed book features detailed descriptions of the cards and the meaning for both upright and reversed positions. Tyson also offers divination guidance and a special divination spread.

978-0-7387-1086-0, boxed kit (5⅜ x 8¼) includes: 78-card deck, 240-pp. book
$26.95

The Lovecraft Necronomicon Primer

T. Allan Bilstad

Elder things. Ghasts. Night-gaunts.

Meet the creatures of the Cthulhu Mythos, denizens of the dark but brilliant imagination of H. P. Lovecraft. The collection of horror and fantasy he penned during his short lifetime is a legacy that has terrified and inspired generations of fans. Lovecraft's tales reveal the horror of seeing what is unknown or hidden for good reason.

Written especially for those with little to no prior knowledge of Lovecraft's work, this book presents detailed descriptions of twenty-nine of the monsters, creatures, and gods that inhabit Lovecraft's macabre fictional universe, without any spoilers that could ruin a future read of his stories.

978-0-7387-1379-3, 288 pp., 5³⁄₁₆ x 6 $11.95

To order, call 1-877-NEW-WRLD
Prices subject to change without notice
Order at Llewellyn.com 24 hours a day, 7 days a week!